CARRION KISSES

CARRION KISSES

KATE LOCK

EBURY PRESS

First published in Great Britain in 2004

10 9 8 7 6 5 4 3 2 1

Text © Kate Lock 2004

First published by
Ebury Press
Random House, 20 Vauxhall Bridge Road, London SW1V 2SA

Random House Australia (Pty) Limited
20 Alfred Street, Milsons Point, Sydney, New South Wales 2061, Australia

Random House New Zealand Limited
18 Poland Road, Glenfield, Auckland 10, New Zealand

Random House South Africa (Pty) Limited
Endulini, 5A Jubilee Road, Parktown 2193, South Africa

The Random House Group Limited Reg. No. 954009

www.randomhouse.co.uk

A CIP catalogue record for this book is available from the British Library.

Cover design by Versha Jones
Text design and typesetting by Textype

ISBN 0091891299

Printed and Bound in Great Britain by Mackays of Chatham plc

Papers used by Ebury Press are natural, recyclable products made from wood grown in sustainable forests.

Permissions:
Extract from 'The Love Song of J Alfred Prufrock' from The Complete Poems and Plays by T S Eliot, reproduced with kind permission by Faber and Faber Limited

Extract from 'Nursery Tale' by Philip Larkin from 'The North Ship', 'Love, we must part now: do not let it be' by Philip Larkin from 'The North Ship' and lines from 'Aubade' from 'Collected Poems' by Philip Larkin edited by Anthony Thwaite reproduced with kind permission by Faber and Faber Limited

'Jacob And Sons' from 'Joseph And The Amazing Technicolor® Dreamcoat' Lyrics by Tim Rice, music by Andrew Lloyd Webber © 1969 The Really Useful Group Ltd London. Reproduced by kind permission of the copyright owner

Lyrics from 'Don't Stop' by Fleetwood Mac. Rights are held by BMG Music Publishing International.

Every effort has been made to clear relevant copyright permissions. Please contact the publisher with any queries.

So every journey that I make
Leads me, as in the story he was led,
To some new ambush, to some fresh mistake:
So every journey I begin foretells
A weariness of daybreak, spread
With carrion kisses, carrion farewells.

From 'Nursery Tale'
Philip Larkin
(*The North Ship*)

INTRODUCTION

How we love defines us. Not wholly, not to the world, but to the people who really matter: our partners and families. They see into our hearts. Prime Minister or parking attendant, we all make the same journey. It is the most basic, and yet the most complex human emotion there is. Our relationships and how we conduct them are fundamental to who we are, even if – especially if – we choose not to show it. But who we love: that's different. That doesn't so much define us as reflect us. Look into your lover's eyes. Who do you see?

This book is the story of a period in my life back in the early 1980s when I met a man called Tim Franklin. The relationship lasted four years. The effect it had on me has lasted ever since. It is a personal memoir, but it is also a biography of Tim and, beyond that, it is an attempt to understand what drew us together and the motivations that kept us in such a destructive relationship. Above all, it is a portrait of an explosive, bittersweet love affair and its consequences. And not just mine and Tim's. There was one who came before me. She was forty-two, the age I am now, when he killed her.

I have written other books (nine in total), which grew out of my background in TV journalism, but they were strictly work, a means of making a living. They were entertaining to do, but frustrating: I was fleshing out the lives of fictional characters while the story I wanted to write was more powerful and disturbing than any television drama. That story I'd lived. I have a file of scribbled scenes, opening paragraphs, chapter breakdowns, going back years, but I didn't write it then, because I didn't know how to. Turning it into a novel seemed wrong; the alternative, to write it as a memoir, was too scary. It wasn't just the prospect of laying myself bare. It meant digging into Tim's past, and I was afraid of what I might find.

It's taken twenty years for me to distance myself enough from Tim to write this. I thought I had put him out of my life for good, but he came back in a way I hadn't anticipated. It became so that I couldn't write any other book. A contemporary novel seemed too glib, thrillers too concocted, romances too normal. Children's books were out of the question. The truth I knew was indeed stranger than fiction. I had to write this one.

Writing this has been at times painful, occasionally

traumatic, not only because I've uncovered some shocking things about Tim's past, but also because it's forced me to take a long, hard look at myself. I've been honest, even when it's made me uncomfortable to admit to things. Other women have similar experiences: you don't have to have lived with a lifer to recognize yourself in this. Some women suffer a lot worse. I was one of the lucky ones, and not just because I got out of it in one piece. Tim changed my life, and in many ways for the better. Things are rarely black and white.

The events I describe in Part One, which tells my story, all happened, and I have diaries, letters, photos and records to back most of them up. I have, though, changed some people's names. There is one person I have deliberately not named, even though her name came out in the press at the time, and I would ask other people to respect that. As to the dialogue, it's impossible to remember detailed conversations from so long ago. Some things Tim said will always stick in my memory, some I wrote down, and some I have had to conjure up listening to that brusque voice of his in my head. I hope I've done him justice. It is easy to recall the words that made me flinch; harder to portray the extraordinary charisma of the man.

Part Two tells Tim's story, and I am indebted to all the people who agreed to be interviewed for it, particularly Tim's sister, Antonia Davy, for being so helpful and open and giving so much of her time, and his daughter Belinda. I would also like to thank Christopher Fothergill, Dave

Upton and Derek King, who worked with Tim and knew him well, and those involved in the original investigation and trial, namely former Chief Inspector Strickland Carter and Gilbert Gray, QC, as well as former PC Harry Codling. I couldn't have tracked them down without my very helpful private investigator, David Farrar, and I'm grateful to my researcher, Barbara Bullivant, for the hours she spent in the archives. Thanks also to Tom and Chris, Hilary, Ginni and Sharon, who shared their impressions of Tim and have been good friends to me over the years. The book wouldn't have come about at all without the enthusiasm and energy of my agent, Sheila Ableman, and the perceptiveness and guidance of Hannah MacDonald, my editor at Ebury. I'd also like to mention the Authors' Foundation, who awarded me a grant for research and give valuable support to writers like myself.

Finally, I'd like to thank my parents for their unqualified support and my husband Stephen for being so understanding about my need to write this, not to mention all the daddy – daughter days he spent being thrashed at Junior Monopoly by a competitive six-year-old while I wrote. He has been my rock, sustaining me emotionally and working all hours to keep us going financially, even selling his treasured childhood collection of Silver Surfer comics on Ebay.

Now that really is true love.

PROLOGUE

Exmouth Beach, 16 May 1987

It was just a rectangular white plastic container. Plain lid. Easy to mistake for a tub of ice cream, one of those economy sizes without a label. There was a slip of paper with it: 'The Cremated Remains of the Late Timothy John Franklin. Date of Cremation: 6 April 1987, 2.30 p.m.' I got a flashback of the unknown pallbearers hoisting Tim's coffin onto their shoulders: the shock at the sight of it emerging from the hearse; the grief, rising like nausea in my throat; my mother, gripping my hand as if I were a child she was about to march across the road. But that was gone now.

I felt calm, sitting on the sea wall listening to the gulls' aerial spats. Calm, but strangely weightless, as if I might at any moment be blown off and bowl along the front like an empty crisp packet. It was 6.00 a.m. and the place was deserted, except for an illegally parked camper van, its windows fogged by sleepers. It would be hot later; the haze had lifted and I could see across the estuary to Dawlish Warren and beyond that to where the Paddington to Penzance line snakes along the bottom of the cliffs. Sun warmed the back of my neck. I was willing to be seduced by its early-morning tenderness: I could have stayed there all day soaking it up, letting my limbs grow heavy with the heat. Putting it off.

A crow jabbed at the contents of an overflowing litter bin nearby, picking over fish-and-chip scraps with its heavy black beak. It cocked its head and regarded me, bright eyes insolent, then hopped onto the wall with a clumsy flutter and took two deliberate steps towards me, eyeing the box. Perhaps it thought I'd got sandwiches. Or perhaps it knew what I'd got. It took another couple of steps, brazening me out. We stared. It knew. I jumped down from the wall, galvanised at last.

Carrying the box carefully, I walked towards the waves across sand etched with ripples and bumpy with worm casts. I stopped just short of the water's edge, watching the foamy fringe of the tide as it dissolved in a hiss of bubbles. I could see the tips of the rocks we used to scramble over at low tide when we were hunting for special shells; shells that were ordinary and dull when we got them home, so that you wondered what beauty you'd seen in them, though we never stopped collecting them. This was our place, out of season. The short drive out to Exmouth became a weekend ritual: we used to come here and trudge the wintry shore, eyes streaming in the wind. Here, harsh words were snatched by stiff breezes and dashed into the Exe, so that by the time we returned to the car, chilled fingers entwined, we were friends again. Sometimes, when the weather was mild, I would run on ahead, run and run, as if my life depended on it, while Tim plodded along behind, stumbling occasionally in the wet sand. But mostly we just pottered, collecting shells that whispered vague promises when you held them to your ear.

It wasn't especially romantic: on a blustery Sunday the oily estuary could look black; the littered beach bleak. But the opening out of sea and sky gave us space; space that reoxygenated not just our cells but our souls. In this place, we could open up to each other without the cross-currents of complications that threatened to drag us under. That's why I'd come. No matter that it was 300 miles from where I now lived, or that the company, who had paid for his funeral, wanted a plaque at the crematorium. I would have driven to the ends of the earth to set him free.

I never saw Tim dead. My father identified the body. I never said goodbye, never kissed his cold lips. I wish I could have done that, made up with him before they closed the coffin on Tim and his secrets. Had I looked in those eyes one last time, would they have told me anything? There's no deceit in death. But of course I would have seen an old man, more shrunken than I remembered, his face, like his past, a blank. Better to keep the image of the lusty lover alive; the man who, even when he was getting on for sixty, could still drag me off to bed and make it last all afternoon. There, only there, he dropped his guard. It was all the power I had, his child–daughter–wife. Until now. I lifted the lid.

I was surprised to see pale flinty chips, like the stuff they put around the base of trees in shopping precincts. I was expecting feathery white flakes or a fine grey powder, proper ashes. There was no smell. No acrid, morning-after hint of a cold grate to catch in the throat. I tried not to think about the cremation process, the offensively functional squeak of machinery as the casket trundled away like a piece of luggage on a conveyor belt. With trepidation, I scanned for bits of bone, or teeth, a giveaway sign that the contents of this box was once a person. The chips were uniform and innocuous. So much for a life. I wanted to plunge my hand into the box and run the ashes through my fingers, to caress him in death with a love I could no longer admit to in life. But I couldn't. Squeamishness about getting a bit of Tim stuck under my nails stopped me and in the end I opted for pouring them in a steady stream into the water, keeping the box at arm's length. The sea swallowed the ashes with a gulp, and he was gone.

I felt I should say something. Not a prayer – Tim would have no truck with Christianity – so I recited 'The Love Song of J. Alfred Prufrock', what I could remember of it. After all, T. S. Eliot was more of a god to him:

'We have lingered in the chambers of the sea
By sea-girls wreathed with seaweed red and brown
Till human voices wake us, and we drown.'

I took pictures of the tranquil scene and picked up a couple of shells for old time's sake. I didn't feel anything much, and although I'd shed a tear with Prufrock, it was more because of the sentimental role I'd cast myself in than out of genuine emotion. Perhaps it was the absence of ceremony or just being alone; the lack of black and organ chords, but the whole thing felt too . . . well, normal. A fishing trawler chugged past me, heading out to open sea, and I spotted a woman walking her dog further down the beach. The day was beginning to wake and I realized I wanted people around me, food, hot coffee. I made my way back to the car, chucking the plastic box in the litter bin. Let the crow have his crumbs, I thought, suddenly tired. I drove to Exeter services. The restaurant was filling up with breakfasting holiday-makers en route to Cornwall. I ate croissants and read the paper, comforted by the clatter of cutlery, the fug of cigarette smoke, children squabbling. The clock said 8.00 a.m. I still had the whole day ahead of me. That's it, I told myself, you've done your bit. You've got a life to live, a fiancé, a future. I walked out high on caffeine and resolve and headed for home.

Two days later, on my way to work, I started crying for no reason and couldn't stop.

PART ONE

LIFE

CHAPTER ONE

I'd known Tim for less than two hours when he told me he was out of prison on licence. Then he offered to walk me home.

'Look,' he said. 'It's late and it's dark. You can't go back by yourself. It's not safe.' He took my coat off the chair and held it open, waiting. I remained in my seat, weighing up the odds. The footpath ran along a bank above the road, and it was narrow and badly lit. Which was riskier: going it alone and chancing being attacked by some unknown rapist, or letting a lifer I'd met in the pub walk me through the shadows? Dawdling over the dregs of my glass, I avoided his eyes, focusing instead on his wrists in front of me, labourer's wrists, brown and muscular and broad at the knuckle. Earlier, I'd found myself wanting to touch them, without knowing why. He extended his arms, offering the coat. A droplet of sweat inched a snail trail down my side. I wanted to bolt, but he was standing in the way. I heard him exhale steadily through his nostrils and sensed he was controlling impatience. Torn between politeness and panic, I told myself he couldn't be dangerous or they wouldn't have let him out. Tim gave my coat an insistent shake. 'Well?' he said. 'Are you coming?'

I met Tim through Mike, a post-graduate I had become friendly with. Mike helped out with our biology practicals and flirted with all the authority that a white lab coat can lend. He had tight fair curls, crinkly blue eyes and a teasing manner, but, most importantly, he was older. At twenty, I was finding it hard to fit in with the other freshers: too young to be a mature student and too old to put up with puking school-leavers. With Mike, at least, there was some common ground – I'd worked with male scientists and could match the banter – so when he invited me to a Biology Society's cheese-and-wine party, I leapt at the chance. 'The others'll be there,' he announced casually, as we tidied up the desks.

'Who? Your harem?'

He flicked agar-agar at me. 'My housemates.'

'Are they nice?'

He grinned. 'They're completely insane.'

I often wonder what Tim saw in me. Youth, mainly, I suspect. Rawness, naiveté. I was so obviously malleable. Like a shark scenting a drop of blood in a vast expanse of ocean, he sniffed out my vulnerability the first time he laid eyes on me. Furthermore, I was wearing a red jumpsuit unzipped to reveal a great deal of cleavage, which demonstrated a willingness to be exploited. (I overheard him joking about this years later – 'There she was, damn thing undone to her bellybutton and pissed as a newt – well, I ask you' – and was dismayed by his coarseness.) It was true that I was drunk, so drunk I could scarcely see, but if all he'd wanted was an easy lay, he could probably have had me that night. It was Freshers' Week, an induction into university life for new students that consisted mainly of trial by alcohol, and Mike and his friends had dragged me to the Philosophy Society's party after we'd drunk the Biology Society's cheese-and-wine dry. He had then abandoned me for a brunette and I had consoled myself with several more glasses of vinegary red, which the cubes of dry cheddar had no hope of absorbing. I remember pouncing on an owlish young man in a sports jacket, who seemed to want to talk about A. J. Ayer rather than dance to Adam and the Ants, and there being some confusion over our interpretations of New Romanticism, but the rest is a blur. I was whisked back to my hall of residence by a couple of sober academics, staggered into my room and was sick in the basin, unaware that Tim had already exerted his influence over me.

Despite my two extra years in the 'real' world (one gap year had segued into another) university life was proving harder to adjust to than I'd imagined. Having survived comprehensive-school bullying – where I'd been picked on for being 'square', a swot and talking 'posh' (the threat of elocution lessons with Auntie Gertie, a retired mezzo-soprano, had done its job) – I had expected students to be more egalitarian. Not so. Exeter University in 1981 turned out to be much more class-driven than my mother, or at least its undergraduates were, and being a police sergeant's daughter, I was now Not Posh Enough. A large proportion of the students were privately educated; Oxbridge rejects from wealthy families with ruddy cheeks and loud voices. They had a nickname, 'Wellies', and a uniform that both sexes adhered to rigidly. The girls wore velvet Alice bands, pearl necklaces, navy pumps and Laura Ashley blouses with the collars turned up; the boys, rugby shirts and brown cords. They were also extremely rude, pushing into the coffee-bar queues and acting as if us comprehensive-school kids were invisible. This created a sense of alienation that drove me further to the political left: I palled up with Matt, a softly spoken Irish Marxist; Lizzie, a lesbian who campaigned tirelessly for the removal of VAT from tampons; and flirted with the Socialist Worker Student Organization (or 'Swizzo' as it was known), mainly, I confess, because I fancied Roger, who was running it. We spent a night drinking Polish vodka and discussing Lech Walesa's Solidarity union, twisting cold tongues and fumbling beneath each other's T-shirts, but we'd climaxed with our mutual hatred for Margaret Thatcher too early, and by the time we climbed under his thin sheets, our passion was spent.

CHAPTER ONE

Being at university was like going back to school, but with one crucial difference: sex was practically on the curriculum. Freshers Week gave a pretty good indication: on the very first evening I saw a theatrical sideshow in which a girl in her underwear simulated fellatio on a groaning, hamming-it-up boy. She turned round to face us, fake spunk dribbling from her shiny lips. 'So good for you, and full of protein,' she mewed, rolling her eyes. The audience roared with delight. I'm not sure which shocked me more: the realistic-looking semen or the flagrant display of her pubic hair, which covered the insides of her thighs like overgrown moss.

I thought I was cool about sex – I had a boyfriend back home who was eager to please – but I was no more experienced than my younger peers, and probably less than a lot of them. I'd been a virgin until nineteen and was busy making up the time: in the space of a summer I had metamorphosed from shy sixth-former into a heat-seeking sexual missile, courtesy of a twice-divorced gardener from Jersey. Boys my own age didn't arouse me; they tended to be immature and grabby. I preferred men with experience and poetry in their souls. I had long legs, a winning smile and youth, which, in that marketplace, seemed to be all that was necessary, and I was naive enough to think that it gave me the power. I knew what they were thinking when they inclined their heads; I saw the glints in their polite smiles. It made me laugh that older men, for all their sophistication, were that transparent, which makes it all the more surprising that I didn't pick up Tim on my radar at that first meeting. But that was his technique, flying under your defences. Tim had a strategy for everything, especially love.

'Max. Nigel. Lindsay. Keith.' Mike waved a hand at the group of post-graduates around the table in the Cowley Bridge, Exeter's 'in' student pub. 'I need a slash,' he added, deserting me.

'Hi,' I said brightly, to no one in particular, trying to appear confident.

'First year?' asked a girl with pale eyelashes. I nodded. One of the lads winked. A student with a thin, serious face raised his glass in sombre salute. The fourth, who was hunched over his pint, belched loudly without looking up. I hesitated, unsure of whether to sit down.

'I'm afraid Keith has a very limited vocabulary,' a voice said behind me, 'especially after a few drinks. His ability to articulate decreases incrementally with every pint of Flowers. Although even when he's sober he talks utter rubbish.'

'Bollocks,' said Keith. I turned round to see an older man bearing a tray of drinks. He set them down and held out his hand. 'Tim Franklin,' he said crisply. 'And you're Kate. Good to see you again.' His handshake was firm, dry, assertive. He was my father's age at least, but fit-looking, as if he worked out, with a taut, tapered torso and bulky shoulders that seemed constrained by his short-sleeved shirt. I had a vague memory of meeting him before, but the image was piecemeal, a Cubist-type collage of sensory snapshots, the features exaggerated and distorted. The thin, white pencil moustache looked familiar and the clipped English accent sounded familiar, but my brain couldn't fit the bits together.

'Freshers' Week. The Philosophy Society's party.' He grinned at my obvious confusion. 'You livened it up no end. The whole thing was a crashing bore until you came along. Lindsay is still recovering. He's never been made to dance before.' Lindsay, with the camel face, shook his head mournfully. A few frazzled synapses sparked for a second, prompting a painful flashback. 'Sorry,' I mumbled, recalling that I'd dragged him, protesting, onto the floor. Lindsay sighed. 'My tutorial group has lost all respect.'

'Nonsense,' Tim retorted. 'Your credibility went up considerably.' Turning to me, he asked confidentially, 'I trust the Masons got you home without incident?' Another connection flared and I had a surprising impression of Tim steering me towards a car, one hand on my arm, the other on the small of my back. The press of his palm had been authoritative and quaintly old-fashioned, as if I were a fine lady being escorted to a waiting carriage, not a silly student who required propping up because she was cross-eyed with drink. Recalling his solicitousness · he had seen me into the car, making sure my seatbelt was done up – I realized that he must have arranged the lift. The funny thing was, I had no memory of talking to him before then. 'Yes. Thank you for . . . well, you know.'

'Think nothing of it.' He indicated a chair. 'Sit down. I'll protect you from Keith.' Mike returned, carrying two brimming pints of bitter – girls didn't bother with halves, I noticed, watching Max drain her froth-scummed glass – and plonked one down in front of me. 'This'll put hairs on your chest.' I sipped it, even though I didn't like the stuff, because it was what the rest of them were drinking, although Tim, I noticed, drank Coke. He was clearly a regular at the Cowley Bridge because he had his own tankard behind the bar engraved with 'Tim's Coke glass' in frosted letters. Everyone seemed to know him and I supposed he was a member of the academic staff slumming it, partly because of his age and partly because he spoke with such authority. Guessing that he was a senior lecturer or, more likely, a philosophy professor, merely compounded the embarrassment I already felt about him witnessing my drunken behaviour at the party. I sat in silence, feeling like the gatecrasher I was, hoping Mike would come to my rescue, but he had already forgotten about me and was larking with Nigel. I downed some more beer, which went the wrong way and made me splutter. Red-faced and wretched, I was preparing to make a dash for the safety of the ladies' loo when Tim passed me a handkerchief. 'Here. It is clean. Would you like me to fetch you a glass of water?'

'I'm all right,' I coughed.

'You're sure?'

'Yes.' I coughed some more, and he patted me on the back, rubbing between the shoulder blades. 'Better?'

'I think so.'

'Good. Mike tells me you're a biologist.'

'Yes.'

'Darwin, natural selection, survival of the fittest?' He looked at me quizzically. I wasn't sure how to respond. Tim gestured around the table. 'Makes you wonder how this lot ever made it. They're definitely mutations, I can vouch for that.' He eyed Keith, who was dozing over his pint, giving a remarkable impression of the dormouse in the teapot. 'I suppose one could argue that he has adapted to environmental constraints.' I started to giggle and he smiled broadly. From that moment, I forgot my awkwardness. Tim talked a lot, but he was witty, and flattered me by asking endless questions. He seemed genuinely interested in what I had to say, wanting to know what my ambitions were and what I thought about things, listening to my answers carefully and treating me like an equal, which, patently, I was not. He picked me up on my answers frequently, but not in a harsh way, and I found myself rising to his challenges as my confidence increased. I had never met anyone like him before: his intelligence was extraordinary. Our conversation made me feel nervous and reckless at the same time. I was having to run to keep up, but the effort was worth it. There were moments when it felt like flying. It was clear from the broadsides he dealt Lindsay and Nigel that he could be intellectually ruthless, but with me Tim was gently teasing, parrying with a presumptiveness that bordered on flirtation. He was attractive, for an older man, and obviously made an effort with his appearance, so I was happy to play along with him. He was too old – late fifties, I judged – even for my taste in men, and I assumed with my youthful arrogance that he was beyond 'all that'. It was harmless, I thought, and anyway, I was having fun.

By this time I was well into my second pint and feeling nicely fuzzy round the edges, so it didn't occur to me that Tim had revealed little about himself. I was astonished when he turned out to be a mature student doing a PhD and not a professor at all. None of the others seemed to find this unusual and he was obviously accepted, despite the age difference and his right-wing politics. Tim seemed equally at home in their company, ribbing them and arguing while puffing furiously on a roll-up. He clearly enjoyed playing the upper-class reactionary to a bunch of credulous socialists (provoking a near-meltdown during a discussion about the student boycott of Barclays Bank), but there was something about the extravagance of his gestures – thumping the table for emphasis, or smacking his forehead in pained disbelief – that seemed almost too flamboyant, foreign, even.

As for me, I sat there soaking it all up, longing to have a share in this laid-back lifestyle. They all lived together in a rambling country house called Barton Place, Tim told me, which the university had taken over for post-graduate accommodation. It sounded blissfully bohemian. By all accounts, life there was one permanent party, with post-pub drinking continuing long into the night, usually in Tim's room. He was obviously the head of their unusual household, an indulgent father-figure who cooked famous Sunday lunches (Tim's roast potatoes were second to none, according to Nigel) and was generous with his booze, if the accounts of his parties were accurate. However, he was rigorous with them, too, challenging any intellectual slacking and criticizing them for their ignorance of history, although his lectures on their lack of morals were accepted as tongue-in-cheek. Looking round at this bawdy, unruly, makeshift family, I envied them their freedom. Life in my hall of residence was depressing and I was spending more evenings than I cared to admit holed up in my room eating Pot Noodles and trying to drown out the noise of competing stereos with my transistor radio.

Of the group, three of them were philosophers: Tim; Lindsay, the gangling young fogey; and Nigel, a Lancastrian who resembled a scruffy puppy. Following a furious argument about Kant's categorical imperative, which might as well have been conducted in a foreign language to me, Tim went off to buy some tobacco and Mike, who I'd almost forgotten about, moved over to sit next to me. He wrapped an arm around my shoulders. 'Well,' he said, blowing beer at me, 'what do you think of our celebrity?'

I glanced around the table. Lindsay and Nigel had deserted us to continue their debate over a game of pool; Maxine, the strapping geologist, was deep in conversation with another girl and Keith, who didn't seem to do anything much except drink, was still slumped in his seat with his eyes shut. 'Who?' I asked.

'Tim.'

'Tim's famous?'

'Tim's notorious.' Mike beamed. 'You don't know, do you?'

'Know what?'

He rocked back in his chair, observing me. 'It's no big secret. Everyone knows. Sociology love him. He's their star turn.'

'Sociology? But he's doing philosophy.'

'He's got a degree in philosophy. He knows his stuff all right. But his doctorate's in sociology. Had to be. Given the subject matter.' He tapped the side of his nose.

'Which is?'

'It's all about prisons. Why the criminal justice system's crap. Like, an insider's view.' He paused for effect. 'Tim's a lifer.'

'A lifer?' I didn't understand. Weren't lifers murderers? The Yorkshire Ripper was a lifer. Myra Hindley, Ian Brady. I assumed Mike was winding me up. 'Very funny.'

'He is, really. You can ask him yourself. Tim's cool.' He swivelled round in his chair. 'Look, here he comes.'

'I'm not a complete idiot,' I said crossly. Mike and Keith had already caught me out by requesting pints of 'Fleurs' (the bitter was Flowers, but I hadn't spotted the pump handles until it was too late) and I was determined not to get stitched up again. Mike frowned. 'I'm not joking. Ask him.'

'Yeah, and my other leg's got bells on.'

'Have it your way.' He got up. 'I'll accept your apology

20

later. I'm going to play pool.' He sauntered off to join the others, leaving me feeling confused. Surely Mike wasn't telling the truth? On the other hand, why make up something like that? It just didn't fit: Tim was a gentleman, besides which he was – well, too old. Too old, and too respectable. And even if this didn't preclude him from being a lifer, the fact that he was so obviously well liked by his fellow students argued against it. Someone that popular could hardly be a cold-blooded killer or an armed robber or whatever else it took to get a life sentence. If Tim had committed a terrible crime, people wouldn't even sit with him. All the same, there had been a secretiveness in Mike's smile that had hinted otherwise, and when Tim rejoined me I found myself unable to meet his eyes. 'I can't believe Mike's abandoned you again. The man's a fool.' He threw a packet of Old Holborn down on the table. 'Still, at least I've got you to myself, now.' He gave me an arch grin. Probably I didn't respond, or perhaps he saw the doubt in my face, because he suddenly became serious. 'Kate? Are you OK?'

'I'm fine, thanks.'

'No you're not. You look peaky.'

'I'm always pale. It's my colouring.'

'Hmph.' Tim looked disbelieving. He studied me carefully. 'Do you feel sick? That beer's strong stuff if you're not used to it.'

'Honestly, I'm OK.' Tears were threatening – where had they come from? – and I stared at the table, concentrating on a ring of moisture left by a glass.

Tim moved closer and laid his hand on my arm. It felt relaxed, heavy, intimate. I froze. 'Kate,' he said softly, 'did Mike say something to you?' I shook my head, biting my lip. 'Come on, I can see you're upset.' He rubbed the baby hairs on my forearm gently with his thumb.

'You're right, I'm a bit pissed.' I decided to play it light. 'Mike was just trying to catch me out again. He thinks I'll believe any story he spins me.' I took a deep breath. 'You should have heard what he just said about you.'

Tim removed his hand and started to tear the cellophane off the tobacco. 'What was it?'

'That you were some sort of criminal. That you'd been in prison.' The words plopped into the space between us like stones in a pool. Across the table, Keith opened one eye and stared at me with lizard-like detachment. The two girls paused to listen.

'I'm a lifer, Kate. Is that what Mike said?' Tim's voice was cool. I felt the back of my neck prickle. I nodded. 'I'm out on licence,' Tim continued. His eyes met mine and there was a challenge in them.

I swallowed. 'What does that mean?'

'It means that I can be recalled to prison at any time, without question. If I was to harm one hair on your head – or even threaten to – I'd be straight back inside, for good.' He slapped his hands down on his thighs. 'That you should know.' The bell rang for last orders and he got to his feet. 'Let me buy you one for the road. A brandy, perhaps?'

I nodded again, dumbstruck. Keith began to cackle,

laughing so much that he had a coughing fit. Max and her friend went back to chatting. Across the room, Mike gave me a cheery wave. I watched Tim go to the bar and order the drinks, joking with Gil, the landlord. My brain felt overloaded with contradictions. The logical side advised caution; the intuitive side told me there was nothing to fear. It was impossible to decide: the information and the image just did not add up. There was nothing in Tim's dress or demeanour to suggest violence; no tattoos, no heavy rings or steel toecaps. He looked less like an ex-con than a favourite uncle.

'I thought you might like some peanuts.' Tim returned with my brandy – a large one, I noticed – and started to roll himself a skinny cigarette. The act, which had earlier struck me as slightly incongruous (the others all smoked Marlboro), suddenly made sense: the eked-out tobacco, worth a week's prison wages. Tim caught me looking. 'Old habits.' He shrugged and licked the edge of his Rizla. It was clear he wasn't going to volunteer any more information.

I took a gulp of my brandy, feeling it burn a ball of heat in my belly. 'If you're a lifer . . .' I didn't know how to ask it. It seemed too crude to just come out with *What did you do?*

Tim's face seemed to close in on itself. 'It was an accident,' he replied tersely, anticipating the question. I felt my mouth open and shut like a goldfish. 'Someone I was with. We had a row and I was trying to restrain her. She fell and hit her head against a wall. I got the blame.' He exhaled smoke through his nostrils. 'Complete miscarriage of justice.

Judge led the jury. The appeal went to the House of Lords.'
He didn't elaborate further and, from the rigidity of his
neck chords, I thought it wise not to ask.

'Time, gentlemen, *please*,' Gil roared, tolling a heavy handbell.
And so, extraordinarily, we left it at that.

The definition of murder is unambiguous. It means the
unlawful, premeditated killing of one human being by
another. Not by accident. Not because they lost control, or
were mentally ill or somehow provoked. But because they
meant to. A verdict of murder carries a sentence of life
imprisonment automatically, unlike manslaughter, which is
judged to have been committed without malice
aforethought and receives shorter sentences. I wasn't well
informed about this distinction at the time, and certainly
not the difference in sentencing. Since Tim had given me
the impression that his crime was essentially a flukish
domestic tragedy, I assumed he'd been charged with the
lesser offence. The fact that he was a lifer should have made
me think harder about this, but he hadn't used the word
'murder' and I didn't appreciate the anomaly.

It was reassuring to discover that Tim wasn't a serial killer
but, despite his explanation, I felt a frisson of unease as I let
him slip on my jacket. He steered me outside, a proprietary
hand again on my back, and we stopped in the car park.
Neither of us spoke. I tipped my face up to the night sky,
watching the moon bowl across it like a pale frisbee. A few
stars winked tremulously through the racing clouds.

'You know,' Tim said quietly, 'what stars are, don't you, Kate?' I turned to him, surprised at the question. He took off his glasses and rubbed the bridge of his nose. His eyes were soft and brown, like a dog's, and he looked suddenly vulnerable. 'I'm not talking about those up there. It's prison slang, what they call someone who's serving their first sentence.'

'I didn't know that.'

'Few people do, except those of us who've had the experience.'

'I suppose not.' I tried to sound casual.

'Prison's a different world from the one you're used to, Kate. But not for me. I had to fight to survive boarding school, which my parents dumped me in when I was six. I had to fight my way through an army barrack room as a seventeen-year-old officer to get the respect of the men. Prison was just another all-male institution; same rules.' He sighed heavily. 'I served eight years, Kate. Eight long, bloody years. I made a mistake and I've been punished for it, even though I didn't deserve what they gave me. And now here I am starting my life again from scratch at the age of fifty-six.' A carload of students drove past us, honking a raucous goodbye. Tim smiled faintly and raised his hand in salute. 'They're a good lot here. Most of them accept me for who I am – although I realize I'm an object of curiosity among the more prurient.' He replaced his glasses, assuming his previous formality. I shivered and he looked at me, concerned. 'You're cold.' He unwound his scarf. 'Have this.'

He looped it around my neck, lifting my hair gently out of the way, then took the two ends and crossed them over. I held my breath for a moment. 'We'll soon have you warm.' His voice was tender. I lifted my chin obediently, like a child, letting him pull the knot tight to my throat, feeling the wool against my windpipe. It was snug, comforting. Our faces were close, close enough to taste the smokiness of his breath, and I kept my focus on the door behind him (there was a hand-painted sign next to it: 'No dogs or muddy Wellies'), too perturbed by our proximity to look at him directly.

'There.' Tim gave the ends a tweak. 'Better?'

'Yes. Thanks,' I stammered.

'Thank you, Kate.'

I lowered my eyes to his face. 'What for?'

He gazed at me levelly. 'For trusting me.'

CHAPTER TWO

Exeter University's main campus is on the outskirts of the city, spread over a couple of small hills. With its woodlands and lake and beautiful views, it is – save for the concrete hulk of the physics tower – one of the most attractive university campuses in the country. A Hepworth bronze stands on the combed lawn outside the Queen's Building, its abstract curves robustly reassuring, and cedars throw pools of shade over the rolling grass, betraying the campus's origins as a country estate. Being in the south-west, the climate is mild, even in autumn when one would expect a nip in the air. Coming from Oxford, where the return of well-muffled undergraduates traditionally marks the turning of the season, it took a while to acclimatize to these balmy conditions. For the first few weeks at Exeter I was always too hot, stomping up the steep paths in woolly jumpers and arriving at lectures overheated and self-conscious about my armpits.

I was studying biology and geography, with the intention of specializing in ecology in my final year. Ever since reading Schumacher's *Small is Beautiful* at school I had set my sights on becoming a conservationist and following in David Attenborough's footsteps (*Life on Earth* had been a landmark). However, I had not reckoned with my complete lack of mathematical ability. Never mind saving the whale, I was barely competent with a calculator, and the 'statistics for biologists' module was beyond me. Unfortunately, passing this was compulsory; those that failed got kicked off the course. The only consolation was that I'd found an ally, Hilary, a frustrated art student who was as bad at biology as I was.

During this time I saw nothing of Tim. Our walk back to my hall of residence had been uneventful and I was too busy trying to juggle a boyfriend back home in Oxford with a slew of social engagements – not to mention coursework – to think much about our disquieting encounter. I had heard from Mike that Tim was seeing a girl my own age, which had surprised me, even though he had flirted with me. It had been a game, or so I'd thought, but now I wasn't quite so sure. I confided in Sally, another friend, whose kohl-rimmed eyes widened when she heard that an aged lifer had been hitting on me. 'Ooh, creepy.' She tossed her black hair. 'Can you get us an invite to one of his parties?'

'I'll see,' I said, unsure if I wanted to get involved with a man with Tim's history. I soon forgot. Someone else had distracted me. His name was Claude and he was a mature student from the West Indies studying drama. He was also a dancer, choreographer and the campus sex-god.

'You start with your legs apart like this.' Claude stood with his back to us, demonstrating. He raised his arms above his head in a fluid, sweeping motion, muscles gliding beneath his gleaming skin, and held the pose, looking up at his extended fingertips. Against the light, his sculpted arms stood out like the boughs of a tree on a winter's afternoon. He lowered them to his sides and repeated the movement in time with the music, swivelling to face us as the jaunty vocals from *Joseph and the Amazing Technicolor Dreamcoat* cut in:

Way, way back many centuries ago
Not long after the Bible began,
Jacob lived in the land of Canaan
A fine example of a family man . . .

'Now, side to side.' Claude began to dance, clicking his fingers and swinging his hips, while we bobbed about trying to copy him and bumped into one another. As a first rehearsal for an ambitious student production, it wasn't going too well. 'No, no, no!' he roared, stopping the music. 'Again, from the top.' The opening chords swelled and we did our best to repeat Claude's instructions, while he prowled around us, criticizing. He circled the group and came up behind me, so close that I could feel his breath on my neck. 'What is your name?'

'Kate.'

'Ket?'

'Kate.'

'Kate.' He repeated my name deliberately, as if making a mental note. I started to turn round, but he grabbed my shoulders and made me face front. 'Your arms,' he growled, running his hands down them and raising them in the air, 'are like a bird flapping'. He waved my arms about, as if I was a puppet. The other students laughed. I could feel my already flushed face turning even hotter, and not just from embarrassment. Claude's body was right up against me. 'What I want to see,' he slid his hands to my wrists, almost folding me in an embrace, and drew them up again, this time achingly slowly, 'is a smooth arc, as if you are painting a rainbow in the sky. You got it?'

'Yes,' I whispered hoarsely.

'Good.' He dropped my arms unceremoniously. 'So next time, do it.' And he strode back to the front of the mirrored studio to restart the music, leaving me burning with a mixture of shame and desire, a desire so physical that it seemed as if every single nerve ending was vibrating on high frequency.

One evening, after a particularly frustrating biology practical, I dragged Hilary off to the Ram Bar in Devonshire

House, the student union building, and we got smashed on cheap beer. There was a disco going on nearby and, attracted by the loud music, we decided to give it a go. 'Look,' Hilary nudged me as we bopped half-heartedly to Spandau Ballet, 'isn't that the choreographer you were telling me about?' She indicated Claude, who was lounging against the bar, propped on one elbow, surveying the room. He caught our eyes and grinned. 'He's gorgeous,' Hilary shouted in my ear. Claude was wearing a black singlet and black trousers, dancer's clothes, as if he'd just come in from a work-out. He looked as predatory as a panther. Tentatively, I smiled back. Ten minutes later, we were getting down to Bob Marley, Claude's hands on my hip bones. When he asked me back to his room for a drink, I said yes.

Claude's seduction technique was both blissfully romantic and deeply sexy; the kind of seduction girls fantasize over before the reality of wet kisses and sweaty hands spoils the illusion. He put on a tape of Percy Sledge singing, 'Let Me Wrap You in My Warm and Tender Love', drew me close and looked deep into my eyes, as if I was the woman he'd been waiting for his entire life. This time it was a proper slow dance, a dance that meant our bodies shared as much surface area as was humanly possible. It was also a dance that I was not very good at, having been a wallflower at sixth-form discos. I kept bumping his knees and standing on his toes, until he gently instructed me to stand off-centre and place one leg between his. Trembling at such intimacy, I obeyed. It worked like magic. Instantly, we were locked together and moving as one while Percy sang 'When a Man Loves a Woman' and my insides turned to liquid with the press of Claude's thigh.

For a few weeks after that, I achieved the exalted position of Claude's official girlfriend. We didn't have much in common, apart from dancing and sex, but it was an acceptable arrangement for both of us. We didn't use condoms, either: Aids had just been officially recognized, but neither of us saw it as a threat. No one did. It was just another news story, something that happened to gay men, and therefore not relevant to us. As for getting pregnant, Claude swore to me that the withdrawal method had never failed him, so when my period was late, I put it down to my erratic cycle. End-of-term tests were approaching, and the problem of the statistics paper was far more pressing. I knew I'd flunk it, and the thought of losing my place at Exeter was devastating.

This was brought home by a sharp word from a lecturer in a biology practical, and I was weeping silently over a petri dish when Mike stopped in front of me and demanded to know why I was contaminating my experiment. 'God knows what'll grow on that now.' He leaned towards me. 'What's the matter?'

'I can't do it.' I wiped my nose on the sleeve of my lab coat. Mike rolled his eyes. 'It's not difficult. You've just to make sure you measure—'

'I can't do any of it. I'm useless. And I hate biology.' I could feel myself building up to a uncontrollable blub. Mike came round the bench and put an arm around my shoulders. 'Hey. It's not the end of the world.' He offered me a handkerchief that smelt vaguely of chemicals. 'You could always try another subject. You'd be surprised how many students change courses, even at this stage.'

'Really?' Hilary, who was sitting with me, pricked up her ears.

'Yeah. Depends what you want to switch to, of course.'

'Art.'

He pursed his lips. 'Not here.'

'English?' I ventured. It had always been my best subject at school.

'You'll be lucky. It's the most over-subscribed course at Exeter.' Mike saw I was starting to well again and added hastily, 'I could be wrong. Check with the faculty secretary. They'll tell you.'

Hilary and I whisked round to the Faculty of Arts the minute biology was over. Mike was right. The were no places to be had in English. Most of the other courses were also full. The only departments left with any vacancies were philosophy and sociology. I didn't have a clue about either of the subjects, but I knew a man who did. Taking Hilary with me for moral support, I went to find Tim.

For a student who was supposed to be the department's star turn, Tim was surprisingly scathing about sociology. 'Load of long-haired layabouts whining about the state of the country and blaming it all on the government. How they have the nerve to call it an academic subject is beyond me. Liebfraumilch? Or Chianti?' He held up a raffia-covered bottle. 'If there's any left. My wine stocks took a hammering last night.' A bearded man who had ambled in through the open doorway said mildly, 'I object to that.'

'I don't see how. You were pissed as a fart.'

'Your remarks about sociology. You can't slate what is, after all, a social science, just because it demonstrates the pathetic inadequacies of capitalism.'

Tim waved a dismissive hand in his direction. 'Kate, Hilary, meet Tom. Note the excessive facial hair. I defy you to guess what he does.'

Hilary and I glanced at each other. Tom held out his hand. 'Someone has to keep the old boy in check.' He had twinkly eyes and a kind face and we took to him immediately. Tom sat down in an armchair and crossed his long legs. 'So what do you think of this place. Bit of all right, isn't it?' He pointed to the window, which opened onto a balcony with white-painted balustrades. 'We take our drinks out there in the evening. Tim likes to keep up colonial traditions. Snifter at sundown, what?' He mimicked Tim's voice.

Tim bared his teeth. Hilary giggled. I looked out at the darkening sky. It was just possible to make out the outlines of trees, a shouldering mass of rhododendrons, distant railings, a field.

'Another night.' Tim drew the curtains. 'Come earlier next time.' He gave me a glass of red wine and clinked his Coke glass against it. 'Bottoms up.'

I took in the room, which was thickly carpeted with patterned rugs, some of them laid on top of each other, and hung with Impressionist prints – Degas's dancers, van Gogh's sunflowers, Renoir's drinkers, Monet's water lilies. Most striking of all was a large framed picture of a naked woman, inked in spare black brushstrokes over a wash of bruised blue. She was seated with her back to us, knees drawn up and head bowed, a pose that was contemplative rather than erotic, although the swell of her thigh and the slight spread of her buttocks hinted at a teasing lushness. But it was the curve of her back that drew my eye; the purity of the outline, the single, assured sweep of the brush. Tim must have noticed me staring at it, because he said, gruffly, 'Picasso's *Blue Nude*. One of my favourites. Before the bastard started giving women nostrils like horses.'

'There's another figure in it,' I said, looking more closely at the shadow of a head lower down, more bowed.

'It's the same one. He scratched out the first version and redrew her. The difference is, most artists cover their workings. Picasso isn't afraid to show you it's not his first attempt.'

We stared at the picture together. It was positioned centrally above the head of the biggest bed I had ever seen in my life. The bed, which took up at least two-thirds of the room, had more than a touch of the Hugh Hefners in its ostentatiousness and was draped in a rose-pink counterpane piled with gold velour cushions. I perched gingerly on the edge and sipped my wine. Tim sat down next to me. 'So you want to study philosophy.'

'Well, I —'

'Excellent choice.' I opened my mouth to protest that I hadn't made up my mind yet, but he held up a silencing hand. 'Seriously. Forget sociology. It's a load of self-indulgent claptrap. And it won't be of any use to you. Unless you want to be a social worker.' He spat out these last two words as if they tasted disgusting. Tom, who was talking to Hilary, caught this, but Tim ploughed on. 'Philosophy, on the other hand, will give you a grounding that can be applied to every area of your life. With a philosophy degree you can walk into any job confident that you have the mental equipment to tackle whatever challenges come your way.'

'If you can actually get a job,' Tom interjected. 'Employers think philosophers sit around contemplating their navels all day.'

'The practice of philosophy gives you a logical framework with which to view the world.' Tim's voice had acquired an edge. 'It gives you the tools you need for thinking, it gives you the basis for reasoning and discussion. And those are the essential requisites for any managerial position.'

'Being able to bullshit, that's all you need to make it in business. Bullshit. Philosophy.' Tom mimed weighing, holding out his palms. 'No, can't tell the difference. Still, you should know. Tim's a management consultant,' he added, for our benefit. He leaned towards me and hissed in a stage whisper, 'He's got a pinstriped suit in his wardrobe.'

'How does that work?' asked Hilary. 'Being a student and a businessman. It must be like having a split personality.'

'I'm a part-time director of an engineering company based in Stockon-on-Tees. I travel up there periodically, but most of the work I can do from home.' Tim got up stiffly. 'I don't find it conflicts at all. Another drink, girls?'

'Someone say drink?' Keith lurched into the room, looking more pop-eyed than when I'd last seen him, closely followed by Mike and another post-grad I hadn't met before called Alastair. Tim handed them tumblers of wine and someone put Steely Dan on and other people drifted in, attracted by the laughter and the noise. It was very late when Hilary and I finally staggered home, our ears ringing with music and our eyes blurry with booze. The next day, when I opened my bag, I found a slim volume of Bertrand Russell's *The Problems of Philosophy* inside it. A postcard had been tucked into the pages, with the inscription, 'Read this! Tim. P.S. I make no apologies for taking this liberty. It was good to see you again. Would you like to come to dinner next week? We can talk about Russell.' I turned the card over. It was a picture of the *Blue Nude.*

'Is there any knowledge in the world which is so certain that no reasonable man could doubt it?' asks Russell in his opening chapter on appearance and reality. He goes on to doubt the existence of the table in front of him, a concept I was having difficulty grasping, since the table in my student room bore seemingly irrefutable proof, not just of its own lively existence (coffee rings, biro scribbles, penknife gouges, cigarette burns), but of someone else's. My baby's. Two blazing blue lines in a circle on a small white stick were confirming what intuition had already told me, even if reason had tried to wriggle out of the truth. I was pregnant.

Dr Jameson, the wheezing physician at the university health centre, corroborated this with the weariness of one who had seen it far too many times before. I don't remember discussing my options with him, or being offered counselling, but I doubt it would have made any difference. I believed fervently in a woman's right to choose, and the alternative meant destroying any chance of getting a degree, and so compromising my entire future. That was how I saw it then, and although I don't hold such clear-cut views now, at the time it seemed the only thing to do. There was some comfort in finding out that I wasn't the only one – many of my girlfriends admitted privately to having had abortions – but no one talked about it publicly. Gonorrhoea, mastur-bation, being gay, these were all openly discussed. We were, after all, broad-minded, liberated, politically correct young people. We had renamed a student union building after Nelson Mandela and banned speakers from the National Front. But some prejudices run too deep. It was easy enough not to buy Cape grapes or to write protest letters to banks, but when it came to terminations, no amount of marching made the subject more accessible. Not, at least, when it was happening to you. Then abortions were no longer a cause to embrace but a desperate dilemma; the political made agonizingly personal.

I didn't expect Claude to want to take on any responsibility – things were on the wane between us – and although he offered to let me go and live with his family in the Caribbean, it might as well have been another planet as far as I was concerned. After some bitter recriminations, we parted. I was twenty years old, six weeks gone, and nine weeks into a disastrous first term. The festive season was in full swing, students were partying to Slade, and, true to form, everybody was having fun. Except me. I sat in my room eating salt-and-vinegar crisps and oranges, which was all that I could stomach, trying to make sense of 'the world of universals' in my philosophy book. I did not take up Tim's offer of dinner and sent some weak excuse via Mike. It seemed pointless to go and talk about the future when I wasn't even sure if I'd be back next year.

The train journey home to Oxford was three hours long and stuffy. My nausea was getting worse, exacerbated equally by the smell of stale coffee and the prospect of telling my parents about the pregnancy. I wasn't sure how they'd react: they were amazingly tolerant when, in my gap year, I'd rung them from Jersey to tell them I was engaged, even convert-ing the garage into a bedsit for my fiancé. They'd been equally supportive when we became disengaged and I decided to go to university after all, albeit two years late. Apart from that, I had rarely given them any trouble, even as an adolescent. Claire, my fifteen-year-old sister, was the one that gave them all the grief, skiving off school and playing loud music and throwing door-slamming tantrums. Debbie, my well-behaved middle sister, and I were the ones Mum set her standards by. 'Kate and Deb never did that,' she would hurl at Claire in menopausal fury. 'Why can't you be more like them?' Since I had two years on Deb, I was the one who, ultimately, was supposed to set an example. I was meant to be the trailblazer, the good sister showing the others how to act, and I had, winning awards and competitions at school, getting good grades, going to university. I had not let them down. Until now.

That afternoon, when I told them my news, Mum threw me out of the house.

CHAPTER THREE

'Did you have a good Christmas?' Tim asked.

I kept my eyes on a puckered balloon, which was hanging limply from a corner of the cornice. In the stark January light, Barton Place had a dusty sadness about it, the drab furniture mocked by an overlooked strand of tinsel draped around a picture. 'Not really.' I shrugged. 'Family hassles.'

'I'm sorry to hear that.' He paused, waiting for me to elaborate. When I didn't, he said, 'If it's any consolation, mine wasn't so hot, either. Had to sleep on the floor. Played merry hell with my back. I was stiff as a board by Boxing Day.'

'You weren't here?'

'Good God, no. I spent Christmas with my daughter and granddaughter. In a squat,' he added.

'*You* dossed down in a squat?'

'North London, Chalk Farm. Not a bad area.'

I started laughing. I couldn't help it. Tim was the last person I could imagine doing such a thing. He gave me a grin. 'It did my image the power of good. Even Tom's impressed. He dropped me off on the way to visit relatives. Now he's trying to convince Lindsay I'm some sort of ageing hippy.'

'Peace, man.' I made the V-sign, swaying in front of him. 'There's a CND march coming up soon. Why don't you join us? You know you want to.'

'Better red than dead? No, thank you.'

'I suppose growing your hair long would be a challenge, at your age.'

'Impudent young woman.' He swatted at my fluttering hands. 'I'm glad to see you've cheered up.'

'Yes.' I stopped messing about. It had been fun to forget, for a moment. Now I felt silly and frivolous. And guilty.

'So.' Tim cleared his throat. 'Are we going to have this philosophy tutorial, or do you want to tell me what happened at Christmas?' He looked at me kindly. I felt my throat closing up.

'I had an abortion,' I blurted, and burst into tears.

The operation had been painless – when I woke up, it was as if I'd just closed my eyes for a second and I couldn't believe they'd actually done it – but when a nice nurse brought me toast and Marmite and a cup of tea afterwards,

I'd felt a fraud. I didn't deserve sympathetic treatment. I spent most of Christmas with a friend who was non-judgemental and caring, and although I did go home and see my parents, something had changed. On the surface, we continued as normal, pulling crackers, drinking sherry and playing Consequences. My termination was not mentioned; neither was Mum's outburst. But underneath, she and I shared the same emotion: a visceral sense of betrayal.

Tim listened without comment while I blubbed my story out, then he said, 'Wait there,' and disappeared. He returned with a glass of something fizzing and put it in my hand. 'Brandy and dry ginger ale. Works wonders. Go on, get it down you.' I took a large gulp and felt it warm me instantly. A few more gulps and I had dried my eyes and recovered my composure. By the time I'd finished it, I was ready to face the world again. I was also slightly drunk. We started our lesson – Tim had offered to tutor me privately, to help me catch up with the rest of the philosophy class – but my mind was like cotton wool. Seeing that I was struggling to understand anything about Bertrand Russell, Tim put his book down. 'I think we could both do with some fresh air. Come and see my garden.'

'Your garden?' I assumed Tim was joking. The grounds at Barton Place were extensive and maintained by a gardener, Stuart. Tim led me round the corner of the house and along a path winding upwards, passing a bank of snowdrops. We walked through an archway into a undulating walled garden, which sprawled across the hillside covering at least half an acre. 'It's not much to look at now.' Tim gesticulated at the rotivated soil, which had been turned over like thick curls of chocolate. 'Stuart does the cultivating. I've got the south-facing wall.'

'What sort of things do you grow?'

'Sweet peas. That entire stretch of wall will be covered with them by June. I have to climb up a ladder to get them.'

'Just sweet peas? Nothing else?'

He shrugged. 'I put in a few runner beans. And tomatoes do well there. But mostly it's sweet peas. I've always been fond of them.' He bent from the hips and tugged at a stout milk thistle. At first it stuck fast in the cakey mud, but then it came out suddenly by the root, showering us both with dirt. Tim crumbled the reddish Devonshire soil between his fingertips, letting it rain down on his boots. 'I enjoy getting my hands dirty. I'd garden all the time if I could.' He fell silent, examining his grimy nails introspectively, then dusted his palms and stuffed his hands into the pockets of his windcheater. A magpie's raucous 'chack-chack' sounded from nearby. I looked around and saw it perched on top of the wall.

'My dad's a gardener, too,' I said, to keep the conversation going. 'Well, not for a living – he's a policeman – but he grows nearly all our own veg.'

'A policeman? Detective or uniform?'

'Uniform. He's a sergeant.'

'That would be Thames Valley, I presume?'

'Yes.'

'Ah.' Tim lapsed back into silence. My mouth was very dry – too much brandy, too early in the day – and suddenly I felt an overwhelming desire to sleep. 'I'd love a cup of tea,' I said.

'Earl Grey or Darjeeling?' he asked, starting to stride up the hill. 'There's Kenyan, if you need a kick-start. Or I could make coffee. I buy it freshly ground from the deli. It's really rather good.'

Studying philosophy entailed a whole new way of thinking. The language was so dense that I'd have to read almost every sentence twice to understand it, which meant my progress was painfully slow. I'd never been forced to use my brain in this way, and it was hard work; the slightest lapse in concentration meant that, by the end of a lecture, I'd be completely bamboozled, having got left behind halfway through. Tim said it was like performing mental gymnastics, and I was painfully aware that I had not yet acquired the necessary intellectual suppleness to do it. I hated formal logic more than statistics for biologists, and epistemology – the theory of knowledge – wasn't much better. The only course I enjoyed was ethics, in which we sometimes touched on real-life issues such as civil disobedience and animal rights, subjects close to my heart, but even then the language was dry and more often the talk was of the objectivity or otherwise of moral judgements. If it hadn't been for Tim, I might not have coped.

As it was, I came to depend increasingly on his unofficial

'tutorials', which usually included a good supper and a couple of glasses of Lambrusco, before rounding off the evening at the Cowley Bridge with the rest of the Barton Place regulars. It was at the pub that I really picked up philosophy: with three post-graduate philosophers in the group, discussions were often academic, but never (unlike my lectures) boring. Partly, this was due to the amount of beer that fuelled the debates, but it was also because they all disagreed violently with each other's standpoints. On one occasion, Tim, Nigel and Lindsay were slugging it out over the possibility, or otherwise, of being able to know someone else's pain. 'Even if it someone acts like they're in pain, there's always room for doubt,' Nigel said. 'Bloke might be making it up. "Ooh, me head."' He clutched his forehead dramatically. 'Always worked for me.'

'Not if he's got a gash on his skull and is lying in a pool of blood,' Lindsay pointed out. 'You couldn't doubt him then.'

'He wouldn't be able to speak then.'

'"Only of that which behaves like a human being can one say that it has pains",' Tim interrupted brusquely. 'Wittgenstein.' He folded his arms.

I absorbed this with incredulity. 'Animals don't behave like humans. Are you saying they can't feel pain? Because if so, that's stupid.'

Nigel and Lindsay exchanged grins. Tim looked as if his patience was being severely tried. 'Take a cow,' he said deliberately. 'A cow can't feel pain, like you or I, because *it has no concept of pain.* To have a concept of pain presupposes language. To quote Wittgenstein again, "If a lion could talk, we could not understand him." Or a cow, for that matter.' He drained his Coke glass.

I found this an outrageous statement. 'So if it's obviously hurt and bellowing in agony, that doesn't count?'

'Not in the context of this discussion. If you're going to do philosophy, Kate, you must learn to stick by the rules.' His tone was curt.

I got to my feet, a little unsteadily. 'Well, your rules stink. And philosophy's just a load of hot air.' I glowered at them all. 'I know about animals,' I added, with what I hoped was dignity. 'I used to have a Saturday job at a vet's.'

I was several hundred yards up the road, Nigel and Lindsay's guffaws still ringing in my ears, when I heard Tim's shout. I broke into a run. He was too far back to catch me up, and I sprinted all the way to my hall of residence at Duryard powered by righteous anger.

The next day, I returned from lectures to find a bouquet of freesias outside my door. 'Forgive me?' Tim had scrawled in his scratchy writing. I divided them between two milk bottles and sat down to do some reading, but it was hard to concentrate: their heavy scent filled the warm room and made me drowsy. I curled up on the bed and fell asleep, only to have a surreal, drugged dream about a laughing cow whose throat had been cut. Its significance disturbed me, until I realized it was the red cow from the processed cheese triangles. That night, I had pizza in the refectory and avoided the Cowley Bridge. Mum had written me a chatty letter, which I read while I ate. They were pleased I was getting help with my studies, she said. Tim sounded like a good friend. I folded up the letter.

I cancelled my next tutorial with Tim, mostly out of hurt pride. He was not, I justified to myself, my real tutor, anyway. A week later, I caught sight of him when I was drinking in the Ram one lunchtime with a group of friends, including Sally and her boyfriend, James. The two of them had just completed a hunger strike outside Exeter Cathedral to protest against Third World poverty and were unwisely drinking Guinness. After a pint, Sally had disappeared under the table and had had to be revived with a chip butty. Tim was standing in the corner, nursing a Coke, cigarette smoke trickling from his lips. He was there with Mike and Alastair, who were trying to perform some trick that involved setting light to Rizlas, and I was uncomfortably aware of him watching me. Eventually, he came over and asked, rather formally, how I was (I had not responded to the flowers), adding, 'We're having a bit of a do at our place tomorrow night, if you'd like to come. It would be good to see you again.' He took in Sally, who was slumped against my shoulder, and James in his tasselled Palestinian-style scarf. 'Bring your friends.' He strode away before I could respond.

'Finally,' slurred Sally.

Barton Place was an eighteenth-century house that had, judging by its elegant proportions and numerous chimneys, seen better days. Jane Austen was rumoured to have stayed there and it was said to have been the model for Barton Cottage in *Sense and Sensibility*. Sally and her friends, who were English students, had been suitably impressed when I regaled them with the house's history en route to the party, but the genteel image was exploded on arrival by a bank of blinding coloured lights set up in the window bay and 'Karma Chameleon' shaking the chandeliers. We found Tim hosting a second, more sedate party in his room. He was in jovial spirits and pecked me on the cheek, the first time he'd done such a thing. Sally, who was wearing a fifties-style floral dress, white stockings, long pink evening gloves and had a large bow tied on top of her head, made herself at home on the Hugh Hefner bed, curling her feet up underneath her. When I introduced her to Tim she raised one hand languidly and he laughed and kissed it. It wasn't long before they were sitting side by side arguing over Ezra Pound, a poet I knew nothing about.

I had been feeling a bit lost when Mike bounced over and hissed in my ear, 'I've got someone who wants to meet you.' He beckoned a foreign student over, announcing, 'Kate, this is Francisco. Francisco, Kate. Don't mention the Falklands. He's from Colombia.' Francisco had a head of thick black hair, a neat black beard and the profile of a conquistador. He smiled broadly.

'You support Argentina?' I asked, to provoke.

'Of course.' He shrugged. 'Everybody in South America supports Argentina. *Arriba* Galtieri!' He gave a power salute. From across the room I noticed Tim scowl. 'Tim Franklin.' Francisco started laughing. I realized he had done it to provoke, too. 'He does not like it when I say this. He is for Maggie Thatcher.' Francisco made a disgusted face.

'He'd be sending the task force right now if he had his way. Not that it'll happen,' I added. It was February, and although an armed invasion had been talked about, nobody thought it terribly likely. Francisco shook his head. 'It will happen. And all Colombians, they agree. Except Tim.'

'He's not Colombian.'

'He lived there, before.' Francisco regarded me, head cocked, as if this was something I ought to have known. 'Have you not heard him speaking Spanish? He's like one of my own. Eh, Tim?' Francisco rattled off something in Spanish which seemed to get Tim annoyed because he made a short, sharp retort that sounded rude even to a non-Spanish speaker like me. Francisco waved dismissively. 'Enough about politics. You like to dance?'

'Sure.'

He turned up the volume on the hi-fi and took me in his arms. It was good to be held again and I was enjoying myself, so when he went off to fetch us more drinks and did not return, I was crushed. I assumed he'd received a better offer downstairs, and Tim, who had just come back up from the kitchen with a litre of red and a stack of beer, confirmed this. 'That Francisco's a bastard. Always chasing skirt.' He poured me another drink. 'Don't worry about him. You're way out of his league.'

'Yeah, in the reject pile,' I said self-pityingly.

'Want me to hit him for you?' I managed a watery smile at the ridiculousness of this offer. Francisco was at least thirty years younger than Tim, and well built. 'I was brought up to defend a lady's honour,' he said gruffly. Suddenly, I wasn't sure whether he was joking or not. I looked at his broad knuckles. I had almost forgotten about Tim's past – since that first night at the pub it hadn't been mentioned – but now I realized he was serious. 'I don't think so.'

'All right.' He took the paper cup out of my hand and pulled me to my feet. 'Then have a dance with me. I promise not to embarrass you. And if that louse dares to show his face back in here, he'll have me to answer to.'

February became March, daffodils draped the campus in yellow blankets and, encouraged by the spring sunshine, the depression that I'd suffered from since the termination started to lift. I still had my bleak moments, and Tim, who had resumed his informal tutoring, was patient and support-ive, listening without criticism when I needed to talk. This usually involved me rambling incoherently late into the evening, tongue loosened by the large glasses of Southern Comfort and lemonade he used to pour me, and then staggering home on his arm. He seemed to know about depression – he called it 'black dog' – and I got the impression he had suffered from it himself. He never discussed his past, but the clues were obvious enough: there were shocking white scars on the insides of his wrists and across his throat, the tyre tracks left by crude stitches clearly visible. When I asked Mike about them, he said Tim had tried to kill himself in prison. The thought of Tim slitting his own throat was ghastly.

By this time Tim had become something of a father-figure to me and I came increasingly to rely on him. He was careful to stay within the boundaries of this relationship and I trusted him. But however indulgent he was of my emotional state, he was a hard taskmaster when it came to philosophy, ripping holes in my ill-thought-out arguments with steely logic. I chafed against it, but his hectoring worked. I began to get a handle on my coursework, even volunteering tentative answers in tutorials, and before long I had caught up with my classmates. I was just starting to relish, rather than dread, the daily mental challenges when something happened that threw me completely.

It was an ethics class, the first lesson after lunch, and I was feeling a little sleepy so I didn't hear Professor Atkinson when he asked me the question, only the, 'What do you think, Kate?' at the end. I must have looked dozy, because he repeated it, rather tersely. 'Is it right to say that a foetus is a person from conception? Or that it is only a *potential* person? And if that is the case, can one say when that potentiality becomes realized?'

'I – I – it's twenty-four weeks, sir. That's the cut-off point for an abortion.' I was blushing furiously. Why was he asking me? Did he know?

'Then are you saying it's not a person?'

I began to wish I could disappear. 'Before that, it's not viable. And if it's not viable, I don't see how it can be a person. I mean, late abortions are wrong, horrible, and nobody should have them unless it's for medical reasons, but if you have them early enough, before twelve weeks —'

'So you think it's OK to play God,' interrupted Thomas, who was predicted to get a first. 'Who are you to deny that foetus its right to live?' I could feel tears squeezing up under my lower lids.

Professor Atkinson glanced at me and said smoothly, 'Bringing God into the argument, even metaphorically, takes us away from the concept of personhood, Thomas, which is what I am trying to get you to define here. Let's try someone else: Sophie?' And I was left to breathe again. I did not contribute to the rest of the lesson. When we got up to go, Professor Atkinson asked me to wait behind, and enquired politely whether I was all right. I said yes, but I could tell he was not convinced. He cleared his throat. 'There are services, you know, for students who are finding – things – difficult.'

'I know.' I thought he was going to dismiss me, but he paused and added, 'Philosophy is the harshest mirror of humanity, more ruthless than religion. It's not God you have to face up to, it's yourself. No rush with the essay. Take your time.'

★

'If only you weren't a damned vegetarian. I could have made you pheasant in red wine.' Tim placed a mushroom omelette in front of me, which he'd served with sauté potatoes and petit pois. As omelettes went, it was a perfectly good one, folded over neatly and golden brown on the outside, but Tim clearly regarded it as an inferior dish. 'Pheasant in red wine,' he repeated. 'I've had a lot of success with that.' Lindsay, who had just entered the dining room, chortled in a knowing sort of way and sailed past us to the kitchen with a coffee mug.

'Don't pheasants have to be hung?' I asked, recalling memories of feathered corpses dangling from the scullery ceiling at my grandparents' farm.

'Very well hung,' Tim said.

From the kitchen there was a snort, followed by an explosion of laughter.

After our meal, we retired to Tim's room for our philosophy tutorial. He asked me about my day and I told him about how I'd almost broken down in ethics, showing him the essay question we'd been set. 'It's too personal. I just don't think I can do it.'

'Poor Kate. I didn't like to say anything, but that subject was bound to come up. Approach it logically. You have the tools at your disposal now. Argue the case. It's no good getting emotional. Take a step back and try to be objective.'

'Some people might say I've committed a murder. Are you telling me it's possible to be objective about that?' I retorted angrily. I hadn't intended it to come out that way, but he didn't appear discomfited.

'If abortion is murder, you'd have to build a hell of a lot more prisons. You had to make a choice, and it wasn't an easy one. You are not unique, so stop wallowing. And for God's sake, let the bloody man take some of the blame. You've got to move on, Kate, or you'll go mad.' This time, his sharpness didn't hurt so much; in fact, it helped. After the trauma of the termination and the schism it had created, I wanted to be looked after and at least Tim's peremptory parenting proved he cared.

We worked on the essay until 11.00 p.m., then he made us tea. 'It's getting late.' He stretched, yawning. 'I think I'll turn in soon.'

'Oh.' I wasn't quite sure how to interpret this. Tim always walked me home; it was part of the arrangement. 'Aren't you going to —?'

'No.' He busied himself clearing away books and papers. 'If you're going to keep me up until all hours, you might as well stop over. By the time I've walked you to Duryard and got back here, it'll be gone midnight, and I for one need my sleep.'

'But . . . where am I going sleep?' All the rooms were taken, as far as I knew.

'Here. You needn't worry, you'll be quite safe.' He opened a cupboard and pulled out a bolster, then he turned the sheets down and placed it in the middle of the bed, dividing it into two. 'See? I can't even roll into you.' He straightened up and looked me in the eye. 'It's this, or you can call a cab from downstairs. Your choice.'

I didn't have the money for a cab. I was tired, and the massive bed looked very tempting. 'OK, I'll stay.' I kept my jeans on, just in case, but Tim was as good as his word. After the initial weirdness wore off, I relaxed and fell asleep, strangely comforted by the sound of his regular breathing next to me.

This became a routine, and from then on I stayed over regularly, always with the bolster between us, though I soon abandoned the jeans. Tim never tried to touch or kiss me, for which I was initially grateful, but after a while I became rather offended by his lack of interest. Didn't he fancy me? Here I was, a pliant twenty-one-year-old girl, lying almost naked just a foot away from him – how could he not want me? I had seen him undressed and admired his toned torso. He had a six-pack that would have done credit to a man half his age. I imagined his muscular arms cradling my body and lay there aching for him to reach out. But he didn't.

Three weeks later, curiosity got the better of me and I climbed over the bolster.

CHAPTER FOUR

I was awoken the next morning by a rasping metallic noise and the sound of Tim grunting 'Oof.' The noise again, like the squeak of bedsprings, then a slap of release. 'Oof.' The rhythm was fast, and whatever he was doing obviously demanded a great deal of exertion because the grunts were getting louder and in between I could hear him straining, as if through gritted teeth, like he was pushing his body to the limit. The repetitions began to slow down and eventually he shouted, 'Argh', as if he was in pain, and something crashed to the floor. I leapt out of bed, sure Tim must have hurt himself, and padded out onto the landing, wrapping his silk robe around me. The door to the adjacent box room was open a crack. Inside, a muted red glow threw hellish shapes on the wall. 'Are you all right?'

'Don't come in!' he ordered, gasping for breath.

'Why? I just want to see if you're OK.'

'You could do yourself irreparable damage. Stay there.'

'Damage? What on earth are you doing?'

He sighed heavily. 'It's my morning routine. I'll be out in ten minutes. Go back to bed and I'll bring you some breakfast.' I did as I was told, stepping out of the robe and sliding between the now-cool sheets. I was intrigued to know what this 'routine' entailed, but there were no further clues: the tortuous noises had stopped and Tim's laboured breathing was no longer audible. I stretched out my legs, enjoying the feel of my body against the Egyptian cotton. Wriggling my toes, I reflected on the unexpected turn of events that had taken place the previous evening. I'd concluded, from the fact that Tim hadn't made a move on me, that he might be impotent. Fifty-six was pretty old in my book and I wasn't even sure that men of Tim's age were still capable of making love. How wrong I'd been.

The sex act itself had been unspectacular. What struck me most vividly was the smell of his skin – he used Old Spice, like my father, which was perversely reassuring – and the taste of his breath, a strange rhubarby flavour, fructose sweet, like overripe fruit on the point of decay. My fourth-form chemistry teacher had once let us sniff a test-tube of ethyl acetate, which smelt tantalizingly of sugar-crusted peardrops, and Tim's breath was similar. Its odour was strangely addictive: I wanted to drink in his juicy breath, and when his mouth closed over mine it was like feeding on nectar.

'Surprised?' he said afterwards, shooting me a sideways grin.

'Well . . .' I didn't like to say yes.

Tim laughed heartily. 'There's no need to pretend. I just didn't want to rush you. Not after what you've been through. First move had to come from you. And it did.' He propped himself up on one elbow and kissed me.

'You set me up!' I tried to sound offended, but it was a very poor performance.

'Hardly.'

'You made me stay over.'

'You wanted to.'

'I didn't know you were going to do – *that*.'

'Didn't you?' His hand stole down my stomach. He wanted, he said, to show me what else he could do.

From that night on, the charade of sleeping over for tutorials was dropped and I stayed over frequently, often tumbling into bed with Tim during the day as well, primed by a lunchtime Cinzano. The sex got better and better as we grew to know each other's bodies, and he had a way of kissing me that would make me go literally weak at the knees ('melty knees' he called it). I was circumspect about telling my parents how far things had progressed, but we made no attempt to hide our relationship from our friends. Reactions varied: Hilary was cautious, my schoolfriend Sharon was concerned and Sally was delighted and demanded another party.

Everyone at Barton Place was relaxed about me and Tim (although Lindsay pretended to be outraged whenever he caught us kissing), and I was grateful for their uncritical acceptance. I put this down to the general laissez-faire, so I was shocked when I discovered that I was far from the first: Tim had a reputation for dating undergraduates. He had not mentioned any former girfriends to me, and although Mike had said something about a girl a while back, I had never seen Tim with anyone. I thought nothing of it when he announced that he was inviting a friend to join us for dinner. It wasn't until I overheard Chris, Tom's fiancée, who was training to be a teacher at St Luke's, fuming, 'How *could* he!' that I got an inkling this was in any way unusual, but by then Ginni was sipping wine with us and Tim had presented me with a *fait accompli*, as always.

I thought Ginni was very nice. She was a second-year archaeology student and had long straight hair, which she had a tendency to hide behind, and a teasing way with Tim that suggested a certain familiarity. She had a passion for motorbikes and heavy metal music, and a particular passion for David Coverdale, the lead singer of Whitesnake – which explained Tim's eclectic tape collection – although she didn't dress like a rocker and was quite shy and serious. I didn't find out that she had been close to Tim until the next day, when Chris revealed that the whole of Barton Place had been agog at our little dinner party and no one could believe how civilized it had been. I went straight to Tim who admitted, unabashed, that he and Ginni had had a 'special' relationship but that it had come to a natural conclusion and she was happy for him. It became clear Ginni had been invited to give me her seal of approval, a sort of handing over the baton to the next girl. Luckily I'd passed, and she and I went on to become good friends, but she was a very private person and never discussed the nature of her relationship with Tim so I never knew how she really felt about him.

Prior to Ginni, there had been a girl from whom Tim appeared to have split acrimoniously, though he was vague about the details. From the comments dropped by Barton Place residents there had obviously been others, though none of them sounded particularly serious. Tim himself was fond of joking about his penchant for 'seventeen-year-old blonde Wellies', so as a twenty-one-year-old state-educated redhead I was the wrong hair colour, the wrong social class and already too old, but since Ginni was a brunette the same age as me and not at all posh, I discounted the teenage toff thing as a fantasy.

There was one person at Barton Place who was not pleased about my relationship with Tim. Francisco seemed to bear a grudge against him, and not just because of the Falklands. By this time, the Argentinians had landed on South Georgia and Francisco was stomping round the house with his brows knitted and had graffitied the communal phone box with political slogans. The exchanges between Francisco and Tim – those that were in English; the ones in Spanish sounded even more inflammatory – were aggressive and personal and although Francisco pretty much ignored me, I often caught him staring in a brooding fashion. When I mentioned this, Tim remarked airily, 'That's because I saw you first', and when I asked what that had to do with anything he said, 'Francisco and I had a discussion about you, the night of the party.'

'But I thought you said – I mean, he found someone else.'

'He may well have, for all I know.'

'Did he or didn't he?'

Tim sighed. 'I don't try to keep up with Francisco's love life. Far too complicated.'

'So why did he disappear so suddenly?'

'I told him to lay off. In the kitchen, when he went to get drinks.' Tim's expression was bland. 'We came to an understanding. Man to man.'

I stared at him, comprehension dawning. 'You didn't really hit him. Did you?' His lips flickered into the faintest of smiles. I didn't know whether to feel flattered or insulted.

After some badgering on my part, Tim revealed that his morning routine involved the use of a chest expander, which was a set of tightly coiled springs with handles at either end that you pulled apart as wide as your arms could go. He rounded off the session with ten minutes under an infra-red sun lamp, stretched out on the floor wearing nothing but his underpants and a pair of dark goggles to protect his eyes from the potentially damaging rays. This explained his tanned torso and impressive biceps – he had the top-heaviness typical of a body builder – though at the time I thought it was rather vain of him. I'd seen these contraptions advertised in the paper, cheesy before-and-after shots showing pigeon-chested wimps inflate into bulging musclemen, and found them comical. I used to tease Tim, comparing him with these oiled and rippling studs, until one morning he snapped, 'It's not what you think, Kate,' in a cold voice and I knew I'd hit a nerve. He put down my breakfast tray and yanked the heavy velvet curtains open aggressively. 'Why can't you get up before eleven? You know how much I detest coming into a darkened room.' Tim normally got up at 6.00 a.m. and pottered about, tending to his garden as soon as it was light and at other times disappearing on mystery missions. These he never spoke about, but he was often in a bad mood when he returned.

I struggled to sit up in bed, shielding my eyes from the sudden glare. He opened the window, letting in a blast of chilly air, and turned to go out. 'What do you mean?' I asked. Tim's face was in shadow, but I could see the set outline of his jaw. 'I'm sorry, I was only joking. Tell me.' I stretched out my arm, but he did not come over.

'It's the only way I can get mobile. If I didn't, I'd be a cripple.' I must have looked puzzled, because he sighed and explained wearily, 'It's pain relief management. I've got a degenerative disease that causes curvature of the spine. Ankylosing spondylitis. It's hereditary, my father had it.'

'What – what happened to him?' I felt afraid to ask.

He used to have to sleep in a plaster cast at night and strap on a steel waistcoat every morning, otherwise he'd have been stooped over. I realized I'd seen old men with this condition, shuffling along, their hands behind their backs and their necks stuck out like tortoises. 'It won't happen to me,' he said, reading my mind. 'I've had treatment to correct it. They fused my vertebrae into a solid rod. There's no way my spine can keel over. It's like having a steel poker up your back.'

'How long has it been like that?'

'A while.' He studied me, a frown creasing his forehead, as if weighing something up. 'It was pretty extreme treatment. They used radiation. It was when I was in prison.'

Apart from that first night at the Cowley Bridge, Tim had never mentioned his past, or prison. I was pierced by a sudden thrill. 'Go on.'

'After I'd finished the treatment they had me outside, stripped to the waist, digging ditches eight hours a day. Did it for months on end. Had to keep moving, or I'd seize up. It's the same now, only the pain's become more bearable. By the evening I'm shattered. When I wake up, I can hardly move. The exercises loosen me up and the Bullworker builds up the muscles that support the spinal column. The heat from the infra-red lamp penetrates the soft tissue and eases the pain. That's why I do it. Not because I don't want sand kicked in my face on the beach.'

'Oh my God.' I got out of bed and ran to give him a hug. He put his arms round me and I felt the tension flow out of his body. 'Why didn't you say?' I asked, touching his face. Tim's early rising – and early bedtime – had already become an issue, not just because he didn't like me lying in, but because I didn't want to go to bed at 10.00 p.m. when he did. I had assumed this was a generational thing. It hadn't crossed my mind that he might be suffering.

'You see me popping Distalgesic. What did you think they were for?' he said, but gently. This was true: by evening Tim would be knocking back prescription painkillers with his Coke.

'I thought you had arthritis or something,' I snuffled.

He sat me down on the bed and took my hand. 'I'm all right, Kate. It's under control. It doesn't stop me doing anything. Does it?'

'No,' I smiled, wiping my wet cheeks.

'In fact, once I've got the old machine up and running, I generally feel pretty good.'

He laid me back on the bed and I watched with a tingle of anticipation as he peeled off his shirt, waiting for the touch of his freshly showered skin and the friction of our bellies.

It was about this time that Tim acquired a car. He had an account with a local taxi firm and used trains for his occasional business trips, so when he rolled up to meet me on campus in a blue Austin Princess, I was taken aback.

'Hop in,' he said. 'I'm taking you for lunch.'

I stood there with my arms full of folders and philosophy books. 'I didn't know you could drive.'

'Of course I can. This is a company car.'

'Oh.' I got in. Tim braced his arms on the steering wheel and shot me a grin. He seemed boyishly excited. 'Ready?'

'Sure. Where are we going?'

'Exmouth. Blow the cobwebs away. It's less than half an hour. I'll have you back for afternoon lectures.' He turned the key. Fleetwood Mac came on the cassette player, full blast:

'Don't stop, thinking about tomorrow
Don't stop, it'll soon be here/It'll be, better than before,
Yesterday's gone, yesterday's gone . . .'

Music pumping, we took off down Queen's Drive, waving to a startled Sally and James as we passed. The volume was up too high to have a conversation, and in any case, Tim was deaf in his left ear (it was best to speak facing him, I'd learned), so I settled back into my seat, enjoying the ride. We drove through the picturesque little town of Topsham – once a Roman port – with its chocolate-box pubs, past the commando base at Lympstone and glimpsed the bizarre, sixteen-sided house A La Ronde as we approached Exmouth. Drawing into the resort, I felt my heart lift at the sight of the sea just as it had when I was holidaying as a child, a flashback to tedious car journeys, squabbling sisters and the lingering odour of travel sickness, instantly allevi-ated by Mum's sing-song announcement, 'We're he-re!'

It was still out of season and there were plenty of parking

spaces along the front, so we stopped opposite a pub, the Deer Leap, and went in. Tim ordered a lager for me and an orange juice for himself, making his usual disgruntled noises about vegetarians when I chose a jacket potato from the chalked-up menu. Afterwards we went for a stroll along the sand, walking hand in hand, all pretence at getting back in time for lectures forgotten. Exmouth Beach is two miles long and extends up to and around a rocky headland, beyond which there are sandy coves and a bird sanctuary. Here, the River Exe oozes into the sea through the narrow neck of the estuary, funnelled between Orcombe Point and the sandspit of Dawlish Warren, protruding across the opening like a valve. The day was dazzlingly bright, with the brashness of early spring, and I inhaled lungfuls of the ozoney air, cavorting and giggling as if it were laughing gas. We soon outstripped the tame beat of pensioners and dogwalkers and had the far end of the beach to ourselves. The tide was out, exposing a seaweed-strewn stretch of rockpools, and when Tim declined to explore them with me I set off by myself, slithering on bladderwrack as I scrabbled between the boulders. Preoccupied with scooping up shells and examining tiny crabs, I was surprised, when I looked back, to see Tim sitting on a rock, writing. I waved, but he seemed not to notice me. When I returned, pockets stuffed with trophies and trainers squelching with water, I asked him what he had been doing. 'Just scribbling,' he said. 'Jotting down a few impressions. That's all.'

We returned to the car, sea-blown and sticky, and Tim

bought a plastic bucket from a kiosk for my shells. 'Remind me to get you a shrimping net next time,' he joked. We ate ice creams sitting on the sea wall and got frozen, and then had scalding tea in a nearby café to warm ourselves up. Tim took my hand across the Formica table and squeezed my fingers. 'Better now?'

'They've gone all tingly.' He raised my fingers to his lips and blew on them gently. I noticed a middle-aged woman across the room lower her head and hiss something at her husband. 'Yes. Feel.' I touched Tim's cheek with the back of my hand. He turned the palm over and kissed it, gazing into my eyes with a look so intense it seemed almost sad. 'What are you thinking?'

'You're so vivid. So alive. So —'

There was a sharp scraping noise of a chair being pushed back and the woman swept past, pausing briefly to spit, 'You shouldn't be allowed' at Tim before exiting noisily. Her husband gave him an apologetic shrug and followed.

We were left with the steamed-up café to ourselves, cocooned in a haze of chip fat and burnt toast, but it could have been the Ritz as far as I was concerned. 'Don't change,' Tim said, getting to his feet and dropping a kiss on the top of my head. We walked to the car, arm in arm, and then I spoiled our perfect day.

'Why did they give you this car now, and not before?'

'Someone else was using it.'

'It would have saved you all that waiting about for taxis. Having a car's much more convenient.'

'I'm well aware of that.'

'You're a director, aren't you? You should have insisted. All those business trips. You're entitled.'

He sighed heavily. 'There wouldn't have been any point.'

'Why not?'

'I couldn't drive then.'

'So when did you learn?' I asked, confused. Was that what Tim's mysterious early-morning disappearances had been about?

He looked at me sharply. 'Get in the car.' I got in and buckled my seatbelt, wary of his change of tone. He sat staring straight ahead, making no attempt to start the engine. Finally, he said, 'I couldn't drive because I was banned.' He lit a Styvesant and rolled down the window. I felt even more confused. 'Was it something to do with you being a – a lifer?'

He almost smiled at this. 'No. It's because I was over the limit.'

'But you don't drink,' I said, without thinking.

He exhaled smoke through his nostrils. 'I do drink, Kate. I'm an alcoholic. I don't touch it now. I can't. If I drink, I'd wind up in hospital. Probably finish me off.' I looked at him, aghast. 'It's not cirrhosis,' he added, catching my expression. 'I take these tablets. Antabuse. If you drink on Antabuse, you're violently sick. They set off a reaction. It's aversion therapy. Pretty nasty, actually. They made me do it once. Once was enough.' He took another drag of his cigarette. We watched the smoke drift out of the half-opened window. I said nothing. No one in my family drank – my parents were pretty much teetotal – and I had no experience of anything like this.

'Isn't it difficult for you, with all of us getting pissed?' I asked, thinking of Tim's parties and our boozy sessions in the Cowley Bridge. 'I could stop drinking, when I'm with you,' I added heroically.

Tim flicked ash at a seagull. 'Kate, you're young. I like to see you enjoying yourself. It doesn't bother me. I don't crave alcohol. Ninety-nine per cent of the time I don't even think about having a drink. I'm what's known as an "episodic" alcoholic. Episodics only drink in response to a specific trigger. Otherwise, they're OK.' He ground the butt in the ashtray and started the car. 'Ready? Let's go.'

If Tim said something wasn't a problem, I believed him. He had an authoritative manner and presented things with a certainty that inspired confidence. I had no reason not to believe him about the drinking, or anything else he told me: he had not, in the several months I'd known him, touched a drop of alcohol and his conduct towards me had been impeccable. He had kept me sane when I was falling to pieces, helped me to keep my place at university and given me back some of the self-esteem I had lost. I trusted him. He was older and wiser than me and had seen the world, including 'things that I hope you'll never see'. His experience so obviously outweighed mine that it was impossible to challenge him. Moreover, he was sweetly

70

devoted, and I knew he had my best interests at heart. Why would I not trust him?

It wasn't just me; Tim was liked and respected by the students at Barton Place and was equally popular with my peers. University life, with its easy acceptance and liberal attitudes, had given Tim a niche that he undeniably exploited, but nobody deferred to him because of his former notoriety. He was valued because he'd proved himself, as a person and as a friend. His generosity with booze and money undoubtedly helped, and some of his entourage were freeloaders, but he had a core of real friends – Tom and Chris, Lindsay, Nigel, Mike, Ginni – who accepted him as he was and remained loyal. Tellingly, he had no friends outside his circle at Exeter.

Of his family, Tim spoke very little. He had been divorced from his wife Rosemary for many years and had two daughters, only one of whom, Belinda, he had any contact with. He also had a sister, Antonia, who was a social worker and lived in north Cornwall with her painter husband, Leo. Tim seemed ambivalent towards Antonia; he told me she had helped him out on his release from prison, but their relationship was strained and he maintained that she disapproved of him.

I felt angry that Tim's family didn't seem to be more supportive of him. As far as I was concerned, he had paid – overpaid – his debt to society for a death that, in any case, wasn't really his fault. I didn't know to what extent their lives had been affected by what had happened, but I thought that if Tim could make a new life for himself, the least they could do was accept that and help him. What mattered now was the future, not the past, and I for one refused to dwell on his crime. That was what I told myself, and during my waking hours I succeeded mostly in doing it, but night-time was a different story. When Tim switched off the light, he would recite, 'Night-night, sleep tight, don't let the booeys bite', but it wasn't the mythical booeys, whatever they were (I imagined viscous darting creatures like vampire bats, only smaller), that ravaged my sleep. It was my own fear of Tim.

However much I believed Tim's assurances of my safety, I couldn't repress my doubts in my dreams. Once we'd begun sleeping together regularly, my subconscious ran amok, screening terrifying nightmares of massacre and murder that continued unremittingly, dream after dream, night after night. It was like being forced to watch back-to-back slasher movies without being able to look away, only it was myself I was watching being stalked and stabbed, myself being chased or gunned down or blown up. I would wake trying to scream, emitting instead a dry-mouthed squeak, my body flooded with adrenaline and my heart hammering fit to burst. My attacker was never Tim himself, not obviously, anyway; more often than not he was not even visible, but rather an evil presence. In one particularly visceral nightmare – set in a large, many-roomed house rather like Barton Place – the killer forced me to betray my friends and members of my family, whom he murdered in cold blood, and then tried to use me to lure Tim into the house. I outsmarted him, using a secret code I knew Tim would recognize, but he caught me and punished me by making me watch as he mutilated a woman. I was to be next, he said, strapping her to a torture table and cutting off parts of her with a long, curved knife, first the tip of a finger and then a hand and then a foot. She didn't struggle or scream; the only sound was the grisly tearing of flesh, like the splitting of an animal carcass. Somehow, I managed to escape and armed police appeared, alerted by Tim, so in this instance he was the hero, although usually he did not figure at all.

I chronicled this dream in my diary because it disturbed me so deeply, and when I described its grotesque imagery to Tim the next morning he looked shaken, as if he'd seen a ghost, and his hand trembled as he poured our tea. My dreams had echoed some curious real-life coincidences of late: a few nights earlier, I'd dreamt about finding the body of an man on the stairs who'd been electrocuted by an electric socket. The very next day I'd switched on a light and the bulb had exploded with a bang so loud that I almost leapt out of my skin. I was convinced I'd been electrocuted and by the time Tim came running I was white and faint and had to be revived with brandy. It turned out all the fuses in the room had blown, so it must have been quite a power surge, though I think the shock was emotional rather than literal. I'd also had an odd dream about naked cyclists, which probably has some Freudian significance. The day after, I read in a newspaper that eighteen naked Friends of the Earth had cycled to Land's End.

Tim's solution to my nightmares was to take me to the doctor, who prescribed sleeping pills. Doc Jameson came up with some psychobabble about me having a subconscious need to experience violence based on the fact that I hated horror movies (I had only ever dared to watch *Carrie*, and that was through my fingers). He didn't know I was sleeping with a lifer and I didn't feel able to tell him, but Tim and I both knew the real reason for my terrors. That night, when we snuggled down under the sheets and had settled into our sleeping position, his knees tucked behind mine and his arms wrapped around me – 'spoons', he called it – he asked if I felt physically threatened by him. 'Of course not,' I said, entwining my fingers with his, but it wasn't entirely true. He was a powerfully built man, and I knew he had a temper, although, apart from a few snappish remarks, it had not been directed at me. He was quick to anger; I had sensed it in the tautness of his lips and the tension in his neck, but mostly it was damped down, barely smouldering, and I believed him when he said he'd never hurt me. Still, I had read Carl Jung, I knew my dreams were trying to tell me something. There was no right time, no right place to ask the question. I drew a deep breath. 'Tim. There's something we've never talked about . . .' I felt his arms tensing.

'I can't, Kate.' His voice caught, as if he was about to break down. 'I'm sorry, darling. I feel responsible for your nightmares. I *know* I'm responsible. But you've got nothing to fear from me. Absolutely nothing.'

'But . . . you – you did kill someone. And you've never told me how it happened. And I suppose, underneath, that's what's causing these awful dreams. It's because I don't know . . .'

'I've told you it was an accident.' He paused. 'That's all I can tell you.'

'But why?'

Another, longer pause. Then: 'Because I made a promise.'

'A promise? To who? I don't understand.'

He sighed. 'I can't say. Don't press me, Kate, because I'm not going to reveal any more. All I can tell you is this: I lied to protect someone.'

'In court?' He was silent. I wriggled round to face him. It was impossible to make out his expression in the dark. He remained silent. 'Tim' I breathed, shocked, 'You can't just come out with that and not explain.'

'No, you're right,' he said gruffly. 'I shouldn't have. It's not something I've told anyone else, and to put that on you –' He sighed again, wearily. 'I only told you because I don't want you to be frightened of me. It tears me up, hearing about these nightmares of yours. I want you to know that I would rather die than harm you.' His fingers gripped mine. 'If I should so much as touch one hair of your head . . .' He buried his lips in my neck.

'You told me. You'd go straight back inside.'

'I'd finish myself off properly. Because I could never live with that.' There was wetness on my shoulder.

His tears made me cry, too. I hugged him hard. 'Don't talk like that. I don't ever want to hear you say that stuff.'

Suddenly it was as if we were at the edge of a yawning black hole, a pit into which at any second we might topple in to. We lay close, without speaking, and then finally he said, 'When I did it before, I had already been released on licence and they yanked me back inside again. I stole a Stanley knife from the prison workshop because I had no hope left. I didn't want to face another day, but they stitched me up and forced me to carry on. And now I'm happy they did because you've given my life a quality I never thought I would find again. You've made me glad to greet each new dawn. I'm not going to lose you.' We made love after that, and it was the most intense emotional connection I'd ever felt with anyone. Still Tim's unflinching attitude towards death haunted me. I didn't want that overwhelming responsibility for someone's life; it was too much, I wasn't worth it.

The next day we were both fragile and at bedtime I took a sleeping pill and slept dreamlessly. I surfaced late, thick-headed and groggy, groping my way back to consciousness like a half-drowned swimmer being hauled out of the water. After a few nights of this the incident faded and I never did ask Tim why he had been recalled to prison, what the trigger was that had plunged him into suicidal despair. I had just about convinced myself that I had been melodramatic about the whole thing when something unexpected brought it all back. I had borrowed an A4 pad of Tim's for taking lecture notes, and when I opened it there was a piece of folded paper tucked inside. I smoothed it out and discovered that it was a poem, written in Tim's familiar stiff italics. It was untitled, and had presumably been composed while I'd been exploring the rockpools at Exmouth:

We sit, among the smooth grey hides
Of sea rocks. Your young sensitivity,
Half-formed, suffers the delight of sun
And salt, the limitless unknown horizon.

Mine, full flat, contained by the past
Accepts the stones which will outlast
My sight, my presence.

We inhabit separate continua. Starting back,
Our steps print the shingle where tide
Moves to erase our brief conjunction.

I accept my fortune, the lack of mystery,
The sun at my back, the end, certain.

And after that, I knew. I knew that this relationship, wherever it was going, would be of a different nature from anything I had ever experienced before.

CHAPTER FIVE

At first, I thought I must have been in an accident. My whole body ached, especially my legs, and my feet were throbbing as if they'd taken especially severe punishment. But worst of all was my head. Even tilting it to the side was painful, as though my brain was rolling around loose in my skull like a bowling ball. I tried to remember what I'd done the night before. I had vague recollections of being in the Ram and getting invited to a party and drinking – oh no – tequila slammers. I'd been celebrating something. What was it? There had been joints going round; I remembered the throat-burning pull, the sudden, silly elevation, somebody's smoky breath. Who had I kissed? Not Tim, he definitely wasn't there. I reached out tenatively to check the space next to me and touched a slimy wet patch. When I opened my eyes I discovered that I was alone in my room in my hall of residence with my hand in a puddle of sick.

The next thing I discovered, once I'd groped my way to the basin and downed three toothmugs of water, was an envelope with my name on it, which had been slid under my door along with some holiday brochures. I bent down to pick them up, supporting my head with one hand, and returned to the bed, chucking a towel over the soiled sheets. Inside the envelope was a letter from Tim. I felt an immediate pang of alarm (had he found me out?), and then guilt (when I realized what he was offering), as I read its contents:

Barton Place
Sunday p.m.

Kate Dear,

Many congratulations on your election. Mike told me that he had met you in the Ram and that you were over the moon about it – with reason! Also that you were coming up here on Monday (tomorrow) evening. I can hardly wait. I've missed you a great deal in the last week. I have an awful lot to tell you (and you me). I got stuck for an extra day up North, as Mike probably told you. An awful bore, but unavoidable. One thing I did get fixed, in between incredibly stuffy board meetings, was that I won't be needed for more meetings until 20 April, and that I can therefore go off on holiday during the Easter break. I have gone and got all sorts of seductive travel brochures with gorgeous pictures of the sunny Canary Islands. Please, dear Kate, give us this time together and come with me. Please. Please! I admit to bringing unfair influence to bear on you, but please . . .

I saw your protest march on TV. Were you one of the girls wearing masks of Mrs T?!

You matter to me. I care for you.

Love, Tim.

P.S. I've been gardening all afternoon.

Now it all came back to me. I'd been on a CND march in central London – hence the aching feet – and a group of us had bonded on the coach on the way back, aided by cans of beer and Billy Bragg songs. We'd managed to catch last orders in the Ram, which was when I'd found out from the noticeboard that I'd been successfully elected to the Guild of Students as a council member. The fact that this was probably unopposed didn't concern me. I felt a moral obligation to stand because I wanted to make a difference, and now I could. My planned career as an environmentalist had fallen through and doing philosophy had forced me to reject religion on grounds of logic, so I'd directed my crusade to politics. (I still have the flier I wrote. It is utterly cringe-making: 'This is not an ego-advert, it's a request that you make the not-too-momentous decision to VOTE FOR ME!') Exeter University wasn't exactly a political hotbed; the Conservative Association had far more members than the various left-wing groups, but Tory students didn't agitate (it was more of a drinking club) so the Guild was staunchly socialist. Tim thought it was a Marxist cabal, so it was generous of him to congratulate me, and to acknowledge the CND march, any mention of which would normally have him frothing with rage.

I leafed through the holiday brochures, which were indeed seductive with their golden beaches and azure seas and page upon page of swimming pools and tanned bodies stretched out in the sun. But Easter! I should be revising hard for the sessional exams, which I had to pass to get through to the second year. And yet . . . I re-read Tim's letter, still clutching my pounding head. I'd only ever been abroad once before, and that was to Canada, to visit an auntie. The thought of a holiday in the Canaries was so tempting, and I could always revise by the pool. I was too fair-skinned to lie about on sunloungers, anyway. Besides, how could I turn down Tim's generous offer? He was literally begging me to go with him. I considered his sign-off line: 'You matter to me. I care for you.' He hadn't actually said he loved me yet. Perhaps he didn't think it appropriate. Or perhaps it wasn't true. But somehow I doubted that. As for me, I was beginning to feel something deeper than girlish infatuation, and I decided there and then to stop messing about with boys. If Tim wanted me as his partner, then I was ready for it, too.

My first sight of the Hotel Buena Ventura in Gran Canaria's Playa del Ingles did not impress me. After a hot, dusty taxi ride – during which Tim conversed with the driver in voluble Spanish – we drew up outside what looked like two tower blocks with balconies set at right angles to each other. The driver, who had a creased face and dark circles of sweat under his armpits, hauled our cases out of the boot and mopped his brow. '*Esta usted Cubano?*' he asked Tim, who threw back his head and laughed. '*No, Inglese.*' There followed an exchange I couldn't understand, although the driver appeared to be emphasizing something by much spitting, and then Tim slapped him on the back, gave him a tip and bade him a cheerful '*Adios*'.

'What was that all about?' I asked, as Tim beckoned a porter.

'He thought I was Cuban, because of my accent. Listen carefully to the Spanish they speak here. It's Castilian, European Spanish. You can tell because they pronounce the *theta.*'

'The what?'

'It's the way they pronounce "c" with a "th". As in grah-*thy*-ahss.' He pronounced the word phonetically.

'That's "thank you". But you don't say it like that.'

He shrugged. 'They don't use the *theta* in South America. I was brought up in Colombia. The accent's similiar.' We followed the heavily laden porter into the vast, air-conditioned lobby, which had a rock formation and a trickling waterfall as its centrepiece. 'Franklin,' Tim announced, slapping his passport down on the reception desk.

The receptionist, an older man with a head of thick grey hair and a bow tie, checked the register. 'Twin room. *Si?*'

'No. *Hemos reservado una doble.*' Tim sounded stern.

The receptionist eyed me curiously. '*Lo siento, Señor Franklin,*' he said, adding in English, presumably for my benefit, 'but there has been a mistake. All the double rooms are taken.' Tim's colour darkened and he barked something at the man, who looked unhappy and said he was afraid he could do nothing to change the situation. Would a fruit basket compensate us for the inconvenience? Tim exploded into another torrent of Spanish, thumping the desk for emphasis. The receptionist continued to counter stubbornly in English. I began to feel a little embarrassed. A queue was building up behind us and, judging by the looks on their faces, everyone else had become interested in our sleeping arrangements. Finally, some sort of deal was agreed which involved us switching rooms midweek and being compensated with a dinner and wine.

'*Bueno,*' Tim said stiffly. '*Gracias.*'

The receptionist handed Tim a key, poker-faced. '*Numero* 569. Enjoy your stay.'

The room was cool and dark, with a tiled floor and heavy wooden furniture. It smelt of polish and lemons and something faintly musty, which I put down to a plug-in device designed to deter mosquitoes. Tim dismissed the porter and opened the curtains, letting in a broad swathe of afternoon sun. We stepped out onto the balcony and gazed down at the S-shaped pool. There was an open-air bar below us with a thatched roof and tables, and sunloungers lined the sides of the pool. The grounds had been landscaped with pine trees and shrubs and conical-shaped palms sprouting fronds like so many arms, but the grass between them was parched brown and the vista – more high-rise hotels, grouped like stacks of Lego – was deeply depressing. We could not see the sea.

'Not bad, I suppose, for the price,' Tim said gallantly. 'But we've got to sort out this bed lark.' He opened his suitcase and burrowed through his clothes, producing a tie, after which he pushed the two single beds together and knotted them at the headboard. 'Old school would be proud.' He rubbed his hands together. 'Needs securing at the feet, though. Pity I didn't bring my regimental tie, too.'

'Fancy you keeping those,' I said. I peered at the tie. It had some sort of crest on it. 'Which school did you go to?'

'Tonbridge. The oldest and stickiest public school in the country.' He grimaced. 'Can't say I've got fond memories of it.'

'So how long did you live in Colombia?' I asked, confused. 'Was that before or after you went to England?'

'My father worked for Shell. We lived all over the place. Typical ex-pats.' He waved his hand airily. 'Come on, let's go down to the pool. I fancy a cold drink, don't you?'

Most of the hotel guests were German. This wouldn't have been a problem had not one of them – a portly man whose oiled brown belly hung out over his obscenely small swimming trunks – caught our accents and turned to Tim with a smug, 'So, the English are at war, *ja*?' He laughed, as if he found the prospect amusing, and the other sunburned Germans at the bar joined in too. I saw a muscle tick in Tim's jaw. The task force had set sail for the Falklands the day before and he was frustrated because he wouldn't be able to keep abreast of the news – all the English papers were two days old – and tired after the flight. To have this man crowing about it was the last straw.

'At least,' he replied stiffly, '*we* didn't start it. Moreover, we know we can finish the job. The British armed forces have a reputation for seeing things through. As your countrymen will recall,' he took in the rest of the group, 'even if you've conveniently forgotten it.' He gave him a cold stare. The man looked taken aback. Tim ignored him and ordered our drinks. It was only when we sat down at a table that I realized he'd bought us two beers. I watched as Tim poured the chilled bottles of Amstel, taking his time and tilting the tall glasses so as not to get too much head. He held his up, examining it minutely – the golden liquid, the pinprick bubbles, the cloudiness of the cold glass – then brought it to his lips.

'What about those pills you're taking? Doesn't alcohol make you ill?' I asked in a panic, wondering how I'd minister to him if he got really sick.

Tim took a swallow and gave a satisfied sigh. 'I've come off them.'

'But . . .'

He looked faintly annoyed. 'It's just temporary, while we're on holiday. I need a break, Kate. Like I told you,' he took another draught, 'I'm not an alcoholic, as such. I'm an episodic. There's a world of difference. I can control what I'm drinking.' He caught my worried face and patted my arm. 'Relax. We're here to enjoy ourselves. So long as that lot keep out of my way.' He shot a dark glance at the Germans, who had gone back to basting themselves in the sun. One of them, a woman, got up from her recliner and walked past us, topless. I looked at her incredulously. Apparently, topless sunbathing was pretty much de rigueur — though I wasn't going to do it — but to sashay through the bar area almost naked . . . She was heavily built, with pendulous breasts, big hips and crinkly cellulite on the backs of her legs, but she obviously thought she looked good because she flicked her hair and strolled over to the bar, flopping her breasts down on the counter. The barman, to his credit, did not turn a hair, but I was horrified. Tim followed my gaze and grinned. 'You don't get many of those to the pound.'

'Tim!'

'Not my style.' He winked at me and dug out his wallet, peeling off a handful of notes. 'I see the hotel has a gift shop. Buy yourself a bikini.'

'I don't want one. I'm not doing that.'

'Rubbish. You've got a gorgeous body. Do you know who you look like naked? The *Maja Desnuda*. It's a painting by Goya,' he added, seeing I didn't follow. 'Very famous nude. Identical breasts. You'll outshine the lot of 'em.' He signalled a waiter, pointing at his beer bottle and holding up two fingers. The waiter nodded.

'I've hardly started mine yet,' I said, but he ignored me. I stood up, feeling slightly woozy with the heat. 'I think I'll get a hat, anyway.'

'Bikini. I insist.' He pulled me deftly onto his knee and kissed me. I couldn't see his eyes behind his dark glasses but he seemed different; happy and carefree and somehow more at home. 'Get some Ambre Solaire too,' he added, slapping my bottom playfully. 'I shall look forward to rubbing that in.'

There is a photograph of Tim stretched out in the sun, a copy of Hamlyn's *Theory of Knowledge* in his lap, and there are more of me sitting in the shade with *Modern Moral Philosophy* propped up against a sugar shaker, so I must have got some work done, though I don't think it was very much. I would manage an hour or two in the morning and then have a swim, and after that we would have lunch followed by a siesta, because it was too hot to do anything else except have snoozy sex and sleep. At least, I slept, usually until four or five, and Tim sat out on the balcony, reading and drinking Fundador, a cheap Spanish brandy that he mixed with 7-Up. He drank steadily throughout the day: in the mornings he drank Cuba Libres – Bacardi and coke – behind an out-of-date *Daily Telegraph* (there's another photo of him shaking his fist in mock rage at some provocative story), and in the evening we shared a bottle of wine over dinner, so I never really knew how much he was consuming. He would become increasingly cantankerous as the night wore on and because I got drunk very easily we started to row, usually over my lack of knowledge or insight or an opinion I couldn't substantiate – something would spark it, I was never sure what – and he would be cruel and cutting and ruthless. Alcohol invoked a Jekyll and Hyde personality in Tim that I found hard to cope with. I didn't know who he was any more, and one terrible, memorable night he got so drunk that he didn't know who I was, either.

I had picked up a few words of Spanish and was very hot with my '*Buenos días*' and '*Buenas noches*' and '*Por favor*' but beyond a smattering from the Berlitz guide I was stumped if anyone actually answered one of my halting questions. I could read a menu and had learned by heart Tim's recitation, '*La senorita no come ni carne, ni pollo, ni pescado*' ('The young lady doesn't eat meat, chicken or fish'), a rollcall that didn't prevent the waiters from suggesting a seafood risotto or a nice piece of veal, vegetarianism being an alien concept to them. I had acquired one piece of colloquial Spanish – Tim had told me how to say 'Fuck off', in case I was bothered by any of the lads roaring past the mini-market on their polluting mopeds – but fortunately I had not had to use it. I had by then bought a bikini and got used to sunbathing topless by the pool, and it was a measure of my new-found self-confidence that the only time we trekked down to the beach, I was more concerned about how to ask the male attendant the price of the sunloungers than I was by the fact that my breasts were bare.

Tim had practically gone native and would chatter away in Spanish with everyone from the maitre d' to the pool cleaner, repeating '*claro, claro*' ('in agreement') and waving his arms expansively. Given the amount of alcohol that was constantly circulating in his bloodstream he had the sense not to hire a car, but he still shouted '*Idiota!*' at reckless drivers in the manner of a hot-tempered taxi driver. He had even made friends with the receptionist, who now treated Tim with respect for his '*machismo*' and made envious comparisons with his own situation ('I have a wife and eight children – we have no TV, you see'). Watching Tim converse with all these people, I felt rather left out. I hadn't made any friends myself; we were such an odd couple, with the age difference and our philosophy books, and the other hotel guests didn't know what to make of us. Most of the time I didn't mind – when Tim was on form he was good company – but occasionally I longed to be with Sally or Hilary, doing girly things and having fun without the stress of tiptoeing around Tim when he'd been at the booze.

It happened on the penultimate night of our holiday. Tim had been drinking since the morning, becoming increasingly taciturn. He seemed to be brooding about something, but when I asked him what the matter was he snapped, 'I'm fine,' in a tone that dared me to challenge him. I went for a swim, ducking under the low concrete footbridge and continuing through the narrow channel, which was dark, like a sea cavern, emerging in the pool on the other side of the hotel. I got out and posed on the side for a while in my leopard-print swimsuit (for some reason it felt wrong to swim topless) but I could sense Tim's impatience, even with a hotel block between us, and after five minutes I returned. Tim gave me a look over the *Telegraph*, ordered two coffees and a brandy on the side, gave the paper a shake and went back to his reading. When the brandy came, he drank it in three gulps. I gathered up my philosophy notes and retreated to the shade. It was best to be out of range when Tim was drinking this much. Despite his line about being an episodic alcoholic – as if this was more respectable than the regular sort – it was plain to me that he didn't need an incident to trigger his drinking. He was clever at constructing a cover of 'social drinking', but even I, trusting as I was, was beginning to see through it.

That afternoon Tim did not make love to me. I had drunk three glasses of rosé wine with lunch – he had insisted on a bottle, but then stuck to rum and Coke so I'd had most of it – and staggered up to the room to sleep it off. When I awoke, sweaty and befuddled, it was almost six o'clock. I expected to find Tim on the balcony, as usual, but he wasn't there. I showered and dressed with a feeling of unease. He was not in the bar or by the pool, and when I asked at reception I was told that he'd ordered a taxi three hours ago and they hadn't seen him since. I waited in the lobby, trying to work out what to do if he didn't appear soon and imagining the worst. Ten minutes later he strolled into the hotel with a bag under his arm. He seemed surprised to see me. 'Kate. You're up.'

'Where have you been?' I hugged him tight. 'I was worried about you.'

'Worried? No need for that. I went into town. I've been gift shopping.' He thrust the bag at me. Inside, there was a jet-and-pearl necklace in a blue velvet case. I let out a gasp. 'Tim, it's beautiful!'

He grinned. 'You deserve it.'

'I thought . . . I thought you'd gone.'

'Gone? Gone where? You thought I'd left you?'

'No, of course not. I just felt a bit panicked because you didn't leave a note.'

'I did leave a note. It was propped up against the camera. You didn't look properly.' He sighed. 'Honestly, Kate, you're hopeless.'

'I'm sorry,' I said lamely.

'Wait here. I'll go and get changed.' He turned on his heel abruptly, the glimmerings of a good mood gone again in an instant.

It was not an auspicious start to the evening and it got worse. Over dinner, when I asked him what else he'd done in town, he accused me of interrogating him, and when I pointed out that he could have told me of his plans beforehand, he said, 'You're not my minder, Kate.' He added nastily, 'If I wanted to be nagged, I'd have got myself a wife.' After that, I decided the best tactic was to shut up and let him make the conversation, but this only provoked him more. I was 'giving him the silent treatment' and being 'childish' and 'moody'.

I felt tears pricking at my eyelids and swallowed hard. 'I don't know what you want from me any more.'

He stared at me coldly. 'Neither do I when you're like this. For God's sake, don't start getting hysterical. Jesus Christ almighty,' as I started crying, 'you're so bloody depressing to be around.'

I got up from the table, my face awash, and blundered straight into a waiter with an armful of dirty dishes. There was a resounding crash, followed by several seconds of audible silence, then a group of pissed-up young men started to cheer and clap. '*Perdóneme*,' I stuttered, which was hardly sufficient under the circumstances, and fled.

I had nowhere to go but our room and waited on the balcony, knowing Tim would be along soon and hoping that the proximity of people on other balconies would prevent him shouting at me. Sure enough, the door burst open a few minutes later. I heard Tim bang into something and curse. This was followed by a muffled 'pop' and furious fizzing, which prompted more curses – he must have shaken the can of 7-Up – and the sound of a drink being poured. I sat on a cane chair, trying to appear composed, although my heart was beating fast. For the first time I felt afraid. He was muttering something in Spanish and sounded slightly unhinged. I looked around the balcony for something to defend myself with, but there was nothing except another cane chair and a low table with an empty glass on it. Suddenly, the curtain was pushed aside and Tim's shadow fell over me. He was breathing heavily. 'Come in and shut the window. You're letting the bloody mosquitoes in.'

'I'd rather stay here.' I wrapped my cardigan round me.

'Don't be ridiculous.' He stepped towards me, as if he was going to haul me out of the chair. I got up and moved behind it, ready to brandish it like a lion-tamer. Tim frowned. 'Look, you can't stay out here. You'll get bitten to death.' He took another step.

I clenched hold of the chair back. 'Get away from me.'

'Cut the melodrama, Kate. This isn't a movie. I'm not going to hurt you.'

'How do I know? How can I trust you? After that.'

'After what? I haven't laid a finger on you. Christ, if that's what you think . . .' He went back inside, yanking the French window shut.

More banging and crashing and swearing followed. This went on for some time and then it fell quiet. I got up and peered cautiously through a crack in the curtain. Tim's suitcase was packed and standing by the door. A wooden screen shielded my view of the sleeping area but I could see Tim's boots sticking out beyond it. Shivering, I crept back inside. Tim had passed out, face down across the two beds. I retreated to the corner of the room and sat on the floor, hugging my knees. I had never felt so alone in all my life.

Tim remained comatose for almost an hour. Then, without any warning, he reared up and glared at me suspiciously, as if I was a complete stranger, and started shouting at me in Spanish. I tried to calm him down, but he wouldn't let me come near him, and the more I repeated, 'Tim, I don't understand, speak English', the more agitated he became. I wondered whether he'd been having a nightmare and hadn't woken up properly, but it was more than that. It was as if he had become a different person. Not only did he not recognize me, or appear to understand me, but he clearly regarded me as a threat. He was red in the face and spit was flying from his lips and I thought he was going to go for me. Terrified, I ran to the bathroom and locked the door, expecting to hear Tim's fists hammering on it at any second. It was like being inside one of my own nightmares. My hands were trembling and I felt sick. I splashed my face with cold water, turning the taps on full to drown out Tim's voice. I needed a plan. I decided I'd wait for a while and then make a dash for the bedroom door, run downstairs and ask the receptionist for help. At least he'd be able to translate. I switched the taps off and listened. Outside, it had fallen ominously quiet. I strained my ears and thought I heard a moan. Yes, definitely a moan. Had Tim fallen and hurt himself? I had a sudden, awful thought: he'd tried to kill himself once before . . . perhaps it wasn't my safety I should be worried about. Drawing a deep breath, I unlocked the door.

Tim was prostrate on the bed, his head buried in his arms. His shoulders were jerking as if he was crying, and he gave another low moan. I kept out of his sightline, not wanting to set him off again, but the fire seemed to have gone out of him anyway. He started to mumble incoherently. It sounded as if he was using English this time, but it was hard to make out what he was saying because he had his face pressed into the pillow. I caught a name, 'Jack', repeated with increasing urgency, and then what sounded like, 'Keep down'. His body twitched, and I thought he was about to have a fit, and then he said, quite distinctly, 'They've seen us. Move.' More twitching and flailing. His head had turned slightly to one side and I could see his screwed-up face, his eyes shut tight. 'They're coming this way. Take cover.' His voice broke into a sob. 'Run . . .' He pounded the pillow like a frustrated child. 'For God's sake, man, run.' Then he froze, and I knew he was seeing something terrible. 'You didn't run,' he sobbed, 'you didn't run.'

I tasted salt and realized that I was crying, too. For Jack and for Tim and for me.

CHAPTER SIX

It was late when I awoke the next morning. I found Tim sitting on the edge of the bed, his hands braced on his knees and his head bowed, as if just breathing required all his concentration. He looked crumpled and old and wispy-haired, more like my grandfather than my lover, and he had the DTs so badly he could barely light a cigarette. He had sweated through the sheets and smelt like a distillery, not just his breath but his skin, too. Showering didn't stop him reeking of alcohol and afterwards he sweated worse than before. He didn't want breakfast, or even coffee, so I gave him some water and told him to go back to sleep, promising to come up later to check on him. 'I'll be fine,' he mumbled, but when I offered him my bed he rolled into it with obvious relief and didn't object when I closed the curtains, despite his phobia of darkened rooms.

It was evening before we talked. I had flushed the re-
maining booze down the toilet while Tim slept and
although he had stayed in our room all day he'd made no
mention of this. He was subdued and sat chain-smoking on
the balcony while I packed my case (and repacked his) in
preparation for our early departure the next day. When I
asked him if he was coming down to dinner, he stood up
stiffly and came back into the room, shutting the French
windows behind him. 'There's something I want to say to
you, Kate.' I felt my stomach lurch. He stood in front of me,
staring into my eyes. It was the first time we'd looked at
each other directly all day, and I was shocked at how grey
his skin was. He cleared his throat.

'Nobody should have had to witness the state I got myself
into last night. Least of all you. It's bad enough that I don't
know what I said or did, but I do know that I upset you and
that is unforgivable. I wouldn't blame you for walking out
on me, but instead you've looked after me, which is
something I don't deserve after my behaviour,' he sighed,
'not just last night, but throughout this holiday.' He removed
his glasses and rubbed the bridge of his nose. 'I've been an
utter idiot, Kate. There's no reason why you should give me
a second chance, but I hope that you will.' He replaced his
glasses, becoming brisk. 'To prove that to you I'm not going
to have a drink tonight and when we get back I will take my
Antabuse as soon as my system's clear. OK? And I swear to
you that I will never touch alcohol again.' He placed his
hand on his heart. 'That you should know.'

It was an expression Tim had used before, the first time he'd assured me of my safety. The irony didn't escape me: less than twenty-four hours earlier I'd been terrified he was going to attack me. *But he didn't*, I told myself firmly, *he was hallucinating*. It wasn't me he'd been shouting at in Spanish, it was someone else, a ghost from his past conjured up by alcoholic psychosis. I'd worked that much out from the flashback that had followed, though what trauma Tim had been revisiting, I wasn't sure. I assumed it was something to do with the war. He had passed out soon after, and I had lain in bed, my imagination working overtime, seeing him lying in a muddy shellhole watching his friend being blown up. I wondered whether the talk of war and the German accents had brought it back. With Tim in such a fragile state, it did not seem the right time to ask. His hands were still shaking and it had obviously taken a supreme effort for him to get through the day without a drink. The main thing, I told myself, was that he wasn't dangerous, he was a drunk. So long as he stayed sober, everything would be all right. He wouldn't risk drinking on his medication. Providing he took it. Tim was looking at me expectantly, as if his declaration ought to be enough.

I cleared my throat. 'How do I know you won't just stop taking them again?'

'I've given you my word, as a man of honour.' I must have looked sceptical, because he stiffened. 'A man's honour is everything. You do not insult his honour unless you're prepared to take the consequences. I've made you a promise, Kate. I would never rescind on that.'

'I'm just saying it's not that easy. As you know. Alcoholism is an addiction.'

He winced. 'I don't need a lecture. If you don't trust me, say so. Although I would have thought seeing me stone-cold sober when I'm surrounded by pissed students night after night ought to give me some credence.'

'It does. I do. But —'

'Look, you can witness me take the damn things every morning, if that's what you want.'

'No.' I started to cry, the stress of the past few days finally overwhelming me. 'I'm not your keeper, Tim. I don't want that responsibility. It's got to be your choice. You've got to want to do it.'

'I do,' he said, more gently.

'But how do I *know*?' I wailed.

He pulled me towards him. 'Because I need you. I need to wake up with you beside me. I need to fall asleep with you in my arms. I need to care for you. I need to make you happy. Without you, I'd – I'd rot. Physically and mentally rot. Don't you understand?' He gripped my shoulders. 'I'm not going to risk that. Not for a drink. Not for the world.' His fingers were digging into the tops of my arms so hard that it hurt.

'I believe you,' I said.

We returned to a Britain gripped by war. Brian Hanrahan's windswept reports from the deck of HMS *Hermes* ('I counted them all out and I counted them all back'), John

Nott's expressionless Ministry of Defence briefings, jingoistic headlines in the *Sun* – people gorged on news, consuming it compulsively until the *Belgrano* went down, and then HMS *Sheffield* and we all started to feel sick. A boy from my old sixth-form class was one of the servicemen killed on HMS *Ardent* and I was more shocked by that, I think, than the daily casualty statistics. It was the first war I'd experienced, only of course I didn't experience it, I watched it on television like virtually everyone else. By June, British forces had retaken Port Stanley and Argentina had surrendered. Tim was magnanimous in victory, but a disgusted Francisco moved out.

I moved on, too, out of Jesse Montgomerie hall in Duryard and into Barton Place. I had my own room, which I used for studying, although I slept with Tim. I loved my room. It overlooked a meadow and beyond that, a row of trees and then hills. Instead of essay writing, I sat and watched the cows trailing down from the pasture to afternoon milking and in the evening, the swallows dipping and diving in the half-light. At night, you could hear owls and foxes, whose nocturnal activities were on one occasion interrupted by me running barefoot over the dewy grass at 4.30 a.m. in my dressing gown, ducking the bats and grinning insanely. My intoxicated state was due to the glories of nature and sleep deprivation, rather than alcohol. I was going through my *Howards End* period at the time.

Tim and I were never happier. Although we had the occasional row – once I'd been prepared to go home there and then, but a rail strike prevented me – it was, my diary blithely reports, 'happiness interspersed with quarrels', rather than the reverse. And the making up was always spectacular. We made love with our window open to the night and once, an electrical storm lit up the sky like a searchlight and we fucked to the clatter of thunder as it bounced off the encircling hills. In the morning we would go down to the common room with glowing faces, the angry words of the previous day forgotten. True to his word, he had stopped drinking, but he continued to show flashes of bad temper. They can't have been frequent enough in those early days to have made a lasting impact, but looking back over my diary I can spot the pattern being laid down. Perhaps I was too optimistic to see it; we were in the first flush of romance then, even canoodling in public places, love's inappropriately young dream.

There was, though, one persistent note of warning that I recognized but chose to ignore. I was still having dreams about death. The horror of these nightmares was reinvented in a variety of creative formats, as if there was an invisible director in my brain. Sometimes they were Dali-esque surreal, sometimes they were like spy thrillers and sometimes they chronicled total annihilation of the planet. I was very aware of the nuclear threat – we all were, then – but most people didn't suffer *The War Game* night after night. You'd think that the recurrent images of corpses might have caused me to reflect on what my subconscious was screaming at me, but I didn't want to listen.

★

Summer term came to an end with a tropical ball, which we all dressed up for in suitably exotic style. Tim, egged on by Lindsay, threatened to wear a pith helmet and khaki shorts, so I was relieved when he appeared in a white tux pretending to be Humphrey Bogart. Mike and Keith were in Hawaiian shirts, Sally was got up like Carmen Miranda and I wore a floaty dress decorated with bright, splashy flowers. (Hilary wasn't there; following my example, she had ditched biology and gone to Goldsmith's College in London to study art.) The ball went on until dawn, with discos, bands, films and a themed bar, plus breakfast for those still standing. The Boomtown Rats were headlining in the Great Hall, supported by The Alarm and The Belle Stars, and a group called Roaring Jelly were topping the bill in the cabaret in the JCR. Everyone was drinking gaudy tropical cocktails and going end-of-term crazy and the Wellies were throwing food in true public-school fashion. Sally and I persuaded Tim to buy us Cordon Negro, which we swigged decadently from the bottle while he sipped Coke. We were keen to last out until breakfast but by 2.30 a.m. Tim was obviously suffering and he and I went home. I was disgruntled at missing the rest and because Tim was tired and I was drunk we went to bed without speaking. His temper was not much improved the next morning, largely because the rest of the Barton Place crowd had arrived home at six singing 'Welcome to the House of Fun' very loudly.

The holidays arrived and my sister Deb came down to Exeter to pick me up with her boyfriend Graham. They were given a taste of student life by Keith, who fell in through the doorway to Tim's room, glared at us drunkenly and said, 'Bollocks' twice, before collapsing in a giggling heap on the floor. We drove back to Oxford the next day in Graham's VW Beetle, but I felt out of place at home, even though I'd long since patched things up with my parents. I became neurotic about sleeping on my own and spent the first few nights of the holiday wrapped up in an eiderdown on Deb's bedroom floor. Tim phoned me every night but still I missed him badly. Until then, I hadn't realized just how much I'd come to rely on him. It was a relief to return to Exeter in August.

Tim's influence over me was considerable. With his tutoring I had passed my exams with a 60 per cent average after just ten weeks of study, which was enough to satisfy Professor Atkinson and get me through to the second year. It was Tim's mission in life to educate me, not just about philosophy, but about art, literature, poetry, history, politics and even how to conduct myself and dress. Some of these lessons I absorbed raptly, decorating my room with Athena prints of pictures by Renoir, Matisse, Lowry and Van Gogh and buying compilations of modern poetry. Others, though, I rebelled against. Politics remained an area of intense disagreement, particularly the activities of the NUS, which Tim regarded as positively traitorous. And my reaction on being told how to present myself for an interview – I had secured an interview for a holiday job with DevonAir, the local independent radio station – was the same as any twenty-one-year-old girl when a fifty-seven-year-old man tells her what lipstick and shoes not to wear. Tim's retort was that, at my age, I couldn't be expected to have developed any dress sense anyway, and when I retaliated he called me 'childish' and stomped off. The nub of his argument was that short skirts were fine if I was with him, but flaunting my legs at radio bosses was out. I wore a short skirt and got the job. They said they were impressed with my enthusiasm.

Tim had an image of how I should look, which I tolerated to some extent because he was generous with his money. While Sally and my other friends were dressing out of charity shops, Tim bought me shoes from Russell & Bromley, expensive perfume (Je Reviens and Miss Worth; not my taste, his) and handed over £20 a time for a haircut, an amount that would have kept me in Pot Noodles for a term in the days before I met him. He paid for me to have expensive private dental work, gave me a clothes allowance – I have a card of his with the inscription 'for autumn plumage' – and topped up my bank balance whenever my grant fell low. I knew there was a contradiction between this and my left-wing principles and felt twinges of guilt from time to time, which self-interest overrode. When my father criticized me for travelling first class on trains, I snapped, 'Being socialist doesn't mean suffering if you don't have to,' but I was stung, all the same. The material trappings were a novelty, but it wasn't the things in themselves that mattered. It was being courted that I liked. Tim was a true old-fashioned romantic: he bought me half-bottles of champagne, ensuring afternoons in bed, fed me smoked salmon and strawberries, sent me little cards and notes. And then there were the flowers he gave me every week: daffodils in the spring, sweet peas in the summer and freesias all year round, subtly scenting my room with their waxy blooms. Every action said 'I adore you' and I felt like a princess. The irony was, I still thought I was a feminist.

What was most seductive of all about Tim was what he expected of me intellectually. He expected more than I knew I had in me and when I found myself responding I felt stronger than I had ever done in my life. The challenge was exhilarating; I never beat him in an argument (it was difficult to find anyone who had) but the fact that he even considered me to be in the same game was itself an aphrodisiac. It was flirting at the highest level and even though I knew he could take me any time, I enjoyed putting up the fight. It didn't always end well – the rosy glow between the first and second glasses of wine I could handle; after that, it wound up in a fight – but it certainly stretched my mind. His intellectual hot-housing changed me as a person and I became more confident and outgoing as a result.

Tim was my mentor, but he was also father-figure and lover, and if he exploited the paternalistic role I was happy to go along with him. Too willing, probably. He used to call me 'hija', Spanish for 'daughter', which I found sweet rather than suspicious. He bought me cuddly toys and we played infantile games and had soppy pet names for each other. 'B' and 'P' (even now I feel I can't give those names up – a peculiar loyalty, considering) lived in a make-believe land, just like Tim and I did in our rural idyll during that baking-hot August. Most of the post-grads had gone home and we had the house and grounds almost to ourselves. It was quiet and peaceful without the others and we pottered contentedly, Tim toiling in the walled garden while I read improving books in the shade of a tree. 'We're very happy, quite ridiculously so,' I recorded in my diary. 'It's frightening – how long can you be on such a high for?'

I should have looked at the books more closely. One of Tim's favourite authors was John Fowles and the first novel he gave me to read was *The Collector*. It's about an obsessive individual called Fredrick Clegg, an amateur butterfly collector, who abducts a young woman called Miranda and keeps her locked up in his basement. Miranda is a vivid creature, creative, passionate and full of life; Clegg is a control freak who compartmentalizes life and cannot relate to emotions. He feeds her, looks after her and gives her everything she wants, except her freedom. Meanwhile, Miranda's diary reflects her feelings for a charismatic older man, 'G P', an artist who is also her mentor and has had a profound effect on her way of thinking. She decides to rekindle the relationship when she gets out – the deal with Clegg is that she will stay for a month – but in the event he does not release her and Miranda falls ill and dies. The book ends with Clegg justifying to himself that he is not responsible and making plans to capture another, more suitable, girl. I found it very readable (unlike *The Magus*). I could understand Miranda's fixation with 'G P'; he sounded so much like Tim. Now I realize I had Tim cast as the wrong character.

A week later the university gave Tim notice to move out of Barton Place and he suggested we get a house together.

All this time, Tim had been reporting to his probation officer once a week as part of the terms of his licence. I didn't find out about this from him, but from Tom, who was doing a placement at the probation office as part of his post-doctorate. Tom had mentioned it casually, presuming I knew; not an unreasonable assumption considering Tim and I had been together for six months. I was shocked, not just because Tim had kept it a secret, but because I thought he'd served his time and was free. He had divorced himself from his past so effectively, or so it had appeared, that it gave me a jolt to realize he was still subject to restrictions. When I told him that I knew about his visits (this was obviously where he disappeared to once a week), he retorted, 'I'm a lifer, Kate. I'm out on licence. What did you expect?' as if I ought to have known what the sentence entailed. He did gradually open up about it, but he never told me what he and his probation officer discussed. It's not hard to guess: other people were monitoring our relationship, although I didn't realize it. Whether the university had decided our liaison was not one they wanted to accommodate, I don't know, but there was definitely an undercurrent and Tom seemed to be concerned.

It's true I was apprehensive about moving in with Tim, but not because of his record. I was worried about how it would affect our relationship. I was aware that the community in Barton Place had provided a buffer for us. We'd had no domestic responsibilities to speak of, apart from cooking, and the almost-permanent party atmosphere had leavened Tim's changeable and occasionally black moods. More importantly, he had been surrounded by clever young people who had given him the constant intellectual stimulation he needed. I was bright, but I sensed I would not be enough. I kept these fears to myself, swallowing the rising feeling of panic I felt whenever the subject came up. Tim, apparently, had no such concerns and seemed to take it as given that we would rent a place together. It was, anyway, too late for me to do anything about sharing with others. Apart from Sally and James, I had left most of my peers behind when I moved into Barton Place, effectively cutting myself off. There was no going back. It was just Tim and me now.

We found a house, eventually; a modern, two-bedroom maisonette just five minutes' walk from campus in a quiet road called Devonshire Place. It was pleasant enough and had lots of light, but there was no garden, just a paved back yard. I was grateful for its plain white walls, clean furniture and central heating; compared to the crumbling Victorian tenement that Sally and James shared with their friends, it was a palace. At £50 a week it was expensive but we could cover it, and when the young Canadian owners – who were obviously amused at our relationship – agreed to rent it to us, we left over the moon. Suddenly, I didn't mind being a couple, with all the commitments that entailed. I was thrilled at the thought of us setting up house and planned our house-warming party all the way home. Tim listened to my excited burbling with a grin on his face, and when I asked him why he was smiling he said he'd been making plans too.

'What are they?' I enquired, as we swung into the driveway of Barton Place.

He parked the car and cut the engine. 'I'm going to convert that yard into a Mediterranean terrace garden, fill it with tubs of geraniums and hanging baskets.' He continued to look at me and smile.

'*What?*' I demanded crossly, thinking he was laughing at me.

He leaned forward and gave me a kiss. 'And I'm going to take you up to bed right now.'

There was one last treat in store for me before we moved – a trip to London. Tim had managed to combine it with a pre-arranged business meeting with Christopher Fothergill, his managing director, and the company was picking up the tab. We were staying at the Park Lane Hotel in Piccadilly, which was very grand and had liveried doormen and a palm court in which we took afternoon tea to the accompaniment of a grand piano. Tim was in a navy pinstriped suit and looked every inch the businessman, while I was in a mini-dress from C & A and looked – well, probably like a floozy. We acted out an uncle-niece charade for the benefit of the silver-haired ladies sipping Darjeeling, which fooled no one. I'm afraid to say that their supercilious stares only made us naughtier.

I was more respectably dressed for dinner, having borrowed a glamorous dress and matching wrap for the occasion. Christopher Fothergill had insisted on taking us to Wheelers in Mayfair, where he kept a flat, and we met up with him beforehand in a pub in Red Lion Yard. He had that urbane, glossy, well-fed look that wealthy people have and appeared considerably younger than Tim. I'd been nervous about being introduced to him, but he turned out to be quite charming. He teased me a great deal about my vegetarianism – Wheelers was a famous fish restaurant – and cracked lobster claws with gusto while I ate yet another mushroom omelette. He was also a wine connoisseur and selected an extortionately priced vintage, which he and I shared sitting side by side on a banquette, arguing loudly and snorting with laughter. Tim indulged our behaviour, though he said we were both 'disgraceful'.

'So how long have you known Tim?' I asked Christopher over dessert, an elaborate ice-cream confection in a brandy-snap basket.

'It must be at least twenty – no, twenty-one years. Nineteen sixty-one, that's when we met. That right, Tim?' Tim nodded. My mind started whirring. Christopher was the first person I'd met who knew Tim from 'before'. There were so many questions I wanted to ask him, but with Tim there it was impossible.

'I was a management consultant at the time, trouble-shooting for businesses. Had a six-month contract with Pickerings to improve efficiency. Took off from there.'

'So you gave up the other consultancy work?'

'Not at first. John Fothergill – Christopher's father – offered me a permanent post a couple of years later, initially to explore the export markets. I'd got the international con-tacts, of course —'

'Hilton Hotel, Malta,' Christopher interjected. 'To name but one.'

'And the timing was right, so I took it.' Tim shot him a look.

'He's being modest, Kate,' Christopher laid his hand on my arm. 'Do you know, he practically saved the company. Up until then, we'd been plugging away making profitless flat-lifts in Scottish tenements. Without Tim's vision, we'd have gone under.'

'Why was the timing right?' I asked Tim, sensing a subtext. 'Because you wanted a family? Was that when you were married to Rosemary?'

'That was over by then.' Tim dabbed his mouth with a linen napkin. 'I wanted to stop rattling around and put down roots. Besides which, I got on rather well with Christopher, even though he was only a pup.'

'I'm only ten years younger than you,' Christopher inter-jected.

'So, you were living in Stockton?' I persisted.

'Near Stockton, yes.'

'By yourself?'

Tim hesitated. 'Actually, I lived with Christopher and his wife for a while. We shared a house.'

'Tim's practically one of the family,' Christopher said warmly. He swilled wine around the bottom of his glass, chuckling. 'Remember that time when you came to stay with us in Redcar?'

'Which one?' Tim looked slightly wary.

'Which one!' Christopher laughed, as if he ought to know.

Tim shook his head. 'Sorry.'

'I can't believe you've forgotten the maggots.' Christopher turned to me. 'My wife always mentions it whenever we talk about him.' I almost choked on my brandy snap. 'Maggots?'

'Yes, crawling with them. Right inside. We didn't spot them until the skin started moving. Then one of them broke through . . . ' He caught my shocked face. 'Are you all right?'

'Where were . . . ?' I was afraid to ask.

'In the Camembert. Just under the rind.'

'Oh.' I let myself breathe again.

'Naturally, my wife was horrified and flung the whole lot in the bin. There was an embarrassed silence, then Tim, quite unperturbed, retrieved the cheese, scraped them off and put it back on the table. And you know what he said? "But this is the way you enjoy best French cheese." ' Christopher beamed. 'He was right. It was excellent.'

Tim pursed his lips. 'Don't remind me.' He waved a hovering waiter away. 'I was going to go for that Brie. I don't think I'll bother.'

We said goodnight to Christopher soon after and he kissed me on both cheeks, congratulating Tim on his 'philosopher girlfriend'. Tim and I returned to the Park Lane Hotel and rounded off the evening with a nightcap in Harry's Bar, where, primed with Cointreau, I continued to probe him about their relationship.

'How did Christopher feel about . . .' I hesitated '. . . about what happened to you?'

Tim sipped his coffee, a thoughtful expression on his face. 'He was surprised. Shocked. Disbelieving. And loyal. Very loyal. I couldn't have asked for anyone more supportive.'

'When you were in prison?'

'Yes. And afterwards. Not many employers would have given me my job back. Mud sticks.'

'So you just took up again where you left off?'

Tim gave a bark of laughter. 'I was in no fit state to cope with board meetings after eight years inside. He made me start all over again, from the bottom. Gave me a job as a fitter's mate. That's how I met Butterball Dave. He was my boss.' 'Butterball Dave' was Tim's affectionate nickname for Dave Upton, the regional manager in Bristol. I'd met him once and had been struck at how easy Tim was in his company. Tim had photos of himself socializing with Dave and his family but he'd never explained their history to me.

'Dear old Dave.' Tim grinned. 'Salt of the earth. He was an absolute tyrant to begin with. Didn't matter that I'd been international director. You should have seen me in my oily overalls and cloth cap! And he made me cart around his ruddy great bag of tools. I got to know every bloody lift shaft in Torquay. It was the best thing I could have done. Learned the business from the inside out. Three years later and here I am back on top with the kind of experience money can't buy.' He yawned. 'I'm dead on my feet, Kate. No more questions. It's been a long day.' He tipped the barman and we took a lift up to our floor.

'So, would you know what to do if this got stuck?' I asked curiously.

'Yes,' he said. 'Press the red button.' He flicked a speck of cigarette ash off the sleeve of his suit. 'Let some other bugger fix it.'

The next day was a whirlwind of sightseeing: Trafalgar Square, the National Gallery (to see the real Monets), Carnaby Street, Buckingham Palace. I was a little jumpy – the terrible bombing of the guardsmen and their horses in Hyde Park had happened a month or so earlier – but Londoners seemed undeterred by the IRA and the shops and streets were bustling. Tim took me to Fortnum & Mason's food hall and bought me handmade violet creams and would have taken me to the lingerie department to look for apricot silk knickers (he was most specific) had I not been overcome by embarrassment. After a drink at the Ritz we took a cab back to the hotel, and then on to Paddington to pick up the 125 InterCity train to Exeter St David.

As the train glided through the golden countryside and Tim dozed, I replayed the conversation with him and Christopher in my head. I realized that Tim had skilfully avoided answering my question about why the timing had been 'right' for him to join Pickerings and had been vague about where he'd lived and why he'd wanted to 'put down roots'. There was only one conclusion I could come to: this was when he'd lived with the woman he killed. The rumour at Barton Place was that she'd been an ambassador's wife. Tim had never given me any clues to her identity and I hadn't thought much about her before. Had she been looking forward to settling down with him in their new home? What kind of life had they led? And why had it gone so tragically wrong? 'We had a row', that was all Tim had told me. I thought about a row he and I had had, two weeks earlier. There was a streak of callousness in him that always took me by surprise because it seemed to come out of nowhere. We'd wiped the slate clean again in the usual rapturous way and I'd forgotten all about it, but now it set me thinking: what kind of a row had they had to bring about such a violent conclusion? It hadn't seemed relevant to ask these questions before, but then I hadn't been planning a future with Tim. Now that we were setting up home together, they suddenly seemed more pressing.

CHAPTER SEVEN

Packing up to leave Barton Place was traumatic. Tim attacked it with a clenched jaw and an expression so grim that I stayed out of his way as much as possible. Watching him puffing and sweating up and down the stairs, I suggested, mildly, that he ease up a little, whereupon he slammed a box down and glared at me, perspiration running down his jowls. 'If you pulled your weight around here, I could. My back's killing me and you're just dithering about. But oh, no, as usual, I have to do *everything*.' His face was very red and his eyes had an odd, fixed set that was slightly unnerving. I noticed his fists were bunched and took a step back. He continued to glare at me, breathing heavily. 'I'm sorry,' I mumbled. He gave a dismissive snort and picked up the box. The bottom collapsed, sending books tumbling all over the floor. 'Jesus fucking Christ!' he exploded, kicking the pile savagely. 'Did you pack this?'

'I'll get you a Coke,' I said, edging past him and making a dash for the kitchen.

The atmosphere remained tense for the rest of the day. That evening we went for a drink at the Cowley Bridge and Tim had another go at me. I stormed out of the pub and went back to Barton Place, locking myself in my room with a bottle of French brandy. I wondered what I was doing, moving in with this volatile man. There had been an perceptible shift in his temperament since we'd returned from London. The stress of moving appeared to have sparked increasingly belligerent outbursts in him, all of them directed at me. Depressed about what I was getting myself into, I downed half the brandy and passed out, mired in a lack of resolve about my future and equally undecided about Tim.

I awoke twelve hours later with a crippling hangover. Tim was nowhere to be found, but there was a note on the table: 'Gone to clean house'. Relieved that I wouldn't have to talk to him, I spent the rest of the day trying to read Ryle's *The Concept of Mind*, which made my headache worse, and sunbathing topless in the garden. Apart from Stuart, the gardener, who averted his eyes (I think), I saw no one until late afternoon when Tim returned. He was withdrawn and spoke formally, as if I was a stranger, and I was stiff and polite in return. Neither of us knew where we were any longer; the gulf between us seemed unbridgeable, communication impossible.

We sloped around in our separate misery until eventually I broke down, unable to bear the sight of his hollow eyes and the tautness of his strained face.

'Oh my darling,' he croaked, holding me close. 'I didn't know if you'd still be here. I've been going through hell all day, wondering.' He squeezed me tighter. 'I've hung the curtains and vacuumed the carpets and scrubbed the kitchen and the bathroom from top to bottom. And I took some vases over and filled the house with those lovely scented stocks from the garden, so we'll have something from Barton Place to welcome us. It's all ready to move in to now. If you still want to.'

He squinted at me, his brown eyes anxious. Blood roared in my ears. I felt suffocated by my heartbeat, the thick thump in my chest, my throat, my skull. I clung onto Tim, not knowing what I felt. My anxiety seemed to have no name. All I knew was that I could not manage without him. He had become my life as completely as I had become his. 'Yes,' I whispered, and the roaring subsided and I heard the splutter of a lawnmower and the world came back. And so we got over that row as we'd got over others, a hug and a kiss and a shaky smile pulling us out of the sea that had threatened to drown us. The relief was overwhelming but nothing was resolved. It was too big a risk to go back there.

It was a pattern that was to become wearily familiar. On 23 September, the day after we moved in to our new house, I wrote: 'This one's for the record, Tim. I am bitterly unhappy, frustrated, and I have no hope. You've quashed just about all I feel as a free individual. I'm tied to your abrasive temper and mood changes and I dance like a puppet for you every time. Until it becomes too much . . .'

I'd lived communally with Tim for three months thinking I was happy; one day into living together as a couple and the reality was hitting home. This time I really did mean to leave him, and locked myself in the integral garage while he raged in the living room overhead. I planned my escape: a train to Portsmouth, then the ferry to Jersey, where I had a friend. Once I was there, I told myself, I could relax and spend a few days considering my options before the autumn term started. There was still time to make a fresh start.

I sat hunched in a corner on the gritty floor formulating this plan, but worries about how I'd cope without Tim kept intervening. Money would be a big problem – my parents would struggle to afford the requisite amount to top up my grant – and accommodation would be almost impossible to find at this late stage, too. I was unsure as to whether I was competent enough to manage the tougher second-year philosophy syllabus without Tim's tutelage, and afraid also of losing my friends, most of whom, like Tom and Chris, I'd made through Tim. Mainly, though, I couldn't imagine living by myself again. Under Tim's influence, I'd regressed to the dependency of a child. The thought of taking on the world by myself cowed me almost as much as Tim's bullying. I felt trapped.

It was creepy, sitting among the empty packing cases and

desiccated spiders with the weak light throwing shadows on the breezeblock wall. Intermittent gusts of rain blasted the garage door like bursts of shot. Not a night to run away. Finally, I could bear the cold and discomfort no longer and went back upstairs. Tim was waiting for me with a face like thunder. 'Had enough of your little game?' he asked maliciously. 'Or do you intend to wring every last drop out of me with your emotional blackmail? Do you know how hurtful you're being? Not that you'd care.'

'Me, being hurtful?' I screamed. 'What about all the things you said? If I was as selfish as you seem to think, why would I stay with a controlling, insensitive bastard like you? I'd have got out months ago and started having some fun in my life.'

Tim's mouth was a thin line. 'You're hysterical. I'm not going to talk to you like this.' He started to walk away.

'I only get hysterical because you drive me to such a state with the things you say.'

He swivelled round abruptly. 'The things I say! That's a good one. You don't know what you're saying yourself, half the time. You're always bloody drunk. That time when you hit the brandy. You staggered into my room with your eyeballs rolling and came out with all sorts of nonsense. I didn't tell you at the time because I didn't want to upset you. But you might as well know. Face it, Kate. You're an alcoholic.'

'I'm not a fucking alcoholic.' I was incensed. 'You're the one who pours booze down my neck. You're the one with the problem. You get your kicks by proxy.'

And so it went on. We continued to ricochet off each other until 4.15 a.m. when the row came to a nebulous conclusion out of sheer exhaustion. I'd developed a thumping headache and Tim dosed me with his Distalgesic and put me to bed. I slipped into a drugged sleep and didn't wake up until lunchtime the next day, missing the train. Even if I had had the courage to go, my plans would have come to nothing: the violent storm that began in the night continued throughout the day and the Channel crossings were cancelled.

My diary doesn't record what started the row – it was usually something trivial – but the complaints were always the same. As I'd feared, the dynamics of living together played a part. Tim seemed to expect me to fall into the role of homemaker, but despite my kitsch fantasy of maisonette living, I wasn't keen on performing housewifely duties. It wasn't that I was a slob, simply that I was a student with more compelling things to do. Tim's lectures smacked too much of parental nagging – a constant source of friction between us – and made me sulk, which made him even madder.

Mostly, though, the problem lay with my own feelings of inadequacy and monthly bouts of depression, for which Tim had very little patience. I suffered from debilitating PMT, which would begin two weeks before my period and send my hormones plummeting. It was a vicious circle: my skin would flare up and I would become even more depressed. I developed all sorts of avoidance techniques to hide my face, walking around with my head bowed and refusing to look people in the eye. However well I disguised the problem with make-up, I couldn't avoid the truth when I washed it off, and when I looked in the mirror I was filled with self-loathing.

To his credit, Tim tried to help with this, paying for me to see a private dermatologist. Throwing money at a problem was something he could do; unfortunately, the effect of the strong antibiotics the dermatologist gave me made my other symptoms worse (I had candidiasis – a systemic fungal infection – though I didn't realise that at the time). That, though, was the limit of Tim's help. He seemed to have no concept of how deeply it affected me psychologically and, what was worse, he didn't seem to care. Whenever I tried to explain how I was feeling, he became angry and confrontational. 'Look at the burden I've got to carry,' he shouted. 'I can't believe you're coming to me with this. Why don't you try helping me out?' He never elaborated on what this 'burden' of his was and I could only guess at the guilt and grief he endured. Compared with my disruptive hormones, there was no contest; causing the accidental death of a partner trumps that easily. The murder of a partner garners less sympathy, of course, but that was never an issue.

My ravaged skin wasn't trivial, though. It was one of the reasons why I had such low self-esteem. I didn't know how Tim could stand to look at me, let alone make love to me, and I was grateful to him that he did. There were times when I thought about overdosing because I hated my appearance so much, and with Tim's penchant for feeding me his prescription-only painkillers, or failing that, a couple of large whiskies, it was a wonder I didn't manage it. I asked him once if it wasn't dangerous, but he said he knew exactly how many Distalgesic were fatal and that you needed to wash them down with half a bottle of vodka to be absolutely sure. Satisfied I would come to no harm, I kept on taking them, grateful for the creeping blackness that blotted out my misery and submerged me in sleep.

Tim found my depression contagious – 'It's like living under a black cloud,' he said frequently – and would become irascible if I moped around, so that I learned to hold back during these times. But the truth was that he didn't know how to help me when I was like this, and his own feelings of inadequacy made him anxious and insecure and his fuse became shorter and shorter. I'd worked this out, but it wasn't much comfort: it was Tim's confidence and capability that had attracted me; I'd wanted someone strong, someone to make things right, and I thought I'd found him. But when I needed to lean on him, he'd crumble, and then he'd want my support and get angry that I couldn't give it. Our relationship was a see-sawing power struggle and there was rarely any equilibrium. We were bound together by mutual need. My mistake was to confuse that need with love.

I spent the rest of the day after the row unpacking the

kitchenware while Tim banged about in the garage. He had a collection of monogrammed silver cutlery that he claimed had been in his family for generations, and I studied the florid initials on the spoons looking for an 'F' for Franklin. There was none. Confusingly, there seemed to be different initials on the dessert spoons and the forks. Besides the regular dinner service, there were mustard spoons and butter knives, fish forks and funny little narrow teaspoons, tarnished napkin rings and scalloped serving spoons, all jumbled up together, a mismatched throwback to another era. They were the only material possessions Tim had from his previous life, apart from the Persian rugs, which his father had collected. I turned the cutlery over, comparing hallmarks. It struck me that I knew almost nothing about where Tim came from. The silver contained clues, but I didn't know how to decipher them. I put it away in the cutlery drawer, reflecting that, despite Tim's love of T. S. Eliot, it wasn't much of a measure of a life to be left with coffee spoons.

It was at that moment that I smelt smoke. I rushed downstairs to the garage – being a maisonette, the kitchen and living room were on the first floor – and wrenched open the internal door. I found Tim hauling papers out of box files and stuffing them into a sack. 'Fire! I can smell fire!' I yelled, forgetting we weren't speaking.

'It's nothing to get het up about,' he replied testily. 'I'm having a burn-up, that's all. Out back.'

'Oh.' I goggled at the papers protruding from the mouth

of the sack. 'Is that what you're burning?'

'Yes.'

'What is it?'

'Stuff I should have got rid of years ago.'

'Like . . .?'

'Notes. Essays. Old . . . jottings. Couple of novels I once wrote. Nothing important.'

'You've written books?' I was amazed. 'What were they about?'

'Crime stories. Thrillers. Pot boilers. They were all trash.'

'Is that why you read all those paperbacks?' Tim had a penchant for bulky novels emblazoned with gold lettering. Given the lectures I'd had from him on English literature, this was something that had always surprised me.

He grimaced. 'I like the genre. It's undemanding, but it's entertaining.'

'But why destroy it all now?'

'It's from a period of my life I don't need to be reminded of.'

I understood then. He'd written them in prison. I wondered what else he was bent on incinerating: letters, cards? I knew he'd written poems when he was inside. He had told me he'd been published in two editions of *Poetry Quarterly*. 'What about the poetry?' He shook his head. 'Tim.' I laid my hand on his arm. It was the first contact we'd had since the fight. Our eyes met. 'You were proud of them. And you should be. They must have been good.' He shrugged. 'You can't burn them,' I pleaded. 'Or the novels.'

I paused, then decided to take the chance. 'At least let me read them first. It would help me get to know you. Then, perhaps, I'd understand you better and we wouldn't have these awful fights . . .'

He pulled away from me and picked up the last box file, emptying it into the sack. 'No, Kate. My life, my choice. I'm getting shot of it.'

I followed him outside and watched him tip the sack into a galvanized dustbin, which he'd turned into a makeshift brazier. Flames leapt and spat, sending charred fragments of paper whirling into the air. Tim moved closer to me. The tension seemed to have drained out of him and he looked younger. He gave me a ghost of a smile. 'New beginnings, eh?' I nodded, though I was still unsure. He put his arm around my shoulders. 'Let go of the past, Kate. Look forward. That's what you and I have got to do.' We continued to stand there, staring at the fire, the heat warming our cheeks. Tim said nothing more. For him, it was an attempt at closure. As for me, I felt a profound sense of loss. I knew then that he would never open up about his past, and I yearned to know him, to fill in the blanks. It wasn't just that I wanted to know about his crime. I wanted to know about his entire life: his childhood, his parents, his time in the army, his mysterious connection with Colombia, his marriage, his children, his other significant relationships . . . I needed to know what had come before me. It was too much to be asked to start with a blank page, like being given a story with the first half of the book missing – except that even Tim's rigid authorship couldn't prevent the odd flashback when he was drunk or angry or off his guard. He'd allowed me a few titbits, but I sensed they were a highly edited version of events and the little I did know only made me want to find out more. It pained me to think that only the previous evening I'd been sitting in the garage, surrounded by his files. I could have discovered his story, maybe, if I'd opened the right boxes.

It wasn't long before Tim and I settled into a routine in Devonshire Place, having reached a compromise on the domestic arrangements. We made a real effort to accommodate each other – me to be more tidy, him to be less temperamental – and our relationship improved, although we still had arguments. I was content, most of the time, and if the spark seemed to have dimmed a little, we were comfortable with each other, and loving, which was enough. Our sex life had diminished, mainly because Tim was so often exhausted by the end of the day, but pouring a brandy and ginger down me at lunchtime usually guaranteed a result. I'd drag Tim off to bed, giggling, and we'd make love all afternoon, falling asleep and waking up and doing it again. It wasn't adventurous sex but he was fit and strong and we had fun and he knew how to please me. I could tell when he was planning to have sex, because he'd sit at the table filing his nails, smoothing them with an emery board and checking each one meticulously for snags.

Autumn term started on 6 October 1982 and it was

good to be back on campus surrounded by familiar faces. I went to the Ram at lunchtime, which was packed to capacity, and found Sally and James. They had colds and looked miserable – their digs had damp patches on the wall – and suddenly I didn't mind if they thought Devonshire Place bourgeois. At least it was warm and dry. There were other bonuses, too. Our house, with its proximity to campus, turned out to be a good choice of location. When I got home that afternoon, Ginni, who lived nearby, came round for coffee, and two other friends, Maggie and Jane, dropped in and swapped vegetarian recipes. Keith had already been over that morning to speak to Tim, ostensibly about Malcolm Lowry, the subject of his thesis, although he spent the time drinking lager and confessing to an alcohol problem. Then Lindsay came over in the evening, looking very gaunt, and Tim plied him with roast chicken, which he ate ravenously. Barton Place, Lindsay reported, was filling up with an odd collection of undesirables. 'You're better off here,' he said, chomping on a roast potato. His comment reminded me that I'd never got an explanation for our eviction, but it seemed irrelevant now. The following day, Sally and James and a couple of their friends descended on us and drank Tim out of Liebfraumilch. Sally fed Tim grapes, which I tolerated because she was pissed, and they left at half past midnight, singing loudly and clutching a fig plant, confirming that our reputation as party-givers re-mained intact.

The first week of term was taken up with the usual

Freshers' activities, including the Freshers' Fair or Squash as it was known, which was the usual mayhem. I spotted Matt the Marxist recruiting for the Hunt Saboteur's Collective and Lizzie the lesbian on the Gay Soc stand. I was making my way through the crowd to enquire about joining University Radio Exeter when I caught sight of Tim. He was having an animated conversation with a young woman I did not recognize. She appeared to be upset. By the time I reached them, the girl had disappeared.

'Who was that?' I demanded.

'Someone I used to know.'

'An ex?'

He pursed his lips. I took that as confirmation.

'The stalker?' He nodded. 'Is she after you again?' I checked over my shoulder.

'Don't worry, I sent her packing.' He lifted a hand, acknowledging someone on the far side of the room. My head swivelled. 'Marguerite. Researcher in Spanish. She's on sabbatical from Madrid.' Marguerite was petite and pretty. I crossed my arms. 'When did you meet her?'

'Last year, at a seminar.' He gave an exaggerated sigh. 'It was when you were with Claude.'

'Is she a nutter, too?'

He frowned. 'Of course not.'

'Really? Are you sure there aren't any more I should be aware of? Because if you're leaving a trail of screwed-up young girls, I'd like to know.'

'Don't be petty,' he snapped. 'It doesn't suit you.'

I turned away from him, eyes watering, hating myself for feeling so jealous and needy.

'For Christ's sake.' Tim took my arm. 'Come on, let's get out of here.'

He led me outside and sat me down on a bench. I was expecting a tirade, but he lit a cigarette, passed it to me, and then lit one for himself, taking a deep drag. Exhaling smoke through his nostrils, he said, 'Look, I had a few flings before I met you. They weren't serious. I was perfectly clear with each of them from the start. Nobody got hurt.' He took another drag. 'She just misinterpreted me. Deliberately, as far as I can make out. Not my doing.' He reached across and took my hand. 'Nobody even comes close to you. I haven't felt this way about a girl since . . .' He paused. I looked up at him. Tim wore glasses that darkened automatically in sunlight, making it impossible to read his eyes. He laced his fingers into mine. 'I have never felt this way about a girl,' he said. 'Ever.'

It was a year since I'd first met Tim – the Philosophy Society's cheese-and-wine marked an anniversary, of sorts – and in all that time I'd deliberately kept him away from my parents. Now, though, I could put it off no longer: some relatives were returning from Canada, and a big home-coming was planned in their honour. It was to be a garden party, a lavish do with a buffet and trifles. All the family were expected to attend and, as my partner, Tim was also invited. It wasn't exactly the low-key introduction I'd had in mind:

launching any new boyfriend at an assembly of uncles and aunts would have been nerve-racking enough, but presenting them with Tim was bound to provoke reactions.

Tim did not share my jitters, or, if he did, he hid them well. He was surprisingly cooperative about meeting everyone, suggesting that we take my parents out to dinner the night before so that they could get to know him. It helped that they already knew his age, and didn't – to my amazement – seem concerned. 'Your father and I are pleased you've got someone to look after you,' was a phrase Mum had used more than once on the phone, as if Tim was an old-fashioned guardian and I was his ward. Had they known he was a lifer they might have thought differently. I hadn't told them, and I didn't intend to. I knew my mother would worry and Tim said my father, as a police officer, might feel obliged to intervene. 'We can tell them once they've got to know me, if that's what you want,' he said as the train approached Oxford station. 'I've never shied away from the truth. But I don't think it would make a very good ice-breaker, do you?'

The meal with my parents was uneventful. My diary keeps a fastidious record of what we ate but says nothing of what we talked about. My parents were easy-going people and I was sure they'd get on with Tim, and so it turned out. Within five minutes of sitting down he had charmed them both. 'Tim was forthcoming and witty and turned on the style,' I recorded. 'Mutual friendship and respect established instantly.' What I had not expected was to feel almost sidelined by the three of them. I was grateful that Dad wasn't doing the heavy-handed father routine, but I hadn't anticipated Tim palling up with him, either. He flirted harmlessly with Mum, who became as giggly as a schoolgirl and allowed him to talk her into an Irish coffee – 'I really shouldn't, it'll go straight to my head' – and all three of them made jokes at my expense. Suddenly, it was like having an extra parent. I kept smiling because I knew why Tim was doing it, but it grated nonetheless. It wasn't just that I felt like the odd one out. Tim was mine. They weren't supposed to like him quite that much.

The party the next day was at my Auntie Libby's house in the country. The scene was chaotic, with relatives embracing, children running between people's legs, a football game going on, dogs chasing after the ball and horses at the bottom of the garden. It was the kind of comfortable family confusion I was used to, but I didn't know how Tim would react. We stood on the patio, balancing teacups, and then Tim said, 'Well, come on,' and sallied into the mêlée with a sociable smile. He talked tomato-growing with my Uncle Rob, played peek-a-boo with baby Richard, admired Libby's horses and impressed Auntie Judy with his knowledge of Canada. 'I like your fella,' she confided in me. 'He's really neat. Very entertaining. He told me he once sold silk stockings door to door in Vancouver.'

By the end of the afternoon, Tim had scored another hit. The only people who seemed wary of him were the older folks, who were arrayed in the living room with their feet up. Granny, who was thin and frail and papery white – but as always, impeccably coiffed – sat watching him through the open patio windows, her lips moving silently. When I went over to talk to her, she laid a rope-veined hand on my arm and said, 'Dear, I think he's much too old for you. And Grandpa says the same. Why can't you find a nice boy your own age?' She looked at me anxiously with mobile, pink-rimmed eyes. 'He's all right, really, Granny.' I kissed her rouged cheek. She smelt of Estée Lauder's Beautiful and face powder. 'You just need to get to know him.'

'I know his type.' She clutched my sleeve, and I felt a tremor in her birdlike bones. 'And they're not suitable for young girls. *He* ought to know that, even if you don't.'

CHAPTER EIGHT

The second year at Exeter was when I really started to find my feet. I joined the university radio station, URE, a glorified cupboard tucked under the steps of Devonshire House which was soundproofed with eggboxes, and learned how to cue up records and drive the desk. It was a bit of a tinpot operation – on one occasion, we were a full thirty minutes into a programme before realizing no one had turned the transmitter on – but it gave me the chance to work on my journalistic skills, such as they were. When Tom King, who was then employment minister, gave a talk on campus, I infiltrated the audience of Wellies and set him up with an innocent question about the value of university education. He took the bait and when I segued into a blast about student loans and unemployment I had him on the ropes for a minute. However, since I hadn't taken a tape recorder, his blustered 'Would anyone else care to comment?' went unrecorded, which rather missed the point.

The introduction of loans was a hot topic and I joined an NUS call to strike over the issue. Being Exeter, the turnout was pathetic, and even worse was the humiliation we suffered at the hands of the Conservative Association, who crossed the picket line jeering and waving in a white Rolls-Royce. Tim, of course, was with the Tories. The political differences between us were a constant rub. He did not approve of strikes – 'Though I'd defend your right to do so, with my life, if necessary' – and we had tremendous arguments about nuclear disarmament. He was the only person I knew who thought that having cruise missiles at Greenham Common was a good idea, and when he volunteered to take part in a debate on the subject, I was torn. As Tim's girlfriend, I owed it to him to attend, but I was uncomfortably aware that being so publicly associated with the 'other side' would do my street cred no good at all.

Tim worked on his speech for days, winding me up by refusing to reveal its contents. He was debating with a sociology lecturer, whom he loathed on sight because he wore a leather jacket and sandals. There was a large turnout – CND supporters were there in force – although I suspect Tim's notoriety as a lifer may have boosted the numbers. Looking around the packed auditorium I felt suddenly nervous for him. I hadn't seen Tim 'perform' before and I knew that if he adopted his usual hectoring tone, the hostile audience wouldn't give him a chance. I was surprised, then, when he stood up at the lectern and, surveying the rows in front of him, announced calmly: 'I do not wish to die in a nuclear war. I am a normal human being.' He paused and looked straight at me. 'I love.' I felt a tear prick my eye. After that, I didn't care that he denigrated the argument for unilateralism as being 'dangerously naive' or demonstrated the logical absurdity of the proposition 'Better red than dead'. So what if everyone knew I was sleeping with the enemy? I was proud of it.

It was while we were living at Devonshire Place that my old schoolfriend Sharon came to visit. Sharon and I had known each other since we were eleven. We'd studied the same subjects, shared the same love of horses, played in a folk group together and supported each other through the usual boyfriend crises. She had wild frizzy hair and dressed like a drop-out and drove a VW called Nuglugger, which had a handpainted dungbeetle rolling a fiery ball of sun across its bonnet. I could tell Tim disapproved of her as soon as they met. He wasn't impolite, but he didn't go out of his way to be friendly, either. I assumed it was her eccentricity; Sharon wasn't a hippy and didn't do drugs, although the police tended to stop her on the assumption that she did, and I guessed Tim may have formed the same impression. It was unusual for him, though. Despite his politics, he was personally very tolerant and it wasn't like him to react to someone in that way. I soon discovered the feeling was mutual.

'I'm sorry Tim's being a bit stiff,' I said, when she and I had escaped to the pub after dinner. 'I think he must be tired. He's normally much better company.'

'It's all right, Kate,' she said, taking a gulp of cider. 'I don't like him much, either.'

'I didn't say he didn't like you.'

'You didn't need to. I can see it in his eyes.'

'Don't be silly.'

'I'm not.' She looked at me levelly. 'There's something about his eyes I don't trust. The minute I saw him, I felt it. The hair went up on the back of my neck. It was like a cat meeting a dog.'

'What do you mean? Tim's got nice eyes.'

'Nice? Does he always look at people like that?'

'Like what?'

'That really penetrating stare, as if his eyes are boring right through you.'

I shrugged. 'Not that I've noticed.'

She shuddered. 'I definitely wouldn't like to be stuck in a car somewhere remote with him. I'm sorry, Kate. I know he's your boyfriend, but I think he's scary.' Since Sharon didn't know Tim's past any more than the rest of my friends or family, her response was a little unnerving. 'No one else has said that,' I said stoutly. 'Mum and Dad think he's great.'

'Yes, well, my mum and dad think it's outrageous. But that's because of his age. I'm not talking about that.' She traced a pattern on the table in some spilled cider. 'The way he was going on over dinner. Those things he said had happened to him in the war. They just didn't strike me as real, somehow.' It was true Tim had been quite expansive over our meal earlier, regaling us with a tale about how he'd been among the first into a concentration camp that the allies had liberated. 'I know people who've been in conflicts,' she continued. 'They don't like to talk about that sort of stuff. To me, his story sounded like bravado.'

'Are you saying he just made it up?' I asked.

'I don't know.' She bit her lip. 'But I don't think he's what he says he is.'

'You just need to get to know him better. He can seem a bit overbearing at times, but he's not like that underneath.'

'To be honest, I can't see us ever hitting it off. And I doubt if he'll want us to stay friends, though he's too clever to do anything overt. Just don't let him undermine us. Promise me?'

'OK, I promise. But I think you're overplaying it. I can't see any reason for him to do that.'

'He's jealous, Kate. I've got ten years on him. He thinks I'm a threat.'

'But why?'

'Because he wants to own you,' she said. 'Completely.'

Sharon left the next day to see her sister Helen, who was at Plymouth Polytechnic. She hugged me before she got in the car. 'Take care,' she whispered. Tim stood at the door, observing her reverse out of the drive. He didn't, I noticed, wave. We watched the Beetle chug away. I felt suddenly, inexplicably lonely. 'I wish she lived nearer,' I said regretfully. 'We hardly had any time together.'

'She wouldn't fit in, Kate.' He deadheaded a tub of petunias methodically. 'Can you see her with Sally and James and that crew? I regret to say it about a friend of yours, but it's obvious to an outsider that you two are poles apart. There's no point in beating about the bush. You've eclipsed her. It's time to move on.'

'You're just saying that because you didn't like her,' I retorted.

'I didn't object to her one way or the other,' he said. 'I didn't *fancy* her, that's all.'

Generally, Tim and I were getting on well, but when he suggested another Easter holiday – this time in Majorca – I was cautious. He'd hit the bottle again since our disastrous trip to Gran Canaria and although it was just the once and he'd been sober for many months, I was worried another holiday would turn into a drinking binge. Talking to him about this wasn't an option – he would have bitten my head off – so I was relieved when he brought the subject up himself. Poring over a brochure, he announced, 'I think we ought to hire a car this time. See some of the island. We can get one included in the deal. I'm thinking of Illetas, it's not too developed. The Hotel de Mar Sol. I've marked it.' He handed me the brochure. 'Five stars. And it's got its own private beach. What do you think?'

'It looks very . . . nice.' I eyed the picture of thatched umbrellas by the poolside bar.

'Of course, I shan't drink this time,' Tim added briskly. 'Don't want to risk my licence.'

'No.'

'Sun and rum. That was my mistake last time. Went to my head. Not a good combination.' He got up and went into the kitchen. I heard him put the percolator on. Caffeine was Tim's drug of choice these days. Sometimes he drank so much of it he'd shake.

The holiday was, amazingly, uneventful. The season hadn't really begun and the hotel was quiet. It had glorious views out to sea and a sweet little cove, although it was too cold to bathe. There are pictures of me posing cheekily in a white vest; I've got shaggy hair and I look slim and my skin's clear, thanks to yet another private dermatologist. Tim looks inscrutable, as always, and very brown. My philosophy books are once again propped up against menus and foam-rimmed coffee cups, and a toy owl called Wol is sitting next to them. There are lots of photos of stray cats and bright geraniums and streaky sunsets, but none of us together. We never made any friends on these holidays; there are no snaps of other couples, or laughing groups raising glasses to the camera. Our relationship was very inward-looking, a twisted take on father and daughter, and people saw that and left us well alone.

The Majorca holiday did bring about one change. I stopped being a vegetarian, or, at least, such a strict one. Fed up with the rigmarole over what 'La Senorita' could and couldn't eat, Tim persuaded me to try fish. I was hesitant, but I was also sick of omelettes, and I finally capitulated. At first, I thought the sea bass might make me sick – after all, my system had been uncontaminated by the flesh of any living creature for four years – but after digesting it with no ill effects I became more adventurous. By the end of the week I was pulling the heads off king prawns, yanking out their feathery innards and dunking them in garlic butter without a qualm.

Sally and James took a dim view of my conversion. They invited us to a dinner party and served up a vegetarian chilli, which had lots of beans in it, haranguing me about the dangers of political compromise. The dinner was in honour of a distinguished poet and literary critic who had addressed the Lit Soc that evening. Sally, as always, looked amazing, her black bob gleaming with hennaed highlights. Statuesque Belle was there, in a short, tight, pink dress, and buxom Linda and pert, blonde Sara, and a number of their friends from the English group had also been asked back. It was a lively, informal meal, the pot of chilli eked out with a mountain of brown rice and washed down with numerous bottles of red wine. The silver-haired speaker was about the same age as Tim, and equally opinionated. Tim tried to talk to him about Larkin, but he was more interested in finding out how Tim had managed to surround himself with so many young girls. Sally, who was pissed, interjected, 'Yes, all this temptation. How do you resist us, Tim?'

Tim gave her a mock-stern look over his glasses. 'You're all absolutely lovely and I'd be delighted to go to bed with any one of you' – whoops from the assembled company and a shouted 'Not me!' from floppy-haired Jonathan, which caused Tim's mouth to twitch – 'but as you well know, I have my hands full with Kate' – more hoots – 'and, frankly, she's quite enough.' He leaned over and kissed me on the cheek. The famous poet's jaw dropped. 'Good God. You old goat.' He stared at me, his face deeply flushed, and drained his glass. Tim frowned disapprovingly as he watched him refill it, sloshing some on the tablecloth. The FP seemed fixated. 'You jammy bugger,' he continued, stabbing a fork in the air. 'Like a pig in bloody clover.'

'He's completely rat-arsed,' Tim said to me in a low voice. 'I'll have to do something.' He tried making conversation with him again, but the FP was having none of it.

'Fuck off, you've got your own.' He put his arm around Belle, who looked embarrassed.

'Actually . . .' said Jonathan, who was her boyfriend.

'You too,' the FP shouted, glaring at him.

Belle leapt up, sending a plate crashing to the floor. Everyone fell silent. 'I'll get a cloth,' she squeaked, fleeing to the kitchen.

Tim stood up. 'I think you've had enough,' he said quietly.

'You what?'

'You heard me. You're drunk. You're making a fool of yourself. And you're upsetting the girls.' He put a firm hand on his elbow and escorted him in a rather military style from the room. It was the first time I'd seen him in a situation like this, and I was impressed by his control. He returned fifteen minutes later, snorting about 'damned idiots' who ought to have the maturity to know how to behave. 'There's nothing worse,' he added, slurping the coffee that Sally held out to him, 'than jealousy. Especially in a grown man.'

With Trinity (summer) term, Part I exams beckoned and I had to come up with a subject for my final-year dissertation. I considered doing something on dreams – nightmares were still plaguing my sleep, less frequently than before, but still disturbing – but I wasn't sure how to approach it philosophically. In the end, I decided to capitalize on my interest in journalism and came up with an ambitious project entitled 'The Moral Responsibilities of the Media'. Tim was derogatory about my choice, maintaining that the words 'moral' and 'media' were a contradiction in terms. Despite his regular consumption of the *Daily Telegraph*, he had a hatred of journalists and regarded tabloids as the lowest of the low.

Undeterred, I wrote to the editors of all the nationals. All said they had no ethical policy. The fullest response was from Michael Molloy, then editor of the *Daily Mirror*, who replied: 'Whether a story ought or ought not to be published on moral grounds depends on its nature. We are not concerned whether an item is controversial or that it might offend people and I think we must be wary of moralizing . . . We believe that it is in the public interest to disclose corruption, crime, hypocrisy and scandal – using the world scandal in its purest sense . . .' which made Tim as mad as a hatter. The *Telegraph* made no comment.

Tim had tolerated my foray into 'steam radio', as he called it, with URE, but when I renewed contact with DevonAir and offered them my services over the vacation he was much less supportive. The job, which had fallen through the previous summer, involved helping one of the presenters, Stephen Ayres, with outside broadcasts, and we had a fabulous time romping round the Devon countryside in the radio car, broadcasting from museums and castles and then stopping at pubs for a ploughman's and a pint of cider. To my delight, he let me conduct the odd interview – I had my big break with the Chudleigh Flower Festival – but when I went home full of what I'd done, Tim merely lectured me about how my studies were suffering. He resented being left alone and was irritable and moody. I resented his possessiveness just as much and felt he was trying to control me. 'He calls it caring,' I wrote in my diary on 11 June 1983, 'but I'm being stifled.' These days he was beginning to look old and grey and tired. The sexual spark between us had diminished and, compared with the banter and flirting that went on at the station, my relationship with Tim was low on fun. The age gap was more irksome than it had ever been and I was forever being ticked off as if I was a naughty child. 'I feel like kicking over the traces,' my diary entry concluded. I've added a question at the bottom of the page: 'How will our futures turn out?'

The question is revealing. It suggests I was waiting for

something to force the situation, rather than take responsibility for my future myself. I could have left Tim at that point, and I should have done. Working at DevonAir had given my self-confidence a boost and I was strong enough to make the leap, if I'd wanted to. But leave an animal's cage door open and they don't always go. It's easier to stay in familiar territory, and I'd grown used to Tim's ways. I knew he could be aggressive, but I'd learned to avoid the flashpoints. I didn't think things were 'that bad'. But how bad does it have to be before you wake up to the truth? In my case, it had to reach danger point.

Tim's first strategy, when he realized I was dissatisified, was to give me what, at one point, I'd most wanted. A ring. It was, literally, an attempt to 'engage' my attention, although it didn't come with a formal proposal. It was, he said, a symbol of our enduring relationship, and it had the initials of our private names inscribed inside: 'To P from B'. I was deeply touched. No one had ever given me anything so beautiful before. It was a 24-carat rolled-gold band, which I wore initially on the third finger of my right hand, although sometimes I'd switch it over to my left hand to see how it looked. When Karen, one of the reporters, spotted this, she screamed, 'Kate! You've got married!' and gave me an odd look when I told her that I'd just fancied wearing it on my wedding-ring finger. I enjoyed showing it off: to me, the ring demonstrated Tim's commitment for all to see. For a while, I was won over by the romance, though I suspect it was more of a branding exercise as far as Tim was concerned. He could have stamped 'Hands off, she's mine' on my forehead, but this was marginally more subtle.

Tim had always made it clear he'd never marry me. I'd wanted him to, in the early days, but he'd said he wouldn't inflict it on me, and as our relationship progressed even I could see that it would have been disastrous. Still, I was curious to know why he was so against marriage and wondered what had happened in his own. 'I made a rotten husband,' was all he would say, refusing to elaborate any further. I pressed him on this once, not long after he'd given me the ring. 'You mean to Rosemary?' He nodded. 'Were you married after that?'

'No.'

'So if you only married once, how do you know you're not suited to it? Loads of people get divorced. It doesn't stop them remarrying.'

'More fool them.'

'What about . . . the other woman?'

'What other woman?' There was a peculiar look in his eyes.

'The one you – who died. Didn't you want to marry her?'

'Why on earth should I?' He looked annoyed. 'She was going to leave me.'

Given that I was sitting on a powder keg of a story with Tim (not that I knew it), it's no wonder that he didn't like me working with reporters. Over the summer, I did a stint in the DevonAir newsroom, editing tapes, compiling listings and being general dogsbody. The newsroom gave me a real buzz. There was a constant tension, driven by the deadlines of bulletins, and rush-editing a soundbite for a breaking news story made me feel at the centre of things. There'd been a couple of major stories, including one about a headless body, that got everyone excited. The race was on to identify the mystery woman and one journalist, who I had down as a future *Mirror* reporter (he had a bloodhound's nose for scandal), came running into the newsroom pink-cheeked, shouting, 'They've found the head! They've found the head! It was on this guy's *mantelpiece*!' He went on to become a sober-suited BBC correspondent.

One of the reporters, Daniel, I liked particularly. He was in his late twenties, good-looking and spoke with a gentle Cornish burr. Part of his job involved reviewing exhibitions, concerts and plays, for which he received complementary tickets, and I was flattered when he invited me to accompany him. Daniel was intelligent, but not bombastic, and unlike Tim, with whom I often felt out of my depth intellectually, I was able to discuss things with him as an equal. It made a refreshing change not to be browbeaten, and the more time I spent in his company, the more I began to realize how one-sided my relationship was with Tim. During those trips, our connection grew stronger, and one evening, after a show, instead of driving me straight home, he drove us to the beach at Budleigh Salterton. We watched the sun going down over the sea and as we stood there, he slipped his hand into mine without speaking. I looked at him, surprised, and he smiled. I could have said something then, but I didn't want to. I'd fantasized about the moment in the safety of the knowledge it would never happen – he had always been quite formal with me – and now that it had, I was breathless with excitement to find out what came next. I knew I was being disloyal to Tim but it felt more like disobeying a parent than being unfaithful to a lover.

We walked along the pebble beach, as tentative as teenagers, neither of us talking, and then he stopped and pulled me into his arms. His kiss was a young man's kiss, hard and urgent. There was nothing polite or politically correct about him now, and the sheer physicality of his tongue in my mouth was a shock. I found myself responding and for a while we stood locked in this embrace, kissing with a kind of desperation, and then he pulled abruptly away.

'We can't,' he said, as if someone had thrown a switch. 'This is madness. I don't know what I was thinking of.' He turned and started to walk back up the beach.

'Daniel.' I stumbled after him. 'Stop. Talk to me. You can't do – that – and then just go.'

He whipped round. 'I've got a girlfriend. You've got a boyfriend. Nothing can come of this. We got a bit carried away, that's all.'

And my heart, which had leapt for joy, felt suddenly as if it had been yanked out and left flapping on the floor like a fish in its death throes. A few minutes earlier, I'd glimpsed a whole new future and it had been liberating. I knew Tim wouldn't let me go without a fight, but with Daniel's help I might have had the courage. Without it, I didn't have a hope.

I took Daniel's rejection very badly. I felt he was cold towards me at work so I got drunk and tried to pay him back by getting off with the future BBC correspondent, despite the fact that he was a head shorter than me and reeked of TCP. We ended up pissed out of our skulls and snogging in a bus shelter, which Tim witnessed from our bedroom window in Devonshire Place. He exacted his revenge in a brutal manner, making me commit sex acts in bed that we'd never done before, frightening me with his intensity. He fucked me as if I was someone else, not his 'P' but a whore, and I was left weeping with shame and bewilderment. Daddy's little girl had been defiled, and after that our relationship took on a different and darker tenor.

CHAPTER NINE

'When you leave, I will be sad, but I will not be destroyed.' This was one of Tim's mantras, although he only said it in the lulls between rows, never during the fights themselves. He repeated it like an affirmation, as if it was something he'd been taught to say, to convince himself as much as me. 'I'm like an elderly knight who has been granted the delightful privilege of escorting a young princess for a few miles down the road,' he said to me once, squeezing my hand. I hadn't read *Alice Through the Looking Glass* then, or I might have recognized the allusion. The fact that the elderly knight in Lewis Carroll's story couldn't stay in the saddle without holding on to Alice's hair is entirely within keeping; I'd seen Tim fall apart too often to believe he could ride on without me to support him, despite his claims to the contrary.

Ironically, the name of the song the knight performs for Alice is 'The Aged Aged Man' (among others), and it brought tears to the eyes of almost everyone who heard it. Alice, who had suffered an excess of poetry that day, was unmoved, but I welled up.

Of course, it is a mistake to imagine a knight's intentions are always honourable. During my third year at Exeter, I wasn't so much escorted on a path through the woods as locked in an unassailable tower.

People abuse the word 'love' all the time, and they abuse in the name of love, too. Tim drew a distinction between *agape*, unconditional love, which comes from the Greek word for charity, and *eros*, which is passionate, possessive and all-consuming. His love for me was, he claimed, the former kind, and he lectured me about its purity. 'Unconditional commitment to another' meant no strings, no demands, accepting the loved one for who they were without terms or conditions; a Christian love – even though he was an out-and-out atheist – that didn't require reciprocation and lasted eternally. In contrast, erotic love was sexual, narcissistic, irrational and jealous, a hot-blooded, hormone-driven condition that was ultimately destructive. If *eros* is all too human, *agape* is a quality that belongs mainly to saints, and Tim was not that. Impressed as I was with his learning, even I could see that he was conning himself. He may have given it a scholar's gloss, but his love was no more unselfish than the next man's.

Being on the receiving end of Tim's 'unconditional' love

often meant suffering. In the wake of my indiscretion, I discovered a cruelty in Tim that unnerved me as much as the callous way he'd treated me in bed. As far as he was concerned, his *machismo* had been dented, and there was no greater humiliation than that. He didn't sit me down and ask why it had happened, or examine the implications for our own relationship. That would have required too much transparency. It was safer to revert to type, thump the table and talk about a man's honour. Probably it was just as well. I couldn't have told him the truth. Had he known of my feelings for Daniel, the fact that I'd, however briefly, fallen for someone else would have been a different category of betrayal entirely. I wasn't sure what he would do, particularly if he'd started drinking, and knowing what I know now, I'm grateful for that instinct to keep quiet. And so I pined in secret, the hurt lying like a lead weight in my chest, while Tim goaded me with the special skill he had for finding my raw spots. True to his word, he didn't lay a finger on me. He didn't need to. The emotional battering he gave me was enough to make me do it myself.

'Why do you eat so much? You fill your plate with food. It's unattractive, watching you shovel it down.'

'For God's sake, take that lipstick off You can't wear scarlet, it makes you look like a tart.'

'I can't see how you'll understand Leibniz's logic when you can't grasp the simplest things I tell you. Only third-class minds make your mistakes.'

'Crying won't get you anywhere. Jesus, you're depressing

to be around. Being with you when you're like this is enough to drag any man down.'

And so on, and so on, insult upon insult, so that the thin carapace of self-confidence I'd built up the year before splintered and cracked, exposing the soft creature that I was. I'd had an eating disorder in my teens which I thought I'd overcome, but Tim's comments only made me comfort-eat more. I drank, too, in an attempt to inure myself, confirming his self-fulfilling prediction that I had a problem by downing whisky until I passed out in the spare room. My self-image deteriorated further when he sent me to Harrods for a make-up lesson. The bored beautician gave me startling eyebrows, spidery eyelashes, hectic cheeks and a deep ruby pout and I rushed straight to the Ladies afterwards and scrubbed off what I could with a wad of tissues. Staring at the cartoon face in the mirror – I looked like a ravaged Betty Boop – I thought that maybe he'd never loved me, Kate, at all. It was as if he wanted to remake me as someone else and I wouldn't fit the mould.

We did get over the recriminations, and there were still good times, but it was no longer 'happiness interspersed with quarrels' but very definitely the reverse. I managed to get my infatuation with Daniel into perspective – he was, I felt, a bit humourless and could appear self-important at times – and I spurned him when he asked to resume our 'working relationship'. However, my love for Tim was no longer a pure thing. Bruised by the fighting, it had acquired a masochistic edge, an almost chemical craving for scenes. It had been coming right from the start and, after two years together, I imprinted on this pattern with Pavlovian slavishness, equating passion with metaphorical beatings that left us limp and drained the next day. Tim was the hard stuff and I was addicted, hooked on the drama and adrenaline highs, a domestics junkie without the fat lip and black eyes. Even though I hated him at the time, the intensity of that emotion had an extraordinary vitality. I felt as if I had never been so much 'in the moment', so aware of myself.

With finals only a few months away and the deadline for my dissertation approaching, the stress of coping with Tim on top of revising began to take its toll. My dependence on the painkillers he doled out increased, and when I couldn't get hold of his Distalgesic I took paracetamol, too many of them, chucking down double the dose. It wasn't just that I wanted to knock myself out; there was an element of defiance, too. Nothing said 'Look what you've done to me' like a siren-wailing dash to casualty, and if Tim couldn't rouse me in the morning, he might realize how deep the hurt went. I always did wake up, though, furry-tongued and groggy, but it would be lunchtime before I could get myself together to start work again. Tim, of course, put my oversleeping down to laziness, which caused more rows, and I was tempted to take a real overdose to prove him wrong. I didn't know that Distalgesic, which is paracetamol with dextropropoxyphene (also manufactured under the brand name Co-proxamol), is highly addictive and it explains a long-standing addiction to painkillers which took several years to overcome.

I also started cutting myself, superficial slashes on the arms, each thin red line a mark of mute frustration. On one occasion, when Tim had just said something particularly vile to me, I'd been in the kitchen washing up the lunch things. I stood at the sink, looking down at him in the garden he'd created, a little sanctuary of troughs and tubs and hanging baskets overflowing with petunias, geraniums, marigolds and nasturtiums. He'd trained sweet peas against the wall, which he was preoccupied with tying up, a reminder of the tender times at Barton Place that were lost to me now. His back was turned resolutely to my teary face, and I was filled with such fury that he could hurt me and then walk away that I seized the nearest sharp object to hand, which was an open meat tin, and dragged the jagged edge across the inside of my wrist again and again, observing the pin-pricks of blood ooze out of my skin with an almost detached curiosity. I remembered Tim describing the time he'd tried to commit suicide and I felt a brief, but perversely satisfying, thrill of kinship.

I didn't tell Tim about the cutting – it would merely have set him off on another 'How-could-you-do-this-to-me' rant – and I didn't tell anyone else, either, because I couldn't explain how he did it; how he got me into such a state that I'd bite the carpet in toddler-tantrum hysterics, kicking and screaming and snotting and frothing like a madwoman. Several times I wound up outside the house, rocking under a bush in the dirt and dark, my fingers numb and my mind empty. I wasn't capable of rational thought on those grim days. I was a jangling mass of untuned sensations, as if I was wearing my skin inside out, my nerve endings protruding like loose wires sparking off haphazardly.

I don't recall seeing much of our friends, or doing any-thing except study, and my 1983–4 appointments diary – which is full of driving lessons and essay deadlines – bears this out. But there are photos that prove we got out, from time to time. There is Lindsay's wedding to his fiancée, Karen, the groom in flapping checked flares. Tim is smiling his inscrutable smile, dapper in sunglasses and suit, and I am hanging on to his arm, tottering in my Russell & Bromley snakeskin heels. Significantly, it's the only photograph of us together in the entire album. There's a dinner party at Devonshire Place where we're eating Tim's famous straw-berries and cream, and other photos with Sally and James at windswept Crackington Haven. There's Tim on the pier at Torquay and Tim on the Cobb at Lyme Regis and some tussocky beach shots that look like Dawlish Warren. The sea, always the sea. We never went sightseeing inland. We needed the coast and the open sky and the roar of the breakers. For both of us, though in different ways, it made us feel free.

One wallet of photographs that didn't make the album is labelled 'Morwenstow, Spring 1984'. There are lots of pictures of steep-sided valleys, tumbling streams and the rocky shoreline, but none of the person we went to visit, Tim's sister, Antonia Davy. Antonia lived in an old stone cottage called Lower Cory at the mouth of the deep inlet with her husband Leo. It was the first time I'd met her; Tim had been cagey about introducing us and I got the feeling there wasn't a lot of love lost between them. Antonia was tall with cropped silver hair and an angular figure and her sleeves were rolled up, revealing a streak of dirt on her forearm.

'I've been pulling leeks for lunch,' she explained, extending her hand to me. 'I hope you like soup, Kate.' She took me in. Her accent was refined and she exuded the same crisp confidence as Tim.

'Yes, yes, I do,' I stammered, shaking her hand.

'Good. You can help me wash the grit out of them.'

She turned on her heel and led us up a path through an overgrown garden. Tim and I exchanged glances. He had warned me that she could be brusque and I was already a little intimidated.

We prepared the vegetables in a long, low-ceilinged kitchen. Antonia's manner was not unkind, but not encouraging, either. She was a formidably intelligent woman and obviously didn't suffer fools, and I felt self-conscious and rather silly beside her. She asked me lots of questions, which was like being interviewed by a headmistress: how had Tim and I met, did he help me with my studies, how did we get on living together? I answered politely, if not always truthfully. 'Your brother has driven me to self-harm' is not what you say when you're trying to make a good impression, particularly to a member of social services. I caught her looking at me with a calculating expression, as if she were trying to make up her mind about something, and then she said, 'What do your parents think of you having a boyfriend Tim's age? Do they approve?'

'They're fine about it,' I replied defensively. 'They get on really well with him.'

'What does your father do?'

'He's a policeman.'

She looked surprised. 'Tim knows this?'

'Yes.'

'And your father, does he know about Tim?' I hesitated. I could foresee an inquisition developing if I told her Dad had no idea Tim was a lifer. 'Yes,' I lied.

'I see.' She braced her arms on the table. 'Well, if your parents are supportive . . .' There followed a long pause, then she sighed and said, 'It's not my policy to interfere in Tim's relationships. I've absolutely nothing against you, Kate, I just don't think the difference in your ages is helpful, for either of you. Tim knows how I feel on that score. But that's my issue, not yours. So long as you're happy . . .'

'I am. We are.'

'Well, then. Subject closed. I'll finish this off; you set the table.'

She was, I noticed, non-committal about Tim, which disappointed me. Tim had told me that Antonia had taken him in after his release from prison, though he'd been vague about how long he'd stayed. I wanted to find out more – not just about Tim's immediate past, but about his background, his family, his upbringing – but the stern set of Antonia's mouth (so like her brother's) warned me this was off-limits.

So I spread the cloth and sipped my sherry while she boiled and stirred, and Tim and Leo, who were both partially deaf, held a shouted conversation at the other end of the kitchen.

I thought it best to keep my head down during lunch. Tim and Antonia argued about everything, particularly politics – he called her a 'bleeding-heart liberal' – but it was obviously well-trodden ground. I got the feeling that their sparring was a way of avoiding a deeper, more personal confrontation; there was an underlying tension between them that excluded Leo and me, and afterwards Antonia ordered Tim to help her wash up, despatching Leo to show me his paintings. The washing-up seemed to take a long time. Eventually, Antonia called us back into the kitchen for coffee. Tim was not there, and I spotted him outside, standing with his back to the window.

'Come and see the garden,' Antonia said, glancing at Tim's silhouette. 'Everything's suddenly come on with this mild weather. The primroses are glorious.' She went outside and I followed, ducking under the lintel. Tim was smoking. He was wearing a red gingham shirt, and his biceps bulged under the short sleeves. The dark hairs on his arms, I noticed, were fluffed up, like an animal's. He exhaled through his nostrils, staring fixedly at the view.

'Watch out for the moss on the path, Kate, it's slippy,' Antonia said briskly. I undertook a dutiful tour of the garden with her, which was wild and rambling and extended some distance from the house. 'This is our boundary,' she said, stopping at a fence. We stood listening to the distant sound of the sea, the warmth of the spring sunshine on our faces. 'See the butterflies,' she said, pointing at a pair of dusky brown ones dancing over the brambles. 'They love this spot. It's a real suntrap.' She grimaced, as if she'd said the wrong thing, and fell silent. I glanced at her, but her face was closed. Uncomfortably aware of Tim waiting by the porch, I turned around. I knew he wanted to get away and suddenly I did, too.

By March 1984, Tim was working for Pickerings almost full-time, his thesis having long since been abandoned. Lent term ended and from then on I was flat out to exams, but the closer I got to finals, the more Tim continued to unravel. I had started to apply for jobs – traineeships with the BBC, journalism courses, newsroom assistant's positions at local radio stations – and had several important interviews lined up during the Easter holiday which Tim proceeded to sabotage systematically. Nothing overt; he was far too manipulative for that. Ostensibly, he was being supportive, paying for a smart, non-student wardrobe of skirts and jackets, a new haircut, new shoes, driving me to Cardiff or Oxford or Bristol or London, wherever I needed to go. But on the way there he'd start to pick and criticize, a campaign designed to undermine my confidence and wreck my concentration. The BBC traineeships were intensely com-petitive – I'd got into the top 100 out of 3,000 applicants – and it was vital to be on top form. Already nervous about the interview, Tim's taunts ensured that, by the time I got to

Cardiff, my face was awash with mascara and my nose was a glistening red. The receptionist took one look at me, pointed me in the direction of the Ladies', and switched my slot to half an hour later. I managed to pull myself together to get through the interview but blew it by attempting to exit through a stationery-cupboard door.

It didn't occur to me that Tim might have an ulterior motive for his behaviour, because I didn't realize his destructiveness was deliberate. I assumed, as always, that it was my fault; that I'd wound him up by saying the wrong thing or misreading the directions or just by being me. It seemed I couldn't do a single thing right in Tim's eyes. He became foul-mouthed and hostile, stamping around the house and swearing, and the more I cringed and cried, the more belligerent he got. Arguing back made him worse. Once, he said, 'You're like a black toad spitting poison at me.' I retreated to my room and tried to revise, but spent most of the time weeping into my toy lion's mane.

I should, perhaps, explain about Bwian here. Bwian was a large shaggy lion that Tim had liberated from Debenhams' window display. I'd found him waiting on the stairs when I came in to the house one day with a packet of smoked salmon and a half-bottle of Moet between his paws. He was very cuddly and very understanding and travelled with me everywhere. I know it sounds babyish but this fantasy was started by Tim, who was also the one that decided Bwian couldn't pronounce his 'R's'. I can only assume this speech impediment was a sop to Wittgenstein's, aphorism about lions and the impossibility of understanding their language; however, it was more likely to have been childhood regression on Tim's part.

It wasn't just that I couldn't understand Tim's vindictiveness: I thought I was about to lose everything I'd worked for. By now, finals were less than a couple of weeks away. I only had three papers, having already sat Part I exams at the end of the second year, but Part II carried a significant percentage of the marks. After taking an extra year out and then switching courses to a subject I'd never studied before, those three papers represented the culmination of four years of my life; four years that would be utterly wasted if all I got was a humiliating third or (the unthinkable) failed completely.

This was one of the lowest points of my relationship with Tim. I was virtually under house arrest and becoming increasingly scared by his unpredictable moods. They would alter in a flash and I was never sure what he would do next. I had never felt so alone. I hadn't seen Sally and James or any of my undergraduate friends in some time – everyone was busy cramming – and besides, none of them knew about this side of Tim. The Barton Place crowd had all left, as had Ginni, who graduated the previous year, and married couples Tom and Chris and Lindsay and Karen had moved out of Exeter. My parents, who'd met Tim a number of times (we'd even spent a family Christmas together), thought he was 'a good influence', although they knew we'd had 'our ups and downs', as Mum called them. I'd never had any contact with Tim's probation officer and it wouldn't have occurred to me to report my fears:

that would be treason, and even if I survived Tim's fury there was a risk he could be hauled back inside. I knew that if that ever happened, he would kill himself for certain.

And then it happened. Six days before my first exam, Tim started drinking. As the evening wore on, he became more and more aggressive and my own hysteria grew in direct proportion. The rational part of my brain, the part that, even while I was screaming on the floor, registered this demeanour with pragmatic detachment (I was, literally, 'beside myself'), knew that I had to get away, however close to finals I was. Tim was sitting in the corner, his face a dark, almost purplish red, a bottle of whisky by his side. He lurched to his feet, staggered sideways and knocked over the coffee table, sending the whisky and his glass flying. 'Fuck it,' he roared. It was a new bottle and he'd already drunk three-quarters of it. Now there was only an inch or so left. He kicked the coffee table, sending it crashing against the wall. One of the legs caught the telephone cable, wrenching the phone off the window sill. It fell with a protesting tinkle and the back came off the handset. 'Fuck it all to hell.' Tim swayed, glaring at the mess. 'I'm going for a piss.' He came over to where I was scrunched up in an armchair and leant over me, bracing his arms either side of my head. Putting his face close, he spat, 'And if you don't fucking stop *carrying on*, I'll . . .' He paused, his features frozen mid-snarl. I had never seen him so ugly and threatening. He had the same glazed look in his eyes that he'd had in Gran Canaria when he'd become psychotic. As with that incident, I wasn't sure whether it was me he was seeing in front of him now, or someone else. Whoever, it felt as if it were someone he hated from the bottom of his heart. I bit my lip, trying not to cry. Tim was breathing rapidly, sweat beading his temples. He hung his head, as if trying to recover himself, and then looked up at me again, his expression fierce. 'Just get out of my sight. That's the best thing you can do for both of us. Just get out of my fucking sight.'

I waited until he'd gone to the bathroom, and then darted for the broken phone. There was no dialling tone. I saw the batteries on the floor and stuffed them back into the handset, but when I tried to put the cover on, my hands trembled so badly I couldn't slide the piece into its slot. I realized I was trying to force it in upside down and tried again. This time, it clicked into place. I pressed 'Talk' and got a line. Shakily, I dialled my parents' number.

'Kidlington 2348.' My father's calm voice.

'Dad.' I started to sob again. The crying gusted out of me, taking all my breath. I couldn't stop it.

'Kate? What is it? Are you all right?'

I gulped. 'It's Tim. He's gone completely mad. I'm frightened he's going to do something.'

There was the sound of the toilet flushing from upstairs.

'Do something? What do you mean?' My parents still didn't know about Tim's past. I heard the bathroom door open.

'I – I don't know. He's changed. He's been drinking and he's got really nasty and he told me . . . he threatened me . . .'

The stairs creaked. A pause. He was listening.

'I can't stand it any longer. I want to come home.'

Footsteps, heavy now, descending rapidly.

'Can you come and get me? Please, Dad.'

'What's going on? Has Tim hurt you?'

'No, but —' I squealed as the handset was yanked out of my grasp.

'Tim here. It's all right, Chad. Kate's just a little over-emotional. Blown things out of proportion. I'm afraid she's had too much to drink.'

'Me, drink? You bastard! You liar! He's lying, Dad. He's lying! He's the one who's drunk.' I tried to snatch the phone back, but Tim blocked me with his other arm.

'There's nothing to worry about, Chad. Everything's under control. Kate's a bit stressed because of her exams and she's had a couple of whiskies and I'm trying to persuade her to go and lie down.'

'That's not true!'

'I'd let her talk to you again, but she's not in a fit state at the moment . . . no, I didn't threaten her, is that what she told you? Well, you know your eldest daughter, Chad. She tends to over-react. I'm afraid she took something I said the wrong way.'

'Give me the phone!' I made another lunge for it. Tim gripped my arm.

'I'm sure you'll find, Chad, that if you ring again in the morning, Kate will have a different perspective on all this. Besides, it's gone ten o'clock – too late for you to set out now. I'm sure Phyl won't want to slog all the way down here in the middle of the night. Really, it would be a pointless exercise. Kate's making a bit of a drama out of what isn't even a crisis . . . Yes, I'll hold.'

I could tell Dad was consulting with Mum. Tim listened, and then gave the phone to me. There was a warning look in his eyes.

'Kate,' Dad said. 'Your mother and I think it's best if we leave things as they are for tonight, and give you a ring first thing in the morning. Have a good sleep and see how you feel then. If you still want to come home for a few days, I'll drive down and get you. How does that sound?' His tone was professional, reassuring. My father used to work in the control room at police headquarters; he'd probably had many a domestic skirmish on the line before. I knew it was a reasonable response; it was asking a lot for him to pitch into the car then and there and Tim hadn't actually done anything to me. At least, now my parents were involved, he wouldn't have the nerve to. 'OK,' I said quietly.

'Are you sure?'

'Yes. But don't forget to ring, will you?'

'I'll call you at nine o'clock.'

'Thanks, Dad.'

'That's all right, lovey. You get to bed now.'

'OK. Night.'

'Night-night.'

Click.

Clink.

Tim had found another bottle. He poured himself a triple measure and threw it back, slamming the glass down on the table. I tensed myself for an explosion, but when he spoke, his voice was surprisingly matter-of-fact. 'You have insulted my honour, *hija*.' He came over to me and took the phone out of my hands. 'Did you not think of that?' He replaced the cordless handset on its base, disconnected the jack and picked up the telephone, wrapping the cable meticulously around it to keep the two pieces together. 'What goes on between a man and his wife is private. Obviously, I cannot trust you not to go shouting about our problems to other people.'

'You've got no right to do that. And I'm not your wife!' I flared.

Tim picked up my left hand, extending my third finger. 'Why do you wear my ring, then?'

'Because I can't get it off.'

'You are my wife.' He caressed the ring with his thumb. '*Mi espousa. Mi hija.*' He tried, clumsily, to kiss me.

I turned my face away. 'Leave me alone.'

'I love you.'

'Well, I don't love you. Not any more.'

It was said. Tim looked shocked. 'You don't mean that.'

'Yes, I do,' I said. 'I'm leaving you. I've decided. I'm going tomorrow.'

He shook his head. 'You're not going.'

'I can't cope with you, Tim. I've had enough.'

'You're not going anywhere,' he repeated. Tucking the bundled-up phone under his arm, he started to walk away.

Panic rose inside me. 'If Dad can't get through at nine tomorrow, he'll call the police. Do you want them knocking on the door?' Tim ignored me. 'You know what they'll do,' I shouted after him. 'What about your precious honour then?'

Tim stopped in the doorway. I saw him check his watch. 'That gives us ten hours,' he said. 'You'd better have a drink. Pour me another while you're at it.'

'What for?'

'You're not the only one who's had enough. We might as well enjoy our last night together.'

CHAPTER TEN

A rescue party arrived the next day in the form of Dad and
Sharon. 'Where is the bastard?' she said, hugging me. 'I put
my geological hammer in my rucksack, just in case.'

'Gone,' I said. 'I don't know where. A taxi came. He went
while I was packing.'

'Good riddance.' Sharon scowled. 'How could he do this
to you when you're five days from finals?'

Dad swung his legs stiffly out of the car. He gave me a
tight squeeze, holding me longer than usual. 'Are you all
right?' he asked gruffly.

I broke down then and cried into his shirt, overwhelmed
with relief. 'I am. But I think Tim's going to kill himself.'

It had been a terrible night. Tim had become so drunk that

he started hallucinating again, seeing people and shouting at them – and at me – in Spanish. I couldn't understand what he was saying, which made him all the more angry; his voice was rasping and harsh and spit flew from his lips and he kept pounding the table with his fist, bringing it down so hard that cigarette butts bounced out of the ashtray. His eyes had the burning stare of a madman, the kind of eyes you avoid on the Tube for fear of them locking on to you. Occasionally, he broke back into English, accusing me of seeing someone behind his back. He refused to believe me when I told him that I wasn't and seemed to connect this fictitious infidelity with some wider conspiracy. 'You've led them to this house and they're watching me.' The more alcohol he consumed, the more paranoid he became. He started shaking and crying. 'They're coming to get me. They're coming to get me.' Eventually, I managed to coax him up the stairs and persuaded him to lie down on the bed. 'Stay with me,' he begged. 'Stay with me tonight. One last night. Please.' He clutched hold of me. 'They can't touch me when I'm with you.' He pressed his body close. 'Tomorrow, when you go, that's when they'll come.'

I lay stiffly in his embrace until he slept, but when I tried to extricate myself I couldn't. His arms were wrapped round me like iron bands. I attempted to push him away, but his body was a dead weight and each time I struggled he grunted and clamped his arms tighter. Miserable and exhausted, I gave up and fell into a sweaty sleep. I was awoken three hours later by the dawn – we hadn't closed the curtains –

and for a few seconds the morning chorus conned me into thinking it was an ordinary day and I couldn't understand why there was this heaviness in my chest, like sadness solidified. And then I remembered.

I rolled over and peered at Tim. He was lying on his front, immobile, his head turned to one side. He looked old and slack-jawed, and at first I wasn't sure whether he was breathing, but when I put my face close I felt the fine hairs on my cheek prickle and the faint dampness of his exhalations. I got up cautiously and crept out of the bedroom and down the stairs, pausing whenever a step creaked. I needed to find the phone. I knew Tim had hidden it in the garage and discovered it easily enough, stuffed in a cardboard box that held fairy lights and Christmas-tree decorations. I plugged it in. To reconnect to the outside world was a massive relief. Never had I been so happy to hear a dialling tone. It was five o'clock: too early to call my parents yet. I made myself a cup of coffee, curled up on the sofa and waited.

'What makes you think Tim's going to harm himself?' Dad asked, as he negotiated Exeter's traffic.

'Because he did it before, when he thought he had nothing to lose.'

He grunted. 'I wouldn't have him down as the type. He always seems together. Very brisk and in charge. I suppose it's his army training.'

'That's the impression he likes to give,' Sharon said darkly.

'He needs to control people,' I said. 'But he's not in control himself. He's an alcoholic. When he drinks he changes personality completely. Then I don't know him at all. It's really frightening.'

Dad looked at me in the driver's mirror. 'Has he ever hurt you?' His voice was sharp.

'He hasn't hit me, if that's what you mean.'

'But do you think he might? Could he be violent?'

I stared out of the window. We were at a roundabout, hemmed in by lorries and cars. It didn't seem the time to tell him Tim was a lifer. My face ached from crying and my brain felt numb and all I wanted to do was sleep. Sharon gave me a questioning look. I closed my eyes. 'I don't want to talk about it right now.'

It took almost four hours to get back to Kidlington, where my parents lived. I dozed on and off, my head bumping against the passenger door, the conversation drifting in and out of my consciousness like background radio. I heard Dad say to Sharon: 'You've met him. Do you think Tim will really do something stupid?' and her reply: 'I wouldn't put anything past him.'

'But why all this now, just before her exams? He's been so helpful with her philosophy. To wreck it now . . . I just don't understand his behaviour.'

'That's the point, though, isn't it? After finals, there's nothing keeping her in Exeter. He's scared of losing her. That's why he's being such a shit. Though it's not a very logical approach.' She gave a bleak laugh. 'He's driven her away.'

Mum and Claire, my youngest sister, were watching out for us and opened the front door as soon as we swung into the drive. 'Tim phoned,' Mum announced.

'What did he say?' I asked anxiously.

'That he's gone to Barton Place.'

Dad put his hand on my shoulder. 'How did he sound?'

'Weird,' said Claire, who had taken the call. 'He was very formal. He's got this posh voice. It sort of sounded right, but when I thought about what he said afterwards, it didn't make any sense.'

As it turned out, Tim did almost kill himself, but not in some showy suicide attempt. He drank a crate of spirits and made himself extremely ill with alcoholic poisoning. Perhaps that had been his intention. He was hospitalized overnight, but discharged himself as soon as he was able to walk. He had a phobia about hospitals, their disinfectant smell, their squeaky-floored corridors, the loss of dignity. I suppose it reminded him too much of being in another institution.

I shut down completely, screening out everything but my books. For the next four days, Kant, Wittgenstein, Ryle, Hume, Locke and Mill took up all my mental capacity. As to emotional capacity, I had none. Tim had left me completely drained. We must have talked – although I can't remember what was said – because he came to get me the day before my first exam. According to Sharon, who chronicled all this in her own diary, he was 'very shamefaced but didn't apologize' and arrived carrying Bwian under his arm. Sharon didn't understand Bwian's significance or she might well have judged Tim shameless as well as shamefaced.

My parents greeted Tim politely, though less warmly than before. Nothing was said about the incident. My mother insisted on making tea, which Tim put three sweeteners in and swallowed scalding hot, and we were off within ten minutes. 'They know,' I said, as we took the Swindon road out to the M4.

Tim glanced at me. 'What, exactly?'

'Everything.'

He pursed his lips. 'I thought Chad seemed reserved.'

'What did you expect? Quite apart from the stunt you've just pulled, he's discovered his daughter's been shacked up with a lifer. It's a lot for any parent to take in.'

'How did they react?'

'They were shocked. But surprisingly understanding.'

'Even Phyl?'

'Amazingly, yes.'

'Hmm.' I could see him computing something. 'She offered me flapjack, you know.'

'There you are, then. Forgiven. Aren't you the lucky one?'

'They are absolute saints, your parents.'

'Yes.'

'They didn't make any comment at all?'

'They wanted to know the facts. I told them what you've told me.' He had obviously been expecting a backlash, if not banishment. With most parents, he would have got it. My parents, however, had a thing for underdogs. I'd painted Tim as a victim of circumstance and, rather than being suspicious of him, they were sorry for him.

'Are they Christians?' Tim asked, as if this was the only explanation.

'Not officially. Not church-going ones, anyway.' Dad was affable, laid-back and the least confrontational person I knew. He had inherited his tolerance from his parents, who lived their lives around the Church of England, but even so, that wasn't his motivation. He had been raised to look for the good in people and make allowances for the bad, and he always did, despite being a policeman. My mother's motivation was more straightforward: she liked Tim. They both had a blind spot where our boyfriends were concerned – exes would continue to drop by for a chat and some boiled fruit cake for years after me and my two sisters had dumped them – and this house policy of liberal acceptance was something other people found difficult to comprehend. Including, at times, their own daughters.

'Didn't they mind that you didn't tell them from the start?'

'A bit.' It had been a difficult conversation to have. They had listened very seriously and asked lots of questions. Dad had admitted that they mightn't have been so accepting if they had known the truth at the outset, but I'd pointed out that this way, they'd got to know Tim without prejudice. His alcoholism was seen as a separate issue; that wasn't acceptable at all. 'They reckon you've paid your dues. "Everyone deserves a second chance." That's what they said. But they're not happy about your drinking and I'm not going to tolerate it, either.' I took a deep breath. 'I'm going back to Exeter to sit my exams, Tim. The rest I can't think about right now. Until then, I think we should stay out of each other's way. I'll sleep in my study room. The first hint of trouble and I'll go to Sally's.'

'You won't need to leave home again, I promise. I'll back off completely. Only you must let me look after you. You won't have to cook, or lift a finger round the house. You just concentrate on work and I'll do the rest. I've been to the supermarket,' he added briskly. 'The fridge is full of spoily things. And I did a little extra shopping. At the travel agent's. For when you finish your exams . . . If you still want to be with me then.'

'You can't buy me back, Tim. Things have changed. All the champagne and exotic holidays in the world won't make me stay if I can't trust you.'

'I know. But . . .' He sighed. 'If this is the end for us, Kate, let's go out in style. Come to Spain with me one last time. You can kick your heels and then, when we get home, we'll say our goodbyes and I shall count myself lucky to have had three such wonderful years with you. It's more than I ever thought I'd have with anyone and I don't begrudge a minute of it, even the bad times. Please.'

I reached for a tape and slid it into the cassette-player. 'We'll see.'

I got a 2:1, in the end. There were two firsts, half a dozen upper seconds apart from me and the majority of the class got 2:2s. There may have been a couple of thirds; I didn't look that far down the list. I was ecstatic. After everything I'd been through, I'd managed to pull it off. I'd proved myself in the examination hall, without Tim. Indeed, despite Tim. I had a brain, a good one, and a single honours degree in Philosophy if anyone wanted the certificate. The only problem was, what to do with it. At a milk-round seminar I attended, the employability prospects of degree subjects had been brutally summarized. Law, one of Exeter's strengths, was deemed excellent. Engineering, Computer Science – any kind of science – were also good. Education, another fair bet.

'And which are the worst subjects, in terms of getting a job?' someone asked. Everyone giggled nervously.

The speaker considered this. 'Archaeology's bad,' he said. 'But Philosophy's definitely the worst.'

My parents came down to Exeter for graduation. I still have the pictures. There's Mum, in French navy, with a white straw hat and matching gloves, looking like the Queen, and Dad, looking younger and trimmer and much more upright than he does now, who is definitely tiddly because he's trying to kiss her. And there's Tim, with his shades and his pencil-moustache smirk, toasting me conspicuously with orange juice. I'm in black robes and a mortar board, wearing my brown heels, which don't quite go, and I'm holding Tim's arm as if he's an uncle, or possibly a grandfather, except that he looks a little too possessive for that. He had managed to hang on to me, after all, and his smug expression states clearly that he doesn't intend to let me go again.

Tim said that the stress of my exams had got to him (making it, inevitably, my fault) and was, for some time afterwards, a reformed character. It was an act; an act he had become adept at over the years, and I was willing – too willing – to suspend disbelief. In my defence, he convinced almost everyone else, too. Mum and Dad were won round, as were our friends and relatives. Those people, like Sharon, who suspected Tim was not what he seemed, I could count on the fingers of one hand. I had a friend called Judith, who was an older woman and very shrewd, and an uncle and aunt, who weren't Tim's fans, either. They only met him on a few occasions, but there must have been an unspoken recognition, because Tim was always very denigrating about them and warned me not to listen to their advice.

Was it just that I had allowed myself to be bought, despite my protestations to the contrary? Looking at my twenty-four-year-old self in the next batch of photographs – I'm posing on the balcony of a five-star hotel with yet another azure pool behind me – it's a question I've been forced to ask. But that girl is smiling and relaxed; she doesn't look like she's compromised herself for a fortnight in Fuengirola. Tim wasn't well-off enough to be a sugar daddy and I knew the grief he was capable of giving me. As a trade-off, it would have been a poor one: it wasn't as if we led a jet-setting lifestyle. The arrangement we had was far more complex. Tim needed me, and he made sure that I needed him, or at least, that I thought I did. Therein lay his brilliance, not to say a degree of brainwashing. Of course I was susceptible, he'd made sure of that when he picked me. There are cult leaders who do the same thing. Their trick is to let people think they've chosen freely.

It went all right, that holiday on the Costa del Sol, after a false start in a grotty hotel, which had dodgy electrics, a shower that didn't work and a view of a plywood bull advertising sherry. I'd thrown a fit and Tim did a lot of shouting into telephones and got us moved to an upmarket golfing hotel favoured by Tony Jacklin. There are the customary shots of Mediterranean scenery and one of Tim with his glasses off, smiling in a slightly embarrassed way and looking softer round the edges, vulnerable even. His face is deeply tanned, apart from a white mark across the bridge of his nose and two paler circles around his eyes, and he's squinting like a mole that's poked its head above the ground in daylight. It makes a change to see him like this. Take away the dark aviator-style specs and his guard is down. In his eyes there's a glimpse of a person beyond the pretence. Suddenly, radically, he's human.

Sometimes, we got up early and went out exploring. We hired a dusty Fiat and drove inland to Ronda and inspected the ancient bullring, and another time motored along the coast to Puerto Banus to ogle the millionaires' yachts. Tim seemed familiar with this part of Spain – he had remarked on some changes to Malaga airport when we arrived – but when I asked him if he'd been there before, he was vague. I didn't think much of it: the relief of not splitting up, of not having to face up to that hell, of not having to make decisions about where to go and how to live without each other was so great that we had rediscovered our passion. We had siestas and lots of sex, feeding hungrily on sun-warmed skin scented with Ambre Solaire. It was survivor sex; our sensations heightened by cheating the bullet, and fucking without the restriction of sheets we made bold silhouettes on our shackled beds in the demi-darkness of the long, hot afternoons.

There is one scene that sticks in my memory, too minor for me to consider noteworthy at the time. Once, I came back up to the room, I overheard Tim on the telephone, alternately wheedling and talking urgently. I didn't understand what he was saying, but I got the impression he knew the person very well. I also got the impression he was talking to a woman. When I walked in, he paused the conversation, covering the mouthpiece. He said he was complaining about the maid service. 'They didn't change the sheets this morning.' I fetched my novel – it was bliss not to have to study philosophy – and left him to it. I thought it an oddly intense conversation to be having with the duty receptionist, but then Spanish was an intense sort of language.

The photographs of me and Tim stop when we left Exeter.

Abruptly. Our relationship didn't, but the urge to chronicle it did, as if I was already subconsciously editing out this final phase. We'd never talked about what would happen to us after university; to get to the end, to have survived three years together, was something neither of us had forseen. We were at a loss as to what came next. Our friends had all gone, even Sally and James, who had unexpectedly split up. Exeter had become a second home to me, but now there was no reason to stay. The only other place I knew was Oxford. So we decided to move there.

Tim was upbeat about this fresh start. It was easier for him to get to meetings in Stockton and London, and he'd been given Christopher Fothergill's blessing to start a new project, overseeing the computerization of Pickerings' operations. Back in 1984, computers were still peripheral to many businesses but the situation was changing rapidly. It was obvious they were the future, and at the age of fifty-nine and with no computer experience, Tim took it upon himself to modernize the company – or, as he put it, 'to drag them kicking and screaming into the twentieth century'. It was also a chance for him to shake off associations with the past. Exeter was where he had been rehabilitated after prison and the move to Oxford represented the next stage in him owning his life again.

It proved more difficult than I'd imagined. The terms of Tim's licence meant that our relocation had to be processed by the probation service. A formal handover was conducted in Oxford and I went with Tim to meet his new probation officer, Penny. The interview was conducted in a featureless modern office with grey carpets and fluorescent strip lighting that made my eyes water. Probably, I was more nervous than Tim: he'd made a point of keeping me at a distance from that part of his life and it was new territory to me. Penny asked me the same sort of questions that Antonia had asked, and in much the same manner. She was pleasant, but I found the formalities discomfiting. Watching her take notes, I realized I was part of the system too, officially linked with a lifer, my details on his file. It was a window onto another, more claustrophobic mode of existence, and the glimpse disturbed me. Penny's airless office had a security lock on the door. Beyond the polite smile there were still prison bars.

It wasn't only dealing with the probation service that marred the move. Some of our new neighbours weren't exactly welcoming, either. We had moved into a close in north Oxford and were renting another maisonette. Some of the inhabitants regarded our age gap as scandalous and stopped their lawn-mowing or car-washing or gossiping to cast dark looks in Tim's direction whenever we walked past. I suspected they thought he was some sort of pervert, and this was confirmed when we discovered we'd been under surveillance. And not just from behind the twitching curtains of the hardliners in Neighbourhood Watch, but by a member of Thames Valley CID.

Unknown to us, one of the locals was a police detective. The police had, as part of the licence process, been informed of Tim's whereabouts, and because this detective lived near to us, he took a special interest in our domestic set-up. The next day, my father received a telephone call at work: 'Sergeant Pitson, do you know who your daughter's living with?' Fortunately, Dad was able to say yes. If I hadn't told him the truth about Tim, the situation would have been a great deal more awkward. I felt guilty enough as it was, but he waved it off breezily.

'I thanked him for his concern and told him there was nothing to worry about,' he said. 'Tim's had a hard life. The man deserves a break.'

As a show of solidarity, Dad helped us move in a heavy three-seater sofa, which had to be hoisted in through the first-floor window because it wouldn't fit up the stairs.

'I hope your colleague is watching this,' Tim puffed, as the sofa dangled dangerously above his head. 'He'll be delighted to report an accidental death if you drop that thing on me.'

We furnished the place with an assortment of second-hand furniture bought through the classified columns, and once we'd got Tim's Persian rugs down and his Impressionist prints on the wall, it began to feel more like home. The downstairs room was turned into an office for Tim, who purchased an Apricot computer. I was the rootless one now. Back in my home town with no job and few prospects, I felt a failure. What had been the point of spending three years getting a degree when it had no currency in the marketplace? I wasn't alone: unemployment was the scourge of Thatcher's Britain. Miners were being laid off in their thousands by the pit closures, and set beside the sacking of entire communities the cause of arts graduates did not evoke much sympathy.

In an attempt to make myself more employable, I knuckled down to acquiring more basic skills. Financed by Tim, I took evening classes in typing and shorthand, resumed my driving lessons and attempted to learn Spanish with a Linguaphone course. An expensive set of tapes ended up gathering dust, but I did learn to touch-type quite proficiently and passed my driving test first time. I also got roped into the local SDP/Liberal Alliance group, out of which grew a useful contact in journalism. I was offered the chance to do some reviewing for a local free newspaper, the *Oxford Star*. I was ecstatic, but Tim was not as delighted as I'd hoped about this career development.

'You said you didn't want to do that any more.' He shook the *Telegraph* aggressively. 'Even this I only read for the international news. These so-called "Home" pages,' he stabbed page three with his index finger, 'they're all titillation. Trampling over people's lives. Is that what you want to do? Because that's what it's about. You want to be a hack, you have to get your hands dirty. And it's not just dirt. Sometimes, it's blood.' He glared at me. The newspaper trembled, ever so slightly, in his hands.

I had heard this tirade before, many times. It was one of the reasons, along with the self-serving conclusion of my dissertation (heavily influenced by Tim's arguments for press regulation), that I had decided against going into hard news.

However, I still wanted to write, and I didn't see how this would put me on the slippery slope to gutter journalism.

'It's a *theatre* review!' I shouted, waving the tickets in his face. 'A play. What possible harm can there be in that?'

As it happened, a great deal. The play was Harold Pinter's *The Lover* and the leading man had a heart attack on stage in the middle of an erotic scene involving some fantasy role-playing. I had read the play dutifully beforehand, so when he missed his cue twice I knew something wasn't right. The audience was rooted, unsure whether this hesitation was part of the play, and then time seemed to stop and the room filled up with the noise of his stertorous breathing. The production, by an amateur company, was in the round, and we were seated so that the audience looked down on the stage. In a few, shocking seconds, the acceptable fiction, the bargain of pretence, was stripped away and there we were, watching this poor man, dying for real before our eyes in an embarrassingly naked performance. After what seemed an eternity, the director hurried on and announced, 'I think he's ill. Is there a doctor in the house?' and people shuffled to their feet, almost reluctantly, as if they wanted to see how this new drama concluded.

I didn't sleep that night. The sound of the man's harsh death-breaths were still echoing in my ears. It wasn't just that, though: I had a journalistic responsibility to deliver some copy in the morning and it wasn't going to be a 150-word theatre review. It was the type of story I'd decided I didn't want to do and precisely what Tim had railed against.

Banner headlines burned behind my lids. 'Sex Scene Actor Dies on Stage!' I knew journalists (one in particular) who would have relished writing an eye-witness account, but I was tortured by the man's untimely and very public end and didn't want the *Star* to make it sound sordid. My contact, when I rang the next day, had other priorities. 'Was the *Oxford Mail* critic there?' he asked urgently, and when I told him I didn't know he said, 'Damn. I'll have to check. If not, we've got the exclusive.'

The *Star*, which was a weekly, came out the following day. The story got a column on the front page but not the lead, because the *Mail*, which was a daily, got the splash. Consequently, our story was brief and to the point and the headline wasn't as sensationalistic as I'd feared. I was surprised to see myself quoted as '*Oxford Star* reporter Kate Pitson', even though I hadn't yet written a word for the paper. It was a beginning, but not the kind I'd imagined. My first journalism job, and I'd already got my hands slightly soiled.

After the initial settling-in period, Tim had again become hard to live with, pulling against any attempts on my part to assert my independence. Although he wouldn't admit it, he was overstretched by his brief for Pickerings, and as a result he was stressed and irritable. He was also suffering a great deal with his back and by the evening his face would be grey with pain. Late fifties isn't considered old these days, but Tim's ankylosing spondylitis, combined with the hammering his body had taken from alcohol over the years, had turned him into an old man. Our sex life was virtually abandoned, and the lack of physical contact and the estranging rows degraded our relationship to such an extent that I began seriously to question why I was still with him. That holiday in Spain had proved to be our last high point and we should have signed off after it, as he'd suggested. Except that it was never a real suggestion on Tim's part; merely an attempt to buy time.

I wasn't even sure I loved him any more. Love was something I had come to regard with mistrust. When a man tells you he loves you more than anyone he's ever loved in his entire life and simultaneously turns you into a miserable, shrinking wretch, you either question the concept, or you question your sanity. By Christmas 1984 the situation between us was so bad that I was afraid I was going mad, and Tim was doing his best to reinforce this. 'You're not in your right mind,' he used to say. 'You're not responsible. You're not the Kate I know any more.' He blamed hormones, hysteria and the full moon when he couldn't think of anything else, but never, ever himself. To do that would have meant holding up a mirror to his own warped psyche. It was a typical inversion: he was by now demonstrably unstable, his behaviour characterized by lightning mood swings, violent rages and paranoia. Our conversations were fraught, full of invisible hair-triggers, any one of which could trip an almighty explosion.

I almost believed him. Tim's ability to portray any

scenario remained so plausible that I would find myself thinking he must be right, even when common sense said otherwise. It was true that I got depressed, though this was due to Tim, and when my depression collided with his destructiveness it had the same effect as two weather fronts slamming into each other, creating a spiralling vortex into which we were both sucked. We clawed our way out in 4.00 a.m. sessions of tears and tea, but each time it got harder to do. 'I can't seem to remember what sort of relationship we had for those three years,' I wrote in my (now resumed) diary. 'I don't feel as if I know this man at all. It frightens me. I can feel everything closing in.' I was on the verge of a complete breakdown, but I had enough strength of will left to realize this was going to drag one, or both of us under. Luckily, some sort of primitive survival instinct kicked in and on 28 December, three days after a calamitous Christmas, I packed my bags and left.

CHAPTER ELEVEN

Tim came round the next day, bleary-eyed. 'The house is like a prison,' he said. 'I can't cope with being there alone. You've got to come back with me, if only for a few hours. I don't know what I'll do otherwise.'

I thought about the short time I'd spent with my family, the relief I'd felt at being back home. So much of the tension in my daily life had dissolved already. After the high-alert state I was always in with Tim, it still didn't feel quite real. Relaxing, watching TV, eating Christmas cake – none of it seemed appropriate, like laughing after someone had died. Talking about my feelings felt equally disloyal. I knew Tim would brand me a traitor. I may have walked out, but his hold over me remained strong. When he said he was finding the strain almost impossible to bear, I knew what he was threatening. A familiar weight resettled itself on my shoulders. What had I been thinking of, imagining I could get away from him so easily?

The house was full of fresh flowers and there was chilled champagne in the fridge, as if this was some sort of celebration.

'I'm not coming back to live with you,' I said, as gently as I could.

He sat down heavily in a chair and put his head in his hands. For a moment I thought he was crying, but then he gave it a characteristic irritable shake. 'I'm not going to pretend I understand your decision, because I don't.' He gave a sigh of resignation, as if being forced to indulge me. 'I cannot comprehend how it has come to this, but I'll accept your terms, because I love you and I need to go on caring for you. So long as you will agree to see me, I'll back off. I won't make demands.' He held up his hands in an 'I surrender' gesture. 'Do we have a deal?'

We had a deal. Another one. The next day, Tim came over to us and stayed most of the day. The day after, he came for tea and spent the evening playing cards with Mum and Dad and Auntie Anne and Uncle Martin. He and I were reserved with each other but he was very jolly with the grown-ups. I sloped off to watch an Ayckbourn play on TV but I could hear their laughter rising from the living room. It occurred to me that perhaps he needed the warmth of our family and our busy house more than me. If I felt aggrieved at him invading my space, it was tempered with a certain amount of relief. At least I could off-load some of the guilt about his well-being. Mum and Dad could look after him instead.

It was harder adjusting to life as a single woman than I'd thought. I missed the material benefits, particularly having a car – queuing in the cold for buses and then queuing in the dismal DHSS offices for my giro and then slithering home on icy pavements wasn't much fun – but I consoled myself that this was how other unemployed graduates lived. There was one encouraging sign: I was getting more reviews to do, which I took very seriously even though the *Star* was a free newspaper.

All this time I had continued to apply for jobs. It was dispiriting, going for interviews and then being turned down, and after eight months of this I was beginning to lose hope. Spying an opportunity to tie me to him more closely – it was a week since our break-up – Tim dreamt up a position for me with Pickerings, inputting data for a 'management information service'. Naturally, this meant working at Tim's house. When, in a moment of weakness, I said that I might be interested, he tried to steamroller me into it, putting plans into action there and then (he was in Stockton at the time), even though I'd told him not to change anything already agreed with colleagues. Once again, I was trapped. To refuse to do it would cause problems for the company and make Tim look unprofessional. 'I feel like a poor, pathetic puppet,' I wrote. 'Tim is always there, inescapable and forever daunting me.'

I was saved by anger. My own anger, this time. It was a new, and unfamiliar emotion and it took me – and Tim – by surprise. His dependence on me, and the endless tricks he used to manipulate me, sparked such a fury that for once it overrode the guilt. I didn't know I had such reserves in me; it poured out of me from a place I didn't recognize, completely unstoppable, as if I was regurgitating all the rage and hurt I'd stored inside. Every time that he told me that he needed me back, that I didn't know how close he was to breaking, I felt instantly furious at him for laying the responsibility at my feet. It stemmed from fear: he had backed me into a corner with his constant guilt-tripping, but this time, instead of submitting, I fought back. Something had changed in me, though I wasn't able to see it for myself then. It was taking all my resources just to keep Tim at bay or I might have realized something that he already had: the balance of power was shifting.

Tim's job was just the start. When I said 'no' to that, he tried another tack. This time, it was something more drastic. He had invited me to lunch at the house. It looked shabby and unkempt. There were patches in the dust where I'd removed my ornaments from the mantelpiece, gaps where my books used to be on the shelves, pale rectangles on the walls where 'my' pictures had hung, even a neat space between the shoes and boots downstairs, all waiting, apparently, to be reclaimed. A month had gone by since I'd left, but already it was like entering a timewarp. I hung about moodily, leafing through old colour supplements, while Tim stirred soup in the kitchen. A glossy new paperback on the dresser caught my eye and I turned it over idly. It was about euthanasia. I could hardly breathe. He was really planning to do it. I stuffed it behind a cushion, shaking. I managed to keep quiet all the way through the soup, but when Tim returned with French bread and cheese I could hold it in no longer. Retrieving the book from the sofa, I thrust it under his nose. 'What on earth do you mean by this?' I screamed. 'Why have you got it? What are you going to do? Well?'

'I should have thought that was perfectly obvious,' he replied, slapping butter on a crust.

'But . . . but . . . you can't.'

'And who's going to stop me? We lead our own lives now, Kate. You made that clear. And what I do with mine is my business, and mine alone.'

'You know I don't want you to do *that*. I mean, of course things are different, but I still care.'

'When I can no longer be of any use, I'm not going to hang on being a burden to anyone. Not my style.'

'No, you'd rather blackmail me with this book.' I hurled it across the room. It hit the dresser with a crash, sending more books cascading onto the floor.

'I'm not blackmailing you. That is an outrageous suggestion. I would never stoop to such a thing.'

'You are always blackmailing me, one way or another. And this – this is just your latest ploy. Well, it won't work.' I was the one spitting at him now. 'You go ahead and top yourself then. Just don't expect me to hold a pillow over your face, or however you're planning to do it. I am fed up with being made the cause of your suffering. I'm not. You do it to yourself.' And with that, I ran upstairs and buried my own face in one of his pillows.

I didn't want Tim dead. I wanted him to be happy. I wanted him to find someone who could handle his insecurities and his volatile temper, an intellectual equal he could spark off who would share his interests, care for him when he was in pain and love him unreservedly. It would have to be an older woman, an academic perhaps, but when I tried to imagine the scenario I realized it would never work. Tim would never cope with a relationship with an confident, emotionally mature woman. And no twenty-year-old was going to put up with his demands now. I was Tim's last chance, and I couldn't carry him any more. I told myself I should just accept that and stop resisting the impulse to save him. It was, as he said, his choice. Perhaps the kindest thing I could do would be to let him go, let him take his life, in a manner and at a time of his choosing. I was appalled at myself for contemplating such a thing – and at the consequences that might befall me – yet it felt right. It was the ultimate, unselfish gesture, a demonstration that, after all and beyond everything, I did still care about him. When Tim came up to me with a brandy, I put it down undrunk and took him in my arms. We held each other without speaking and the touch of our bodies, after such a long time, said more than words ever could.

'Don't do it by yourself,' I whispered. 'When the time comes, let me be there with you to hold your hands.'

He wrapped his arms around me tighter but did not reply. I thought we had a deal. Our final one, this time.

That avowal – I hesitate to call it an avowal of love, and yet I think it was – brought about a small breakthrough in those dark February days. We became more relaxed with each other and even managed a few civilized 'dates', driving out to the White Hart at Wytham, which became our local. Tim capitalized on this by suggesting a weekend break in Exeter. After a month of freezing weather, it had turned unseasonably mild – 'Perfect for a stroll on Exmouth beach,' he pointed out, 'we could revisit a few old haunts and go to the Ship at Cockwood for one of their seafood lunches.' I wasn't sure, but he'd been looking so much brighter that I hated to turn him down. 'We could look up Nigel,' Tim prompted, 'and James.' That swung it. We'd had a mysterious invitation to Sally's wedding – she was marrying someone I'd never heard of – and I wanted to hear all about it.

Tim drove us to Exeter in a hired BMW, doing 100mph most of the way. We found Nigel, covered in mud, playing football, looking as scruffy as he always did, but everything else had changed. Ginos, our favourite Italian restaurant, had moved, the Cowley Bridge, once the 'in' pub, was deserted, and Barton Place had been sold. We walked round there and inspected the crumbling stucco, cupping our hands to peer in through the dirty windows. The house had an abandoned air. I remembered sunning myself on Tim's balcony, revising on the daisy-strewn lawn, the parties and the laughter, and felt heartsick for that simpler time. Three years on and the past had acquired the golden glow of that country-house summer in *The Go-Between*. As to the future, I had no idea. Tim and I were booked into the Imperial Hotel. It meant sharing a room and, therefore, a bed.

As I was undressing that night, the telephone rang. A 'Mr James' was in reception to see us. It was 11.30, typical of James, but we didn't mind. He told us all the news, including the revelation that Sally was marrying some up-and-coming trade unionist, which caused Tim to snort in disgust. He'd already had his fill with Nigel, who had argued Scargill's case over spaghetti and clams, and to rub it in we were sharing the hotel with a delegation from the TGWU. They had rough accents and beer-bellies and bushy sideburns and had been in the bar all night getting progressively louder. I suppose he'd envisaged a more romantic atmosphere in which to reclaim me.

We did make love. In my heart, I'd known we would. It had obviously been Tim's plan all along – go back to where we'd started, rekindle the flame – although I hadn't liked to admit it, I wanted it, too. Sex, anyway. I was emotionally battered by the fighting between us and craved the comfort of physical contact, the reassurance of being held. To be naked, to touch and be touched, to feel your body responding – there is an honesty in that, even if it is not a wise move. It sounds contradictory, but many 'estranged' couples sleep together, and besides which, I thought I could handle the consequences. It was painful physically and emotionally but the next morning, warm and silky from sleep, it was easier and more natural.

'This a new beginning for us, darling,' Tim said, nuzzling me. 'We won't let things slip back again, ever.' We were cuddled up, his knees in the crook of mine, one hand on my belly, the other cupping a breast.

'No,' I whispered, although even as I said it, I didn't believe it. I'd already slipped back, after all.

'I've been so desperately lonely without you, Kate.' I heard the croak in his voice and turned over. He looked haggard, as if he hadn't slept well. 'I didn't tell you before, but this is only the second time I've lived by myself since I came out of prison.'

'Oh.' I hardly dared ask, but I knew I had to. 'What did you do the first time?'

'This.' He held up his wrist. I stared at his raised white scar, the crude blanket stitches. 'And I was close to doing it again this time, too. If you hadn't – come round – I'm not sure I'd be here now.' I traced the scar with the ball of my thumb, trying to imagine what it would have been like to discover him. The trail of crimson, the bloody bath, Tim's wrists gaping open like bleeding lips. Holding his hand while he slipped painlessly away was one thing; discovering his mutilated corpse was another. How would I have felt if I'd found him like that?

Responsible, said my conscience. 'It would be your fault.'

Free, a small voice inside me whispered. *You would be free.*

199

I didn't move back in. I didn't need to. By now Tim was having most of his meals at Kidlington, and felt like one of the family. He got on extraordinarily well with my parents, forging a weird, *Last of the Summer Wine* kind of threesome. It was a curious arrangement. There was no discernible jealousy on Dad's part, despite the fact that my mother came over all giggly and girlish in Tim's presence. He still had the old charm and would flirt with her and chivvy her by turns, bringing her flowers, taking her shopping and chastising her in a masterful manner over the *Guardian* quick crossword, which had become a daily ritual for them. Tim seemed to provide something different for both of them. In Dad's case, it was a mate. My father was a gregarious man and he enjoyed having Tim as an ally. They bonded over the gardening, digging and planting companionably while arguing about the role of the Police Federation, which my father was active in.

It was an ideal arrangement for Tim, who got his meals cooked, people around him and a release from the pressure of his job. But it wasn't just that our house provided Tim with convivial company. By hanging out with my parents, he was able to keep an eye on me. I was going over to his house regularly, but it was more or less to keep the peace. There were moments of tenderness and, providing we stuck to non-inflammatory subjects, we got along, but it was a patched-up job, a relationship worn threadbare, held together by denial on his part and guilt on mine with occasional sex to salve our loneliness. The lovemaking, at least, was still good and it seemed a small price to pay to keep Tim reasonable. He had agreed, in principle, that I should be allowed to make 'other friends', but his presence at home cramped my style so effectively this was virtually impossible. I couldn't expect normal people to understand our set-up. It barely made sense to me.

I first fully understood that Tim was losing control when he directed his anger very deliberately at someone else. Until then, his destructiveness had been contained. I was the one who always caught the force of the blast and although my parents sometimes got the fallout, Tim had never, to my knowledge, involved other people. However, when I started campaigning with Evan Luard, the Alliance's candidate in north Oxford, Tim became obsessively jealous. Evan, a highly respected former MP, was a bachelor the same age as Tim and after canvassing he would invite me back to his house in Observatory Street where we'd discuss poetry and drink sherry from dusty glasses. Our little chats were quite innocent, but Tim resented the time I was spending in his company hugely. One evening he delivered a furious ultimatum: 'If you don't get back over here for the night, I'm ringing Luard and chucking all your SDP stuff out of the house.' I refused, never thinking he'd do it. Forty minutes later, I received a worried phone call from Evan. Tim had emptied the contents of our campaign office, which I ran from his house, out onto the driveway, in the rain.

I thought at the time his response was out of character: it wasn't just that he'd verbally attacked a stranger; I had a legal responsibility, not just to my candidate, but to the ward, and he'd done his best to wreck it. It was embarrassing, too; although ironically, Evan found it flattering to be regarded as a love rival and began kissing me along with the Coleridge. He subseqently came to view himself as a kind of rickety protector, regularly proposing marriage. It wasn't the first time Tim had behaved so impulsively, but his over-the-top reaction showed an unusual lack of judgement and I feared he was suffering some sort of breakdown. He had been under increasing pressure with his job, working all day and half the night with two computer consultants. Donald Fothergill, Christopher's son, had been there, too, and there had been some conflict at board level that seemed to stress Tim out a great deal. But that wasn't all.

'I'm spitting blood and I've been coughing it up for three days,' he said, when I went round the next day to have it out with him over the business with Evan. As a pre-emptive strike it was brilliant. I couldn't berate a sick man, and when he told me he thought it was lung cancer I was beside myself with worry. A check-up revealed a small lesion on the back of his throat – nothing serious, apparently – but a few days later he was back in the casualty department of the John Radcliffe at 3.00am with uncontrollable shaking and a racing heart, for which they had to tranquillize him. It was being by himself, he told me; he couldn't cope with being alone at night. And so I dutifully slept over, organized his shopping, did secretarial work for him and cancelled an interview, my eyes puffy from (now habitual) drugged sleep and my feet dragging their invisible chains. There was no point in objecting; I was now a daily witness to his manic behaviour, as were my family and his colleagues. 'I can't leave Tim, no matter how badly he treats me. He's too unbalanced and it would be dangerous,' I wrote despairingly.

And then, like some sort of deus ex machina, a way out was presented to me. I was unexpectedly offered a job on the *Oxford Star*.

Getting the job – I was to be editor of the arts and leisure section, which entailed a crash course in subbing – forced Tim to relinquish his control over me. He knew this, and he hated it. That first week, his behaviour towards me was intolerable. When I went to visit him, he attacked me verbally, without provocation, becoming so hostile that I walked out. By now he was struggling to maintain a façade of professionalism at work and people were beginning to talk. I couldn't look after him because I was at the *Star* and, once again, my parents took over the role. When Tim had a panic attack, my father would drive over and walk him round the block, talking him down on laps of the estate, and at home Mum fussed over him like a mother hen.

I avoided Tim's visits whenever possible. He was a liability and, after his recent outbursts, I didn't want to risk him coming near the paper. However, when he realized he couldn't prevent me doing the job he became more conciliatory and one day I let him run me to the office. When I sat down at my typewriter, Carolyn, one of the journalists, looked up. 'So who's the old guy?' she asked. I realized she must have seen us through the plate-glass windows.

'Friend of the family,' I answered, inserting two sheets of copy paper and a carbon and bashing out a catchline. I felt her green eyes assessing me. I hit the carriage return with unnecessary vigour and it ratcheted up with a clang.

'I do believe,' Carolyn drawled, 'you're blushing.' She leaned her chin on her hand. 'Do we have a secret here?'

'There's no mystery,' I snapped. 'Honestly. He's no one.'

Wednesday, 22 May 1985, my first week at the *Oxford Star*, marks my penultimate diary entry. The final one doesn't come for another seven months. I was getting on with my life at last, and although I still saw Tim, he had apparently given up trying to control me. Until, that is, I got a proper boyfriend. Sam was an American, and a gentle giant of a man. He was also, according to Tim, gay. When I rubbished this, he told me he'd hired a private detective to follow Sam who could confirm this, and suggested I get an Aids test done. The implication that Sam was HIV positive was cannily timed – Rock Hudson had died barely a fortnight earlier and Aids was headline news – but Tim's claim to have hired a PI sounded pure Raymond Chandler. Nonetheless, he had succeeded in planting a doubt. Sam was thirty-nine and had never been married, something I had wondered about myself. He'd said it was because things just hadn't worked out, and I'd believed him, but that evening, at the late-night showing of *Body Heat*, I couldn't help wondering whether it was Kathleen Turner's breasts or William Hurt's sweat-drenched body that turned him on.

I continued to see Sam, convinced by his healthy appetite for sex that he couldn't be gay, so Tim took his revenge by trying to pick up another young girl. He was sixty; she was twenty. Lucy was a blonde, bubbly student and a friend of my sister Deb's. Tim had helped her with her sociology studies a couple of times and the relationship had been strictly pupil-mentor, but the third time they met, at a party, he had offered to drive her home and then whisked her back to his house without offering any explanation. Concerned and suspicious of his motives, she'd become even more apprehensive when he'd shown her into my old study-bedroom and pressured her with offers of rent-free accommodation, extra tuition and a holiday together, all the while making 'certain innuendoes'. Lucy, who didn't know Tim's *modus operandi*, had been worried and scared. It was now the early hours of the morning and all she wanted to do was to go home. Instead, she was being kept at Tim's house while he tried to persuade her to move in with him and dropped loaded hints about a sexual relationship. After taking her there without warning, Tim's inappropriate suggestions and obvious desperation to hang on to her must have seemed very sinister indeed.

Tim was in Stockton by the time I heard this, at a board meeting with Pickerings. Rather conveniently, he wasn't due back for a couple of days. I was absolutely furious. It was difficult to know what I was angriest about: the fact that he had frightened a friend, or the fact that his mentoring routine was just that – a system, a patter, a tried-and-tested formula – designed to get young girls into bed. A routine that I, at Lucy's age, had been gullible enough to fall for. When he rang, unexpectedly, late that night, I blasted him on the phone. Shaking with fury, I asked him what he thought he'd been doing. 'You practically abducted and terrorized poor Lucy.'

At these words, Tim went berserk. I was used to him overreacting about things, but this time his response was off the scale. 'You're not going to get me like that,' he screamed. 'I won't let you destroy me. I'm coming back now.'

He drove back from Stockton there and then, without stopping. The next morning, he demanded to see me. I was wary, but I went.

'You had better be very clear,' he said grimly, 'about why you're doing this. Because I can tell you now, you're not going to win. I shall make sure of that.' The threat in his voice was new, and nasty. I had never heard him be so deadly cold. 'I'm not doing anything,' I replied, 'I was upset about the way you treated Lucy. You were completely out of order.'

'And accusing me of abducting and terrorizing a young girl isn't?'

'Look, I'm sorry I blew my top,' I said, trying to pacify him. His demeanour was disturbing, more so because, unusually, he was in control. He seemed to have gone beyond anger. 'Maybe it was a bit extreme, but – well, she didn't know what was going on. You took it too far.'

'*I* took it too far?' He gave a harsh laugh. 'Oh, no. Not me. You have.' He took a step towards me. 'You know why I was recalled to prison that time.'

I shook my head. 'No, I don't. You never said.'

'Come on, Kate. Tom must have told you.'

'He hasn't told me anything.'

Tim came up close. I could see the deep furrows in his forehead, white bristles on his chin. His eyes were trained on me, the black beams of his pupils fixed on my face. It was like staring down the barrels of a shotgun. 'You're lying.'

'I'm not. Really.' I tried to step back, but there was a table behind me. I gripped the edge with my fingers, bracing myself.

'That's strange,' he said. 'Because someone else used those same words against me once before. She accused me of abducting and terrorizing her, too.'

My mouth went dry. I didn't need to ask if it was true. One look at Tim's face told me anything was possible. 'That's why I was recalled. So you see why, Kate, I can't let you go around saying things like that. If the authorities get to hear about it – and I assume that's your intention – I'll be hauled straight back inside again. And this time, they won't let me out.'

I saw then that he was a man with nothing to lose, and the consequences terrified me. 'Get away from me. I want to go.' He caught hold of my arm. I started to struggle and scream, 'Let me go, I want to go', but he had me in an iron grip.

'Where? To the police? What is this, some sort of signal? What are you scheming? If you've set me up . . .' He looked around wildly, as if expecting the doors to burst open. I continued to scream, hysterical now. 'I know your game. What is it now? Rape? Is that what you're going to tell them?'

'No,' I howled. 'Just let me go. I won't say anything, I promise.'

'I can't let you go. I can't trust you.'

'Tim, please! You're hurting me.' He let go of my arm. I edged away, my eye on the door. 'I'm not going to the police,' I gulped, 'I'm going home.'

'You are not. You're staying here. I need to think this through.'

'There's nothing going on. Honestly. It's all in your head.'

He spotted me sidling towards the door and moved to block my escape. 'Kate. Don't make me commit a terrible sin.' His words made my blood run cold. I stared at him. I did not recognize Tim behind those hollow eyes. He had the look of a man who had played this scene before. Suddenly, everything made sense. The woman he had killed had wanted to leave him, too. I'd always believed it was an accident.

Until now.

CHAPTER TWELVE

It's no surprise Tim called himself a 'lifer'; it tells you his sentence, not his crime. I don't think I ever heard him describe what he did as a murder, hence my complacency. The truth that I had lived with a murderer for three and a half years, only hit me now, when it was too late to run. Here was a man who had not only killed intentionally, but, I now discovered, had been accused of abducting and terrorizing someone else. When he said, 'Don't make me commit a terrible sin', it was his uncharacteristic use of biblical language that made me realize this was no empty threat. He didn't believe in God, the connotation was for emphasis. We both knew what terrible sin he was referring to, and the 'Don't make me' told me he knew he was capable of it. And the only way you know that is if you've done it before.

Fortunately, instinct took over. Something told me that the worst thing I could do would be to go on the offensive. Tim's paranoia was such that to provoke him, or attack him physically, would almost certainly trigger a violent reaction. His behaviour before my finals had been frightening enough, but on that occasion he'd been drunk and the pattern was at least predictable. This time his psychosis was undiluted by alcohol and seemed much more dangerous. I took a deep breath and, looking him in the eye, said as calmly as I could, 'I'm not taking that blackmail, Tim. And I'm not staying here a moment longer. Let me out, now.' I had to press my lips together to stop them trembling. He scanned the room behind me, as if still expecting the SAS to abseil through the window. I kept my gaze on his face, aware of his chest rising and falling, the silence amplifying his ragged breathing. The moment seemed to go on for ever. Then he said, 'Very well.' He wore a peculiar, twisted smile as he opened the door, as if he had scored some kind of victory. I stumbled out and ran all the way to the bus stop, making it just in time to hail a Barton bus. 'Kidlington, please.' I handed the driver a five-pound note, which was all I had on me. He looked at it and sighed grumpily. 'Return?'

'No,' I said.

That wasn't the end of it. Tim said he had secretly tape-recorded our encounter. He then telephoned me at work to tell me he was serving me with a writ, and told me that his solicitor had a copy of the tape, which would be sent to my employers as 'proof' of my guilt. His charge was that I had committed slander against him, a crime so grave that, according to Tim, the Home Office had had to become involved. The accusations came thick and fast on the run-up to Christmas, so that my father was having to keep a daily record of Tim's increasingly bizarre allegations, culminating, at 11.00pm on Christmas Eve, with a phone call from him announcing that he was going to see the Chief Constable and complain about police harassment. His paranoia was now totally out of control and his unpredictable and threatening behaviour was menacing us all. Contact had to be restricted to our solicitors. Tim had successfully cut himself off from everyone who had loved and supported him.

It turned out that the whole thing was another of Tim's fantasies. There was no writ and no tape had been sent to his solicitor, or indeed anyone else. By then I had apologized, in writing, for using the words 'abduct and terrorize', even though I hadn't used them to bring him down, as he supposed. Nonetheless, his vendetta continued, and I was haunted by the feeling that he would do everything in his power to destroy me. The last entry of my diary begins: 'Death weighs me down. I sense tragedy, there seems no other way out. He wants to drag me down, and go with me.' It ends with this long overdue statement of recognition: 'The man I knew no longer exists. But the man he has become was there all the time.'

★

211

On Tuesday, 31 March 1987, Tim was found dead in a hotel room in Bristol. My parents drove round to the cottage I was by then living in to tell me the news.

Mum fell into my arms, weeping. It was the first time I had ever seen her cry. 'He left you this,' she said, fumbling with tissues and a handbag. She produced a little gold-coloured box and handed it to me. 'He gave it to me before he left yesterday.' She blew her nose loudly. 'He didn't say why. Just, "Give this to Kate." He seemed to think you'd understand.' The box rattled when I took it. I opened it and tipped a small white seashell and two five-peseta coins into my palm. We studied these innocuous treasures. 'Do they mean anything to you?' Mum asked.

I closed my fingers around them. The message, if there was one, was mixed. Spain? Tim's honour? His roots? Our holidays? There was something that drew him back there, some link that I didn't understand. The shell was easier; it must have come from Exmouth, the one place where we were always at peace with each other. I turned it over, stroking its pearly smoothness with my thumb. Were these all the clues I was to get? Out of habit, I put it to my ear, even though it wasn't really big enough. There was a faraway sound, a faint whooshing noise: whispers of the sea – or the dull roar of nothingness? Blood pounded in my head. 'She'd better sit down,' I heard Dad say. He sounded a long way away, as if we were at opposite ends of a tunnel. Hands guided me to a chair. The world was upside down and I was enveloped in blackness. When, at last, I opened my eyes, the ceiling had stopped spinning. I was surprised to see the familiar lampshade, the artex swirls, the seismic crack in one corner, a spider web. For a moment I'd expected to arrive somewhere else.

There was, inevitably, a mystery surrounding Tim's death. After discussions with Christopher Fothergill he had retired from Pickerings a few weeks earlier and had told Mum and Dad that he was moving to Spain to start up his own business. Something about this story didn't ring true to me, but after all the intimations of tragedy that I'd had, the obvious didn't occur. When Tim rang to say goodbye, his voice stiff and formal, I replied sarcastically, 'So you're finally going, are you?' It turned out to be more apposite than I realized. He was spending the night before his flight in Bristol, at his usual hotel, the Swallow. I wasn't the only person to get a call that evening. Mum got one, too, but she wouldn't tell me what he'd said, only that it was 'personal'. The following day, a maid found him lying dead on the bed, a half-empty bottle of vodka and a packet of Distalgesic on the floor. There was no note, though the 'Do Not Disturb' sign on the door might have been a hint. They tried – and failed – to resuscitate him anyway.

Because it was a sudden death, the coroner's officer had been brought in to investigate and a date was appointed for an inquest. No one was talking about suicide officially. It was thought possible that Tim had overdosed accidentally – a couple of extra pills to ease his aching back, a few rash vodkas to see off the old country – and the absence of a letter seemed to confirm that. Tim was a man who liked to do things properly. He'd given my parents no clue that he was unhappy. Pickerings had offered him a generous retirement package and he'd been enthusiastic about setting up the business in Spain. No one had any doubts that that was what he was going to do. He proposed to set up a consultancy advising companies who wished to penetrate the British market, for which he certainly had all the right qualifications. It sounded ideal. People were happy for him and wished him well.

The idea that Tim might have taken his own life was anathema to Mum and Dad. They didn't like to think that he'd given up hope. I had moved out of home a year earlier because, after everything, they had continued to help him and I didn't want to be around Tim anymore. After I left they had become his carers, worrying about his deteriorating health and even sleeping with the bedroom door open in case he rang at 3.00 a.m. He was having seizures and had been hospitalized on a number of occasions; epilepsy had been investigated as a cause, but they were subsequently found to have been triggered by a magnesium deficiency, which can occur in alcoholics. After they'd nursed him, fed him and daily kept him company, the implication that Tim had taken his own life suggested a rejection of everything they'd done for him. And, more painfully, everything they'd been to him. I think my mother felt that especially.

I wasn't surprised. Tim had talked about suicide often enough, and I also knew that he was capable of using people ruthlessly. After the initial shock had worn off, my reaction was seething, boiling anger. The following day was 1 April, April Fool's Day. Another of Tim's little ironies, I thought bitterly. I had an interview in London for a job on *Capital* magazine, and I was determined Tim's death wouldn't stop me attending. With his history of attempting to sabotage my career, I was beginning to think this was his ultimate ploy, which shows how persecuted he'd made me feel. I took the train to Paddington and the Bakerloo Line to Oxford Circus and strode into the interview with my chin up, resolving not to break down.

'I'm afraid I haven't had much time to prepare,' I announced, 'but my boyfriend killed himself yesterday.' The editor, Caroline Stacey (who is now a well-known restaurant critic), looked taken aback. 'It's OK,' I added. 'We'd split up, anyway.'

She eyed me doubtfully. 'Why do you want this job?'

'Because I want to move to London. I want to get away from – all that.'

Half an hour later saw me sloping round Liberty in a Paisley-print depression. Caroline had been very sweet, but I didn't want sympathy, I wanted a new job, a new life. And with an opening gambit like that, I didn't rate my prospects very highly.

The next few days passed in a blur of telephone calls as the news spread about Tim. Even in death, he couldn't escape the notoriety that comes with being a lifer and the police did indeed attempt to make him a scapegoat (the subject of his abandoned thesis) until my father put them right. He was contacted by Bristol CID, who were following up possible suspects for a brutal murder that had occurred locally. An elderly woman had been beaten to death two days before Tim died. Did he think Tim could have been the perpetrator? Dad looked resigned. 'I would forget that line of inquiry,' he said stolidly. His normally ruddy face was grey with exhaustion. In the absence of Tim's family, Dad had taken charge and it was he who travelled to Bristol to identify Tim's body. He was taken to a mortuary, where Tim had been laid out in a coffin. 'My main impression was how small he looked, compared to the robust man he used to be,' he said later.

I didn't ask to go with Dad; I was in another relationship then with someone I'd met at the offices of the *Oxford Star* in Osney Mead, and we were engaged to be married. It had been over a year since I'd broken the connection with Tim and it didn't seem appropriate to go chasing off to view the corpse of my former lover. Besides, I didn't want to. Perhaps because of that, Tim's death didn't seem quite real. I knew he was gone, but somehow I still expected him to come stomping into the kitchen at home and brew up coffee, or make a fuss of the cat. I kept catching glimpses of him in crowds, and every time I saw an older man wearing a trilby hat like Tim's my heart would skip a beat. It wasn't until the coroner's office released his personal belongings that it really hit me. They were jumbled together in a heavy-duty polythene bag: his boots, expensive, high-sided leather boots that he'd worn to support his collapsing ankles; glasses, wallet, watch, a washbag, specially bought by me for business trips. I unzipped it and inhaled his scent. Inside, his flannels, toothbrush, hairbrushes, Grecian 2000 ('You can't walk out with an old man with white hair'), Old Spice aftershave. I unscrewed the top and it taunted me with memories of warm skin, a broad chest, lusty arms, afternoon siestas. Snatching his flannel, I buried my face in it, gulping the rancid smell. In the senseless moments that followed, I realized even the dead could live on . . .

Typically, there is another layer of subterfuge surrounding Tim's death. He made one more telephone call that I know about that final evening. He rang Dave Upton, who he'd worked with on his release from prison, and asked him to come to the hotel. When Dave got there, he found Tim eating a supper of smoked salmon in his room. He spent several hours with him before leaving quite late. His remark to me was: 'Had I been a Roman Catholic priest, it would have been like taking confession.' Tim gave Dave a sealed Jiffy bag addressed to me, with strict instructions that it was to be delivered into my hands. Dave motored up from Bristol the next morning, which was when we first learned of this mysterious encounter. Mum rang me at the *Oxford Star* to tell me and I dashed back, sure that the package contained a suicide note, and dreading it.

I was right. And I was not. There was a letter, but a letter that had to be read between the lines to discern its true meaning. It did not refer to me by name. It opened 'Hija. Espousa. P,' and continued, 'The only circumstances under which you will read this will be if I kick the bucket rather suddenly, either here or in Spain.' It went on in crisp, unemotional language to describe Tim's failing health, his increasingly frequent seizures, which he claimed to have concealed from my parents and everyone else, apart from a neuroscientist at the Radcliffe Infirmary, who had confirmed a diagnosis of epilepsy, something his GP had always denied. ('Goody for old Dr R. He never was much use, was he?' Tim had added, to counter this.) He continued: 'I shall carry on as long as I can without letting people down, endangering them or otherwise becoming a burden. I have an instinct that I will not last long enough to settle down in Spain. No matter. You know my philosophy on that.'

I certainly did. I suspected the business about epilepsy was a cover story, and this proved to be the case. (Tim had actually stolen headed writing paper from the eminent neuroscientist's desk and forged a letter diagnosing his 'epilepsy', which my father, recognizing Tim's distinctive scratchy hand, destroyed.) It was obvious Tim meant me to see through this excuse, but the letter had been carefully couched so that I would not be in the position of receiving a suicide note. He continued by saying that, should such an event occur, Belinda and her family were provided for, 'and therefore you need have no hesitation in taking for yourself what is your right, the little that I have left (but it was such fun spending the rest?) and my household effects . . . I like to think of you breathing a sigh of relief over credit cards and car bills as you clear them. But then I have always been incurably practical/romantic rather than romantic/romantic?' He had paid for his furniture to go into storage for three months, and enclosed a rough inventory. The letter ended: 'Sell them if you want. Use them if you want. You owe me no duty except to benefit from what little I have to leave you, *hija*. Your always loving B.'

I re-read the letter in a mist, unable to take it all in. There was a card with the letter, one that I'd originally given to Tim. It had been sent from our pride of toy lions, too, and it had a picture by Pissarro, one of his favourite Impressionists, on the front. Inside, Tim had added: 'Darling P. Thank you for the best years of my life.' The anger that I'd felt over the past days and months dissipated in an instant. Most heart-wrenching of all, though, was the inventory: bed sheets, glasses, the record player, light fittings, bath towels, photograph albums . . . the writing, scrawled on ripped-out sheets of notepaper, grew looping and almost illegible, sliding down the page at a sloping angle as if tailing off in distress. My B had been sobbing as he wrote it, and the ink was splodged with tears.

An open verdict was recorded at Tim's inquest. He had not taken enough pills for suicide to be proven. Mum and Dad were now convinced, though. 'I should have guessed,' Mum said. 'When he rang, he said . . .' She hesitated. 'He said, "Love you, Phyl." I don't think he meant it *that* way,' she added hastily. 'It was more like a sort of – I don't know – a sort of "thank you for everything". But you know how formal he was.' She laughed a little nervously. 'It wasn't the sort of thing he would have said if he'd been coming back.'

I don't think I'd ever needed convincing that Tim had taken his own life, but that letter removed any doubts. The thought of him dying alone in a hotel room made me despair. Tim hated hotel rooms. No matter how luxurious they were, they inevitably reminded him of a prison cell. Just four walls to call his own space. Lying on the bed, it must have been familiar – too familiar – territory. Had he been frightened, I wondered, as he waited for the darkness finally to dissolve him? I had not been there to hold his hands after all. I felt guilty about that, as if I'd reneged on my part of a bargain, even though we'd been estranged for over a year. Not that Tim had paid any notice of that: on the few occasions we had spoken since Christmas 1985 he'd continued to call me 'darling' and '*hija*', despite my coldness towards him. As for the letter, it blithely ignored our fifteen-month hiatus, forgoing apologies or explanations and addressing me as if we were still as close as ever. But then that was part of his game plan: I suspect he knew he'd reel me in with it. There's nothing like a big dramatic gesture to wipe out the past. I was hooked all over again.

Ordering the flowers was the most difficult thing I had to do in preparation for the funeral. Tim had sent me a message, and it was my turn to respond. I took the company minibus into town, which was loaded with telesales girls, tuning out of their chatter. When Jack, the driver, braked and swore at a cyclist in front, I was jolted back to reality. What to write? But I knew really.

The florist put on her discreetly sympathetic face when I told her the flowers were for a funeral. 'We have a minimum charge of ten pounds,' she said, pushing a laminated ring-binder towards me illustrating their range of bouquets and wreaths.

'I don't want those. I just want some freesias – the coloured ones you've got outside,' I replied carefully, a lump blooming in my throat. I chose a simple spray, unwrapped. 'And what message would you like?' she asked, pen poised.

'Can I write it? It's rather . . .' My voice tailed off. Personal? Difficult to explain? She passed me the pad. I leaned over it, blinking, and wrote: 'B. *Te amo*. P.' I did not cry. Signing the cheque with trembling hands wasn't easy, but I managed to carry off the rest of the transaction without disgracing myself. I walked out, swallowing hard. It seemed as if everyone was looking at me with curious eyes as I swam through the crowds of shoppers in the reeking covered market. Whole rabbits hung outside the butcher's shop, paws crossed, glassy-eyed. Sometimes, at Christmas, there were deer. Usually, I circumvented this shop, avoiding the carcasses, but today I'd walked right up to it without noticing. Choking on the intimate smell of blood, I held my breath and bolted. Reality receded and reappeared as I climbed back into the minibus, which was rustling with purchases from Top Shop and smelt of damp hair and warm bodies and the sulphurous whiff of egg sandwiches.

The funeral was two days later. I bought 24-hour waterproof mascara and dressed in black from head to toe, including underwear, suspender belt and stockings. The matching lingerie was a tribute; I knew Tim would like it. I would play the young widow after all. Once arrayed, it was easier to carry off the role, though by mid-morning I was feeling sick and Dad had to administer whisky. 'Are you sure you wouldn't like a nice cup of tea?' Mum asked, but I said I needed alcohol, and for once I didn't care if they knew it.

Friends arrived. Chris, heavily pregnant, but looking beautiful, and an unusually sombre Tom. 'The doctor didn't want her to travel,' he said anxiously, putting an arm round Chris's shoulders.

'And I said I wouldn't miss saying goodbye to Tim unless I was in labour,' Chris joked. 'So if my waters break in the middle of the service the vicar can get hatching and despatching over in one go.'

She and I embraced, giggling, and I felt her huge bump rear up against me. I was reassured by their presence. We'd been through so much together at Exeter and they'd known Tim in a way that no one else but I did. Ginni turned up next, serious and restrained, with a new boyfriend in tow.

He looked bewildered. I didn't blame him. Tim was a tough act to follow. My fiancé wisely wasn't coming.

My father insisted on calling the crematorium 'the Crem', which made me wince every time he said it. Everything about the crematorium made me wince. The whole, production-line smoothness of it, factory-processed, date-stamped death. It operated on a snappy turn-around, one group of mourners entering the chapel pale and tense while the previous group left through a different door tear-stained and quivering. Standing in the grim car park awaiting our turn, I noticed Tim's daughters. Belinda, who I'd met several times before, was looking stoic; Julia (whom Tim had always referred to as 'Pookey') was sobbing. Antonia did not come, she had lost Leo shortly before and told Dad she was not up to her brother's funeral.

'It's better for you to cry,' an aunt said, and I saw a vein green in Deb's left temple and that Claire's face was red and blotchy. 'I still miss the old bugger,' she sniffed, which, for a second, almost made me smile, because she and Tim were always clashing. Many of my relatives had come, as well as our friends and a sprinkling of Tim's business colleagues, including faithful Dave. 'Good turnout,' Dad said briskly, as a hearse drew up in front of us. A coffin was slid out and borne aloft. 'Those are our flowers on top,' Mum whispered. I stared at the burnished wooden casket. Tim was in there. My Tim. And I didn't want to share him with anybody.

The first hymn set me off. As the chorus swelled, so did I. I slumped against the pew, head bowed, shoulders shaking, swamped by a grief I didn't think I could feel, not after so much hate. Mum's hand, blindly reassuring, gripped my arm, or I would have slid to my knees in an undignified heap. I could hear Uncle Martin singing valiantly behind us, his voice cracked with emotion.

I didn't take to the priest. He reminded me of a smug professor I used to have, whom Tim had nicknamed 'Old Jollywobbles'. He took Dad's typewritten notes to heart, relating Tim's degrees, his career as a businessman, his intellectual ability. 'He was a highly intelligent man who loved to challenge ideas,' he read, unaware there was a subplot my father had seen fit to omit. 'I can see he and I would have had a lot to talk about. We would have sparked each other off,' he added in self-congratulatory tones. (So he would, I thought, sniffing angrily. But you don't know how.) 'Most of all,' the priest finished up, 'he was a gentle man.' I glanced at Dad. He smiled at me. It was more than Tim deserved, but in terms of a secular pardon it was the most forgiving, the most generous accolade Tim could ever have hoped to have got.

As a ceremony, cremations lack finish. I would have preferred a burial; I wanted a handful of earth to fling, to hear the soil rain onto the casket, to see grave-diggers lifting their shovels, but failing that, a blazing funeral pyre would have done. Something dramatic, something gutsy. Something. Instead, we trooped out and stared at the flowers, which were stacked in their own little marked bay on a concrete porch outside. I spotted my freesias, half-hidden behind a waxy wreath from Pickerings; they'd got the message right, which was all that mattered. '*Te Amo.*' I love you. Pickerings had paid for the funeral and Christopher had wanted Tim's ashes buried at the crematorium, with a headstone, but I'd refused. The seashell Tim had left for me was in my handbag, wrapped up in tissue paper. If he wanted to go out with the tide, then that was what I would do for him. This charade wasn't goodbye. I would travel down to Exmouth, and then I would be able to let go of him properly.

That's what I thought. But that was before I decided to find out about Tim's past.

PART TWO

AFTER LIFE

CHAPTER THIRTEEN

A few months after Tim died, I used my contacts to obtain cuttings of the story from newspaper archives. When I read about what Tim had done, I realized why he'd been so against my going into journalism. He knew this day would come, that I would find out, and he did everything he could to deflect me. That it never occurred to me to investigate his background while he was alive is a mark of the influence he had over me — had over us all — and perhaps, had I taken up some other career, I might have continued to accept what he'd told me. But I didn't; I persevered with my ambition and became a journalist, and journalists ask questions.

What I discovered shocked me, but the revelations only raised more questions. I was left in limbo with these unresolved issues eating away at me, unable to move on. The following year, I planned a pilgrimage to Exmouth on the anniversary of Tim's death, and when that fell through I went the next year, which caused a row with my husband. My first marriage, which I had rushed into on the rebound, never stood a chance. The damage caused by Tim's domineering personality and emotional abuse had a knock-on effect: I'd wanted the antithesis of Tim, or so I thought, but I was forever comparing, drumming up dramas, trying to replicate the formula. Tim hovered over us like a ghost.

After that marriage broke up, I went wild, skittering around London drinking too much and getting involved with other older and unsuitable men. I was desperate to feel something. Sex gave me no particular pleasure, it was simply part of the package. It was as if, ever since I'd parted from Tim, I'd become numb. 'I want him back,' I confessed in my diary. It's a testament to the consuming nature of my obsession that knowing the details of Tim's crime didn't affect this yearning. If anything, it intensified it. Dangerous men are a lure and attraction to lifers is well documented. I didn't place myself in this category at the time, naturally; our relationship had become elevated in my mind to something much rarer. That ability to selectively edit the past astonishes me now, but that's how I was back in the late eighties. No one could follow Tim and I thought I'd never fall in love again. My diary – it's the last one I ever kept – concludes despairingly, 'I just can't bear these ordinary blokes.'

Stephen, a divorcee three years older than me, proved to be my saviour. I thought he was another ordinary bloke when I first met him, but within ten minutes I realized he was an extraordinary man underneath. He's needed to be; I've given him a rough ride at times, especially in the early days when I was still suffering the backlash from Tim. Stephen, who has a very black sense of humour, cultivated by sitting through murder trials as a law clerk at the Old Bailey, dealt with this rather mockingly. I was outraged – Tim's story demanded reverence, not jokes – but despite some tantrums on my part, it had the desired effect. I stopped romanticizing Tim and, with Stephen's chipping away, the pedestal I had put Tim on was gradually whittled down to a stump. Then, in 1994, Stephen was relocated to York and I went with him. Suddenly, Tim's story was in my face again. Not only had his trial been at York Assizes, but we ended up living five minutes down the road from the court.

When, eight years later, in September 2002, York Crown Court (as it is called now) had a rare public open day, I booked on a tour. The bewigged clerk told us to sit anywhere, so, prompted by an urge to experience the ancient court as Tim had done, I chose the dock. I stared across the huge leather-covered table around which the prosecution and defence normally sit and tried to imagine how he must have felt, facing the judge. The clerk made a jovial reference to 'the prisoner' and all eyes swivelled towards me. A shaft of sunlight flooded through pantheon skylights in the ornate domed ceiling and I sat there, illuminated, like an actor frozen in a play. I looked up at the tiered public galleries, which surround the courtroom on three sides. They had been packed back in March 1971; Tim's five-day trial for murder was the hottest ticket in town. It was theatre in the round, with Tim centre stage, and by all accounts it was a bravura performance. Being in the dock made me realize something I hadn't, in my self-absorption, given much thought to before: I knew how the drama ended; what I didn't know was how it began.

As the tour group shuffled out of the room, I went across to the cramped jury benches and sat there out of curiosity. It immediately gave me a different perspective, and not just on the room. Glancing across at the dock, I asked myself a question: would I have found Tim guilty? He'd never denied being responsible for causing the woman's death, but he had always denied any intention to do it. The version of events he'd given me was incomplete, that was undeniable, but he had stuck to that basic story throughout the trial and afterwards. The jury didn't believe him; they found him guilty of murder and, given the evidence, most reasonable men and women would have done the same. But I knew Tim, I knew how he thought, how he operated. Was it just feasible that he had been telling the truth? Something he'd said to me, very early on in our relationship, came back to me: 'I lied to protect someone.' Who was that 'someone'? Why would he lie? And had that lie cost him his liberty? It was there, in the courtroom, that I vowed to find out.

In a sense, what follows is something of a personal retrial of Tim, an attempt to let him redeem himself – or not. I'm not concerned about protecting his reputation now. I don't feel angry, or vengeful, or bitter. I just want to know the truth. When I started to write this book, I didn't know how it would end. I knew what was in the cuttings, but that was all. Originally, it was going to be just a memoir, but then I decided to turn detective, to reconstruct not just the murder, but as much as I could of Tim's past. And the more I dug, the more overwhelmed I became.

Talking to the people who were closest to Tim – Antonia, Belinda, his colleagues, his friends – it became clear there was a big part of Tim that no one ever knew. Least of all me, in my solipsistic naivity. But it was when I began talking to the professionals whose lives Tim crossed – the detective who arrested him, the barrister who defended him – that something even more disturbing became apparent. The reports in the papers only tell half the story. If you believe the motives the police were considering, it may have little to do with the truth at all.

That visit to the court was what finally committed me to writing this book. Tim's past was a mystery, a mystery that I needed to solve, whatever horrors I had to face about him, however unpalatable the reality. My living in York had brought me full circle back to him, and there was a kind of karma in that. There were too many coincidences to explain it logically, too many dates and times and people and places that fell into a pattern during the investigation. It started with the date of the murder, which was thought – although no one can be absolutely sure – to have been on or about 28 January 1970. My ninth birthday.

CHAPTER FOURTEEN

'This is a rather strange and certainly a gruesome story you are going to hear,' the prosecutor, Mr Geoffrey Baker, QC, said to the jury at the commencement of the trial of Timothy John Franklin at York Assizes on Wednesday, 3 March 1971. The newspapers were rather more straightforward. The *Northern Echo* said it had 'overtones of Alfred Hitchcock and Agatha Christie', and called it 'one of the most sensational and horrifying crimes the North has ever known'. The trial lasted five days and the description that follows is based on coverage by local and national newspapers, including the *Yorkshire Evening Press*, the *Sun*, the *Daily Express*, the *Daily Telegraph* and *The Times*. This is how I first properly encountered Tim's story, and it was the starting point for my own investigations.

The story, as it was told to the jury, begins in early 1963 in the exotic atmosphere of the West Indies. Timothy Franklin, who was described by the prosecution as 'a man of hitherto impeccable character, of undoubted high intelligence and no mean intellectual and commercial ability', was a business consultant and had been sent to Jamaica to do a survey of the banana industry. There he met Richard Strauss, an agricultural consultant, who lived in the capital Kingston with his wife and eight-year-old daughter. Franklin was looking for a confidential secretary to help him prepare his survey and Mrs Strauss, at her husband's suggestion, offered her services. She was 'a very cultured and pleasant woman and, by all accounts, good-looking,' said Mr Baker, and so began what one newspaper described as 'a women's magazine love affair', which was to result in Elizabeth (also known as 'Tina' or 'Betty') Strauss filing for divorce. She left her husband in June 1963 and returned to England with her young daughter. Franklin followed on ten days later. They lived with Tina's aged mother in Droitwich Spa until 1966, when the three of them moved into a large house called The Garths in North Otterington, near Northallerton, North Yorkshire.

Franklin occupied a self-contained flat in the house, but, said Mr Baker, 'there was no doubt that Mrs Strauss was his mistress'. A secret means of communication was discovered by police officers, who found a hole in the wall covered by hinged wall mirrors on both sides. One door was in Franklin's flat; the other opened into Tina Strauss's dressing room. Ostensibly the couple lived separate lives, while continuing to meet in secret through the mirrored doors. This charade was necessary to hide their relationship from Tina's husband, with whom she had had a long legal battle over maintenance payments for her daughter. Richard Strauss had continued to pay his ex-wife a 'substantial income', but had reportedly sent over investigators to check out the precise nature of her domestic arrangements. There was a great deal of money at stake: Richard Strauss was extremely wealthy and their daughter was heiress to almost half a million pounds, a fact that was emphasized repeatedly by the press.

Outwardly, at least, Timothy Franklin and Tina Strauss appeared to have settled into village life in North Otterington. He commuted daily to Stockton-on-Tees, where he was sales director for a lift manufacturing company called Pickerings, while she took part in local cultural life, taking French lessons in Darlington and becoming treasurer of next-door St Michael and All Angels church. But their life of 'concealment and subterfuge' had been marred by Mrs Strauss's volatile temper, claimed Gilbert Gray, QC, defending. In his evidence, Franklin said that Tina had thrown things at him and had once threatened him with 'a kitchen knife or scissors'. Nevertheless, he did not consider himself to be in constant danger of attack. Despite her flashes of temper, they lived 'a peaceful life' and she showed, he said, 'considerable love and affection' towards him.

However, by the beginning of 1969, Tina Strauss appeared to have tired of living in this rural backwater. She was a society hostess with 'a sophisticated international background' said Mr Gray, and to her the North Riding was 'dull, lacking bright lights and gay activity'. She also wanted to live in a hotter climate, but Franklin was happy with his job and did not want to move abroad. It was then that Tina told him she was going to leave, a proposition that made him 'hurt and extremely sad and depressed' and which was compounded by jealousy. He thought she probably had another man lined up, or the intention of finding one. 'She would not have taken off in a vacuum . . . She was not a solitary woman. She was attractive to men and enjoyed [their] company.'

But Tina didn't attempt to leave for another year, despite her repeated threats to do so. She was last seen on 23 January 1970, when she picked up her daughter from the cinema. After that, said Mr Baker, 'Mrs Strauss simply vanished into thin air and nobody saw her again.' On 29 January, Franklin told company director Christopher Fothergill that Tina had left him. Mr Fothergill, who knew the couple well and was a frequent visitor at The Garths, said Franklin appeared 'in his usual calm, cool, collected manner'. However, the next day the prosecution recalled Mr Fothergill to the stand after he admitted recalling further details of their meeting. He said that Franklin had a noticeable bump on his forehead and his hands were swollen and grazed, injuries, he had claimed, caused by digging in the garden. Mr Fothergill's wife, Elda, who appeared for the defence, confirmed this. In March, several weeks after Tina's disappearance, the Fothergills invited Franklin and Tina's daughter to stay with them after he showed signs of being depressed. He and the girl, then aged fifteen, went on holiday together to the Canary Islands in April, the same month that telegrams signed 'Betty' were received by Tina's mother and her solicitor respectively. They had been sent from Malaga, in Spain. Her solicitor received another letter in June, postmarked Stockton-on-Tees, this time signed 'Tina'.

Franklin was still living at The Garths with Tina's daughter, who attended a private school in Darlington, when word of Tina Strauss's abrupt disappearance reached the ears of Detective Superintendent Arthur Harrison, deputy head of the area CID. No one had questioned Tina's absence too closely at first because villagers knew the couple were not married and did not want to embarrass Franklin, but as time went on, gossip surrounding the circumstances at The Garths had reached fever pitch. Among the speculation, one piece of information that grabbed Harrison's attention was the fact that Tina Strauss had been key-holder for the church. Whenever she had gone away before, she had left the key with a neighbour, something she had failed to do this time. The talk was, what had she done with the key? Harrison decided to investigate and on 26 August 1970 police paid Franklin an informal visit.

Franklin told them that Tina had gone off with a wealthy

man and would probably be abroad, but he was sweating profusely and had 'a haunted look in his eyes', which prompted DS Harrison to suspect his story. Franklin said some 'very strange things' during the interview and dropped dark hints about 'watchers from Jamaica'. He was also alleged to have said, 'You have stumbled on something very big', suggesting that some dire fate might have befallen Tina, possibly at her husband's instigation.

The following day, the police went to see Franklin again. In a long interview, recorded in shorthand, Franklin gave detailed answers, which were, said Mr Baker, 'nothing more than a sustained and deliberate lie'. They included a 'fanciful account' of meeting a representative of Mrs Strauss at Malaga airport in April and handing over to him her mail. 'It sounded very much like some fictional spy drama.' Harrison was still not convinced, and when he learned that Tina's solicitor had received a cable from her on 17 April, he decided to check again with Franklin. This time, he asked to see his passport. It showed an entry for Malaga on the same date. Franklin was taken to the police station for formal questioning, but stuck to his story. The interview went on all night and into the early hours of the morning. 'I had almost given up,' Harrison admitted later. 'I didn't think he was going to crack. He was impressive.'

At 5.10 a.m., after hours of interrogation, Harrison finally got his break. 'Franklin said, "Superintendent, can I have your assurance [Tina's daughter] will be taken care of?" ' Harrison agreed and Franklin admitted, 'The body of

Tina Strauss is in the windshelter. I have done it.' When asked if her body was buried he replied that it was about six feet underground. Detectives went out at first light to excavate the area, a patch of ground that had been screened off for private sunbathing with four sections of 6-foot-high trellis, covered in climbers and roses and accessed by an archway. They dug down and gradually uncovered the body, which, from the state of decomposition, had been there many months. It had been wrapped in a bedspread and there was a ligature around her neck, consisting of a length of blue plastic clothes line, which had been wound twice around. A scarf had been stuffed into her mouth, apparently as a gag. She had injuries to the skull, nose, cheekbone and jaw and her voice box had been broken. The damage was so severe that her identity had to be confirmed from dental records.

'If the police had not made diligent and persistent inquiries, this violent death and disposal of Mrs Strauss might have remained uncovered for all time,' Mr Baker told the jury. When questioned again after the discovery of the body, Franklin admitted sending the cables and forging the letter. He told police he had thrown the typewriter away in a hedge. Asked why he had killed Tina, he said, 'It was simply that we had a row. She hit me with something just above the eye, and kicked me. I got hold of her and the next thing I knew, she was dead.' After that he said he was tired and did not wish to say any more and asked for a solicitor to be appointed.

The question of motive was impossible to establish, said

Mr Baker, who put forward three possible theories to the jury. 'It could have been jealousy, if there was some truth about her going off with another man, or it could have been anger if she was going to leave him. It could also have been that he was casting a greedy eye towards [Tina's daughter], the heiress. Perhaps the mother might have stood in the way of him benefiting.'

In his opening address for the defence, Mr Gilbert Gray, QC, said that the case 'did not seek for its explanation a lust for gold, a lust of any sort or wickedness. What happened was so hopelessly unlooked for, so horribly unreal.' Franklin, he said, had not intended to harm a hair of Tina's head. What happened was self-defence, and Franklin, who had pleaded not guilty to murder, should be found not guilty of the lesser charge of manslaughter, too, and indeed 'not guilty altogether'.

Describing the incident that led to Tina's death, he said that they had started to argue about her leaving, an argument that had escalated into a vicious fight. 'She picked up a box of nails in a downstairs hall where Franklin was adjusting the central heating system. She hurled it at him, and hit him. She then went for him with an iron bar and he was in fear for his life. His hand was struck, he grappled her and struggled as he tried to throw her off . . . as he was spinning to get free, he was struck on the head. Eventually all became quiet, and Tina fell, apparently lifeless.'

Afterwards, he said, while Franklin was in a state of 'utter, abject misery, heartbreak and pain', Mrs Strauss's daughter came in and said, 'Where's Mummy?' Mr Gray went on, 'What could he say but, "Gone away"? Once he said that, there was no going back on it. With the passage of time it became impossible to go to the police.' When darkness fell, he took Tina's body outside to bury her, but before doing so put a clothes line round her neck and tightened it. 'Not in a callous way, but with the tenderness of a motorist who has run over a rabbit and then goes back to make sure it is dead.' Mrs Strauss was still, cold and lifeless, Mr Gray said, but Franklin had a horror of burying somebody who was not completely dead.

Called to the stand, Michael Firth, of the Forensic Science Laboratory, Harrogate, said he found blood splashes on a wall 4 feet 10 inches from the floor and further blood splashes on the wall beneath the staircase and on the floor. He concluded that, 'a sustained attack had taken place on a person lying on the floor near the staircase'. He was followed by Dr David Gee, pathologist and senior lecturer in forensic medicine at Leeds University, who had assisted with the excavation of the body. He said that the cause of death was strangulation. 'The head injuries would not necessarily have proved fatal, but the ligature would inevitably have proved fatal very rapidly.' The fractures, he said, could have been caused by one single impact of 'considerable force' or several blows of lesser force. Iron bars were also found buried at the scene, but he thought it 'unlikely' they had caused the head injuries, which were more likely to have been caused by the head hitting a broad flat surface. Asked by Mr Gray whether the fractures were consistent with the head hitting a wall, Dr Gee replied, 'If the impact was very violent, possibly so, but it would have to have been in [such] a very restricted space.'

In his evidence, Franklin recounted the build-up to the argument in January. He said he had been 'in despair' at the thought of Tina leaving him and although he had not threatened her, he had said he would 'spill the beans' to her ex-husband about their life together. He explained that, despite Richard Strauss's monthly alimony payments, he himself funded most of Tina's lifestyle and had paid for the house, the car she drove and her expenses. He had hoped that, by saying this, he would appeal to her basic sense of security. 'It was the only thing left that would stop her. Money was so terribly important to her independence from any one man.' At that point, he said, Tina had 'completely lost control of herself'.

'She called me, "You bastard." She was in a terrible rage. She rushed towards me with an iron bar. It was a very frightening weapon. We struggled and she kicked me in the balls. She was like a wildcat. She appeared to be trying to kill me.' He was unable to give a blow-by-blow account, but he thought he had swung Tina round to get the bar away from her. 'I did not swing her round intentionally to bang her head on the wall, but I have a recollection that she and I hit the wall.' Afterwards she had fallen to the floor and he noticed she was bleeding from the nose. It was then he had realized she was dead. 'I was shattered. Everything was in a whirl. I do not think I really knew where I was for some time.'

Tina Strauss's body laid in the hallway for the rest of the day. Franklin said he drank heavily after her death and went for a walk by the river, a place where the couple had often strolled. At 5.00 p.m. he had picked up Tina's daughter from school and brought her home, using the front entrance of the main house (his flat, where the murder occurred, had its own separate entrance at the back). He dug the grave about 9.00 p.m. or 10.00 p.m. after she had gone to bed, working by the light of a bedroom window. 'There must have been an awful lot of digging.' He wrapped Tina's body in the cover of their bed, called a *matrimonial*, which they had bought from Spain. 'I tried to lay her decently in the grave . . . I wanted to give her a Christian burial,' he said. The ligature he had applied because he did not want there to be a 'million-to-one' chance she could be buried alive. He said he had put the cloth into her mouth to prevent earth entering into it, which was an old custom and still practised abroad. Asked why he had buried the iron bar, he replied, 'I wanted to forget it. It had the most appalling associations for me.' He could not explain why two other iron bars were found nearby. He did not think he 'logically' chose the windshelter, or suntrap, for Tina's grave because it was pro-tected from public gaze, but he remembered it was a place that had bought her great happiness. (He had built it as a birthday present for Tina some years previously.) Replying to a question from Mr Baker, Franklin said it had not disturbed him to know that Tina was lying close to the house. 'It was a comfort to me.' Neither he nor Tina's daughter had used the suntrap after that; he had told the girl that the area had suffered some damage and was unusable. Asked if he had not found it macabre that the young girl could, in theory, go and do her homework over the ground where her mother was buried, Franklin replied, 'That didn't occur to me.'

Quizzing Franklin about the ligature, Mr Baker asked whether wrapping a clothes line twice around someone's neck suggested that she had been decently laid to rest, as he had claimed he had tried to do. Franklin said that although reason told him Tina was dead, he had 'an animal or historical interest', that made him feel horror at the thought of burying anyone alive. He continued that he had buried people before on a number of occasions in South America, some of whom had been shot as a result of guerrilla warfare. Asked if he had put ligatures around their necks, he said, 'No . . . the people were shot and sometimes badly mutilated and in that climate you had to bury them very quickly.' He couldn't explain why he had not called a doctor if there was any chance of Tina being alive, claiming instinct had overtaken reason. He had continued to drink throughout the burial process, which was 'appalling in retrospect'.

When Mr Baker asked him whether he had been trying to drown feelings of horror at what he had done, Franklin said, 'I was certainly horrified, but horror is too small a word for it.'

Summing up for the prosecution, Mr Baker said that Franklin's claim that he wanted to give his mistress a

Christian burial was, 'one of the worst pieces of hypocrisy you may ever hear' and referred to the explanation about the ligature as 'pure fantasy'. In his closing speech he told the jury: 'This was a brutal murder. There cannot be any room for provocation in this case.' He added that Franklin's experiences abroad had shown him to be 'a man who could cope with most situations that a man meets, situations which perhaps most men had never experienced. He seems to have been in the thick of things in some guerrilla fighting and burying people . . . Do you really accept his account that when Tina came at him – if she did – with an iron bar, that those injuries, and by that I mean the degree of fracturing in her skull, took place simply because he was trying to disarm her? Did she really represent that threat he asks you to believe?'

The true position, Mr Baker said, was that Franklin had reached the end of his tether because he knew Mrs Strauss was leaving him. He conceded that Franklin had been depressed afterwards, but it had not prevented him going abroad with Tina's daughter. If he had gone alone, or with friends, it would have been more credible, he said, but Franklin had gone with someone who would remind him of Tina Strauss all the time.

In his closing speech for the defence, Mr Gray said it was not a death that had been plotted, planned or designed. He said Franklin was not a murderer, but a man who had been 'caught up in a hopeless chain of cause and effect which escalated and eventually resulted in tragedy'. Franklin had loved Tina Strauss and 'there was no motive at all for him to kill the person he loved more than anyone in the world'. The ligature was 'not a strangler's knot, it was more of a lover's knot'. He told the jury to discount newspaper headlines referring to large sums of money. All marriages had rows, he said, but in the final row between Franklin and Tina his remarks about 'spilling the beans' to Richard Strauss had been dynamite.

The all-male jury reassembled on Monday, 8 March to hear the judge's summing up. They retired at lunchtime, returning just ninety minutes later to find Timothy John Franklin guilty of murder. The judge gave him a sentence of life imprisonment. The press had a field day. 'It's life for director who murdered mistress' screamed the headline in the *Northern Echo*, which carried sections on the 'Christie-style murder that rocked village' and 'The remote executive' and gave the story its own little logo (a profile of The Garths) with the strapline 'The Body in the Garden Trial'. 'Boss murdered mistress in house of secrets' said the *Sun*, following it up with 'My stormy love life with a wildcat', while the *Daily Express* went for 'Web of deceit that hid a killer's secret'. A magazine was even produced about it, entitled *The Near-Perfect Crime*, though this was only published in the US.

However, it was not the end of the story. In May 1971, two months later, Timothy Franklin made formal notice of appeal, claiming that Mr Justice Griffiths had misled the jury, and in October 1971 he was granted leave to appeal against the conviction by Mr Justice Wrangham, who agreed that pauses made by the judge indicated to the jury the importance they should place on certain bits of evidence. Franklin was once again represented by Gilbert Gray, QC. He fared no better second time around, however, and the appeal was dismissed on 13 April 1972.

The appeal was fortunate in one sense, in that it meant the judge's original summing up was transcribed in full. I managed to procure it at the start of this investigation and it is all I have officially of Tim's case file, which has been selected for long-term preservation at the Public Record Office. The files, I am told, contain 'sensitive information' and have been closed to public inspection until 2056 under the Public Records Acts to protect 'named individuals'. That is why I have not named Tina's daughter, who did not give evidence, although she was named in court and her name appears in all the cuttings.

The transcript of the summing up gives a very full description of the prosecution and defence cases and includes a great deal more detail than the newspaper stories. It makes disturbing reading, particularly the forensic evidence, and by the time I'd finished reading it the first time my hands were shaking and I felt physically sick. There were things I hadn't known – for example, besides the ligature, there was a loosely knotted man's necktie around Tina's throat – and when questioned, Tim said that he thought he'd tried to throttle her with it as well as the clothes line.

Given that he used to use his necktie to secure our beds together, I found this versatility chilling.

The information that the actual ligature had been wound so tightly that it forced Tina's voice box against her backbone was an image I found even more upsetting. Even if you accept Tim's story that Tina was already dead, the deliberate nature of the act, and the brutality that it would have involved, show that Tim was a man who was not afraid to do what he deemed 'necessary'. This picture of Tim physically strangling Tina, not in rage but as a calculated decision, was the one that appalled me the most. I tried to reconcile it with the Tim that I knew, but I could not. I could, though, believe it of the man in the cuttings. The mugshot of Tim carried in all the newspapers is a passport photo of a forty-ish bull-necked man with dark staring eyes, low brows and an obstinate mouth. He looks frightening. He looks like a murderer. He just doesn't look very much like Tim, although the set of his lips is familiar.

One of a number of issues that Mr Justice Griffiths made a point of raising was Dr Gee's statement that Tina's head injuries were consistent with hitting a broad, flat surface, such as a wall, which was the defence's assertion. There seems to have been one main fracture on the side of the head and a number of subsidiary ones spreading into the nose and around the eye orbit as well as over the top of the head. These were fissured fractures penetrating the entire thickness of the skull and could, said Dr Gee, have been caused by one very considerable impact or a number of blows of a lesser degree of force. Justice Griffiths had questioned how one blow on the side could produce the fractures on the front of the face as well and Dr Gee explained that if the blow was of 'sufficient violence' the fractures would spread out in all directions from the main injury. Equally, they might have been started by one blow and spread out as a result of repeated blows in the same place. There was another, separate injury on the opposite side of the skull that he thought was a 'contra coup' injury, caused by an echo effect from the force of the main blow.

Then we get to the nub of the argument, which is that for the injuries to have been caused by the head smacking that hard against a wall, considerable velocity would have had to have been achieved, a velocity that, given the restricted space in the hallway, would have been hard to build up. 'I would really have thought you would have needed more room,' said Dr Gee, a claim that Gilbert Gray, giving him the dimensions of the hallway (6 feet wide by 15 feet long with a distance of 8 feet travelling diagonally across), dismissed. But as the judge pointed out, nobody then had heard Tim's account of where the struggle took place, and when he gave evidence he said it occurred with him backed up against the wall by the bathroom and hemmed into the restricted space between the stairs and the wall, a space, measured on a scale plan of the house, of only 3 feet. 'He made the point of the restricted space, so it is a matter for you,' the judge said to the jury, suggesting they 'consider very carefully' the velocity that could be achieved in such a confined area.

I had never before realized there was any significant difference between a splashing and a spattering of blood, but forensically there is, and it is a difference that could determine whether Tina did indeed fly head first into the wall, as Tim claimed, or whether she was repeatedly beaten with a weapon of some sort as she lay stricken on the floor. The blood splashes, which were about the size of a pinhead and in the shape of an exclamation mark, were on the wall opposite the stairs. According to Mr Firth, the scientific officer, they were the tiny splashes you get from falling, hence the streakiness. Other blood splashes were discovered on the wall beneath the staircase and underneath the treads of the third to the sixth stairs. There was also a large circular blood stain 20 inches in diameter on the vinyl covering the floorboards. All the blood was type O, the same blood group as Tina.

Mr Firth's conclusion, that the blood splashes indicated a violent attack on a person lying in the space underneath the stairs, was based on two key indicators. Firstly, he said, it was 'inconceivable' that you would get such a scatter as a result of one blow – three blows would be the minimum to produce such a wide distribution – and secondly, the blood on the wall and under the stairs had a different characteristic pattern to the blood on the opposite wall. The difference, he said, was between a splashing and a spattering, the latter breaking the blood up into smaller droplets. His interpretation was that somebody lying under the stairs had been struck a number of times with some object, which had first caused the scalp to bleed, and then, as further blows were struck, spattered the blood upwards and downwards. The fact that the blood on the wall opposite had a different character was consistent with blood coming off some weapon as it was flung up.

Mr Justice Griffiths was under an obligation to mention the defence's objection, which was that, had somebody been repeatedly hit on the head when they were lying on the floor, the bulk of the spattering would have been lower down, which it was not. However, Mr Gray's theory that the blood was flung off Tina's hair during the course of the struggle appears just as fallible, given that there was blood underneath the sixth step from the bottom, a height of 3 feet 10 inches, which doesn't tally with Tim's account that they were fighting and she suddenly fell to the ground dead.

One other, perhaps crucial, piece of information that did not properly come to light, as it were (and this is where the judge's so-called 'dramatic' pauses were noticed), was the discussion about how Tim could have seen to do the digging in the dark. Instructing the jury to study photographs of the relative position of the suntrap to the upstairs bedroom window of the house, Justice Griffiths pointed out that the curtains were drawn, as, apparently, they always were. Tim had claimed that the light from that window had been sufficient to dig by because the curtains were of a light texture, which allowed it to come through. 'Photographs 30 and 31 show the bedroom, and they show those curtains,' Justice Griffiths states baldly. Since I haven't seen the photographs, this meant nothing to me when I read it. However I've since discovered that the curtains shown were heavy-lined red velvet drapes – the very red velvet curtains, by the sound of it, that used to hang in Tim's room in Barton Place, and went on to furnish our houses at Devonshire Place and north Oxford – which not only scandalized me, but it also explains why the curtains were so significant. No light could possibly have penetrated them. Conclusion: Tim was lying. The fact that this photograph was taken seven months after the murder was not brought up.

It is pretty clear what the judge thought of Tim when he reminded the jury to 'consider the nature of the man with whom you are dealing'. He said Tim was entitled to have it weighed in the balance that he was a man who had not been in trouble with the law and had held a number of responsible positions. 'On the other side of the coin . . . he has shown himself to be capable of a sustained and skilful course of deceit since the time he buried Tina Strauss.' He pointed to the deception Tim and Tina practised against Richard Strauss over the maintenance payments, which continued to be received after Tina's death, although Mr Gray said that Tim had not stood to gain 'a penny piece' financially from her death. There was also the fact that Tim had hidden Tina's jewellery and share certificates in his office the day after the police's first visit, so as not to arouse suspicion. This duplicity is compounded by the revelation that, despite being in a state of deep mental depression and alcoholism after the killing, Tim was capable of forging convincing business letters and telegrams and had taken Tina's daughter away on holiday.

The picture, one has to admit, is not good. Tim himself wrote to his sister shortly after he was arrested and taken to the police station. In the letter he said, 'the charge is justified' and continued, 'I should have taken your advice years ago and gone to a psychiatrist. I've known I am mentally ill for a long time and been afraid of accepting it.' The judge fell on this, saying, 'That is not what you would write if you had accidentally killed Tina in a struggle. That is the sort of thing you write if you knew you had completely lost control of yourself and really gone berserk.' Tim, as always, had an answer for this – that it was his way of explaining his 'disgraceful and unbalanced' behaviour in concealing Tina's body – but his sign-off in the letter does not help his case. 'It started off as self-defence and ended in a blackout' is not what he said on the stand, and his assertion that, 'I did not lose my temper at all, I was too frightened, I was terrified' was deemed questionable, given that Tim was a physically powerful man ('You have seen him,' remarked the judge) who had, on a previous occasion, apparently disarmed the slimly built Tina of a carving knife in an open room.

As to the 'unreasoning sense of fear' that had apparently prevented Tim from taking 'the elementary step of seeing if he could get medical aid', Mr Justice Griffiths sounded dubious. He reminded the jury that Franklin was 'not a man of timid intellect' and that his experiences of guerrilla activities in South America showed that he was a man of the world who was 'not apparently a stranger to violence'.

Concluding, the judge said there had been some sensational headlines about Tina's daughter, adding that any fortune she may come into 'would appear to be a long way distant', contingent as it was on the death of her father and her aunt. He continued that there were some odd, unexplained features in the case, namely, 'How would [Tina's daughter] accept her mother had gone away when nothing of her effects had been removed?' Specifically, her jewellery, which was not taken away by Tim until 27 August. 'But, members of the jury, these are loose, untied ends and you may think with me that it would be very dangerous to enter into too much speculation about that matter.'

The question, the judge reminded the jury at the commencement of his summing up, was not whether the accused man had killed Tina Strauss, but whether he had intended to, or whether it had been an accident during the course of which he was defending himself from attack with an iron bar. In self-defence, he said, a man was entitled to use force to prevent self-injury, and it was also 'sometimes necessary to kill'. But no one was entitled to use more force than necessary to meet their attacker. 'You are not entitled to go further and use the occasion to take vengeance on the person who has attacked you.' As to whether it was a case of murder or manslaughter, the latter would apply if they thought Franklin had been subject to a high degree of provocation. 'He may have been provoked by fearful violence. Can you do better than ask yourselves the question, "Would it have affected me in that way?" ' If they believed Franklin's story of how Tina died, he was entitled to an acquittal. However, if they were not convinced they had heard the true explanation from Franklin's lips, then they could not acquit him.

They did not.

That, until I embarked on this book, was all I knew about Tim's past. It was hard enough finding out that he had strangled Tina Strauss and buried her body and laid a carefully planned trail of deception for seven months, all of which he'd omitted to tell me when he announced, 'I'm a lifer.' Those weren't the actions of a normal person who had accidentally caused someone's death. The extensive head injuries that Tina had suffered seemed to call that into question, too. But even if I accepted Tim's version of the fight and that he'd panicked and done those things because he'd become committed to a course of action, it still didn't take into account the most astonishing fact of all: that he had continued to live in the same house after the murder with Tina's fifteen-year-old daughter. I hadn't even known she existed.

Tim had never hidden his attraction to young girls; on the contrary, he was proud of it. His joke about 'seventeen-year-old blonde Wellies' made us laugh because of its preposterousness, but it wasn't a joke to Tim. Of course, seventeen is just above the legal age for sex. Tim was careful to keep his jokes clean. I knew all this and yet I still thought

I was 'the one', the original. I discounted the ones who had come before as meaningless flings, because that's what Tim had told me and it was easier to believe that. When I learned about Tina's daughter, I didn't know what to think. Had he been in love with her? Surely not; she was too young. And yet, I'd sometimes felt Tim was repeating a pattern, that the things he'd bought for me, the flowers, the perfume, were bought with someone else in mind. Then there was the way he wanted me to look, to behave, the places he'd taken me to. Gran Canaria? He took Tina's daughter on holiday there, too. Malaga? That's where he sent the forged telegram from. When I read the cuttings, the shock at finding out about her was so great that the real question didn't occur to me at first. It wasn't a question of what he might have felt about her. It was a question of what he had really felt about me. And now there was no way of finding out.

Who had I been to Tim? That was the hardest thing to face up to. That was the killer blow he dealt me.

CHAPTER FIFTEEN

Timothy John Franklin was born on 8 April 1927, in Trinidad. His sister, Antonia, was born two years later, in Albania. I owe much of what I've learned about Tim to Antonia. She was a social worker when I met her twenty years ago and has since become a counsellor and continues to practise and teach in her seventies. Her choice of profession speaks volumes about their childhood: 'I'd always been drawn to childcare, and to childhood deprivation, and it affected me a lot. I didn't realize, until I got into social work and was so concentrated on childcare, that what I was looking at was my own deprivation. The lack of any family life, the lack of a home.' But while Antonia faced up to her early traumas, Tim fled them. Or, at least, he tried to. He never succeeded, and the shadow they cast over him eventually consumed him.

No one, I suspect, ever knew the real Tim, and the version of himself that he presented was just that: one possible version. The fact that he turns out to have been fifty-four when I met him, not fifty-six, as he told me, is a typical anomaly. (This age is recorded in my diary at several points so it's not down to a failure of memory on my part). There was always a bit of a mystery about Tim's actual birthday – he was coy on the subject, admitting he had two passports which gave different dates – although he didn't explain why. It doesn't make sense, surely, to pretend to be older than you are, particularly if you want to pull young girls, but there it is. As the mysteries surrounding Tim go, this is one of the minor ones.

This is an attempt to get, not just behind the headlines, but behind the smokescreen of charisma Tim blew in our eyes. That was the witty, charming, generous Tim people liked and respected – 'the perfect gentleman' as he was so often known – but there was also the Tim that one only got to know through prolonged exposure, the violent, raging, unpredictable and potentially dangerous Tim. 'I think there were two of him,' Antonia says. 'I don't mean he was schizophrenic. He was a very divided person.' She describes her brother with a candour and clarity that comes from having extensively analysed their shared past. 'I'm all for truth,' she told me at the start of our first interview. 'There was a lot about Tim that was magnificent, but there was a lot that was not.'

★

Tim's family history gave him a lot to live up to. His father was a geologist who took up the profession on the promise of an inheritance from his own father: a mine. Tim's grandfather was a Russian aristocrat, a sometime writer and civil servant who owned mines and railways and was married to a princess. He was also chronically unfaithful: Tim's father was illegitimate, the product of an affair with an English-speaking governess. The governess, Tim's grandmother, had her own, incredible story: she was actually part-English, part-French and part-Russian and came from an extremely wealthy family. After the death of her father they fell on hard times and their improverished mother was forced to farm her five daughters out to friends and benefactors. Tim's grandmother was brought up by the Bishop of Ceylon. In terms of scandal and drama it's a hard story to beat. 'There are some parts of our family that seem to come straight out of Dostoevsky,' says Antonia.

Their father, who was named Waldemar Anthony, was born in St Petersburg. He lived there until he was six, by which time the playboy nobleman had lost interest in the governess and had taken up with a Russian ballerina, whom he subsequently left the princess for. Waldemar moved to Bournemouth with his mother, attending prep school and then going to Marlborough. Despite this thoroughly English education, he kept his Russian nickname, and was known throughout his life as 'Boun', short for Bountik. Roughly translated it means 'bad boy' or 'little villain', a nickname he earned early on. 'He had a strong will and there was obviously something of him that fought back,' says Antonia, pointing out that illegitimacy, in those days, was not easy. 'But it meant our mother could say, "You know, your father really is a bastard." And he was. He could be absolutely bloody and he was very bloody to Tim.'

Tim, she remembers, was born with a fierce squint, a squint that must have given him a ferocious expression because in later years their father claimed, 'That boy was born hating me.' It was, she says, 'pure projection' on his part, but as a first take on his son it did not bode well for their relationship. Things did not improve. 'Our father had a dreadful temper. Tim would get formal beatings over trivial stuff like table manners. He was always being criticized by him. I don't remember any good times between father and son. The only contact Tim got from his father was rejection.' Tim did not take this lying down. 'He fought back. He might well have been called Bountig, too . . . He had a fearsome temper like his father and a fearsome tongue. He could be very rude and sharp and he was a difficult child.'

Having parents who were always travelling meant that Tim and Antonia never knew a family home. When Tim was three years old and Antonia just fifteen months, they were placed in a children's home while their parents went abroad again. They were reunited with them on their return to England, but continued to live an itinerant lifestyle in company accommodation and rented houses. By the ages of six and four respectively the pair were at boarding school full-time after their father accepted a post in Persia. Antonia was sent to a 'home school' for children of ex-pats and Tim to St Andrews, a preparatory school in Pangbourne, where he was a founding pupil. In the holidays, if they were lucky, their mother would return and they sometimes stayed with their grandmother. She did not always make the effort, in which case Tim would join Antonia at her school. 'We never had a community, a place in the world, other than school,' says Antonia. 'It cuts out a lot of easy socialization and certainty about where you come from.'

The lack of parenting had a profound effect on both of them. Young Antonia became less and less sure that she had parents at all − 'sometimes I thought I'd made them up' − while Tim lashed out at everyone around him. 'I can't say he was bullied at school, because he was so aggressive no one could bully him, even though he was small for his age. But he was quite targeted because of his glasses and his squint.' She recalls seeing him being cornered by some other boys behind a table. 'It was agony.' He was also singled out, she believes, because of his inability to interact normally with his peers. 'He was OK with schoolwork, good athletically, but socially, life was not good to him . . . He found relationships very very difficult.' Unable to make friends of his own, he latched onto hers, when he joined her for school holidays. The other children did not like her possessive older brother and he alienated them with his behaviour. If Antonia had divided loyalties, she was not allowed to show it. With Tim, you were either for him or against him; there were no half measures.

The two children were close out of necessity as much as kinship. 'We got on well because we had to, but the relationship was that he was in charge.' Tim handled the pocket money – his and Antonia's – and made sure his younger sister knew that he had power over her in a variety of unsubtle ways. 'He'd go off to buy ice creams and come towards us licking one and hand that one to me.' He was vicious, too, and frequently hurt her physically, although she gave her best back. When he beat up a cousin who had hit her, 'it was only because I was his younger sister and if anyone was going to hit me, it would be him'. All the same, she was the only certainty in his life, and with their parents away so frequently it was Antonia around whom Tim's life pivoted. Antonia he could control. She was all he could control. An obsession with dominating younger women was born.

Antonia recounts an example of the isolation Tim endured: 'When he was six he was taken into hospital to have his tonsils out. He was put on an adult ward, had the operation and was taken back to boarding school. No one came to visit him.' In the early 1930s, such treatment wasn't considered unusual or callous. No one would have dreamt of a mother keeping a 24-hour presence in a hospital ward. As to the rest – separating siblings at such a tender age; depriving them of love and affection, a home; putting them in regimented boarding schools and not even visiting during the holidays – it's not considered good parenting these days, but no one questioned it then. 'Before the

Second World War, it wasn't considered that mothers were vital to children,' Antonia says simply. 'That had not been professionally stated.'

Even if the literature on child development hadn't yet recognized this, it seems to go against human instinct. However, as Antonia points out, their mother was brought up with the same expectations. 'It was absolutely normal to leave very young children in England when [the parents] went back to India and my mother's family were all British India so she wouldn't have had that back-up, that feeling that she was important.' There was another snag too: their father's infidelity. Boun was charming, good-looking and, like his Russian father, an incorrigible womanizer. 'The dilemma was that, if she had stayed with us, Dad would have got himself a new relationship and the marriage would have gone.' As it was, even staying with her husband didn't guarantee their mother security. Persia was a disaster. 'Father sunk a well in the wrong place and ran off with somebody's wife.'

Their parents returned to England for a short time, then relocated to The Hague in Holland. Antonia, who was herself showing signs of disturbance, including running away from school, was sent to join them. She was eight years old. 'It didn't really work out. Both parents were having affairs. They had no idea of how to deal with a child at home.' She was made to get herself to school by tram. 'Mother, although she was a dear, wasn't very maternal.' Despite her obvious unhappiness, Antonia was sent back to her English boarding school. 'That was the culture in those days . . . It wasn't deliberate cruelty. It was thought perfectly ordinary and natural and didn't do children any damage.' This was demonstrably untrue in her case, although Tim had so internalized his emotions that superficially it may have been less apparent. Life was better for him at Tonbridge, by which time his squint had been corrected, but by then the psychological damage had already been done. His remarks to me about his upbringing rendering him 'an emotional cripple' was an insight he gained too late in life to help him through the biggest crisis of all. 'Until he got into that total mess, he never acknowledged his emotional inadequacies. He had this myth of our happy childhood.'

Tim joined the army as an officer straight from school at the age of seventeen, but it was 1945 and the war was almost over and he did not see action. He signed up to join the rifle brigade, but significantly was not taken on. Psychiatric testing for officers had just been introduced and Antonia believes this was why they failed him. 'Any psychiatric test should have shown that he was a deeply disturbed person.' She is puzzled when I mention Tim reliving an incident in which he witnessed a friend being blown up (this was the night he got drunk on our first holiday). He had been deafened by a shell going off near him on a training exercise, she says. It blew one eardrum in, but as far as she knew there was no one else involved. Tim had told me and Sharon that he'd been involved in liberating a PoW camp, and although that particular heroic fantasy doesn't appear to have been true, he was involved with such a camp. He did his service in Germany where, because of his deafness, he was seconded from his unit to oversee the trains that were taking displaced persons to the Soviet Union. It was a heartbreaking job and he hated it, but got on rather better when he was moved to a camp near Hamburg. This was a holding place for Jews who wanted to go to Israel. They had organized themselves and become a thorn in the side of the British in Palestine, and as a result, most of the British army didn't go into the camp. Tim, who was then nineteen, was one of the few who did. 'He had enormous sympathy and respect for them and really got on with the Jewish people.'

Tim was demobbed at the age of twenty or thereabouts, though never formally (he suffered from terrible seasickness and couldn't stomach the trip over the North Sea to return to Germany). Faced with the choice of what to do with his life, he opted to follow in his father's footsteps, joining Shell as a management trainee. Boun had retired from Shell by then, but it's interesting that, given the friction between father and son, Tim should have so deliberately invited comparisons. Did he want to upstage him, or was he hoping to finally gain the old man's approval? 'He wanted his independence and he wanted money,' says Antonia. 'He could easily have gone to university but he wasn't inter-ested. He saw himself as not being bright enough, which was completely untrue.' She explains that Tim took the school certificate at sixteen but didn't matriculate, whereas she took it at fifteen, a year after him, and did well. 'We now know that girls just do. But in our family it was a disaster. Father wouldn't believe it. He thought we'd taken different exams.' That failure, she says, was 'appalling for Tim. He was constantly needing to compete with me, to be better than me, and it distorted his image of himself.'

Shell sent Tim out to Venezuela in South America, where he started to learn the oil business. He was twenty-one then, and after the years of torment in public school followed by the harshness of life in the army ('I had to fight my way through school and I had to fight my way through a barrack room' is a phrase that comes back to me), the vividness and spontaneity of the Latin culture must have felt like stepping into a world of colour after a lifetime of institutionalized black and white. It was his first taste of freedom and he embraced it wholeheartedly. This must have been when he developed his Spanish-speaking alter ego, because he did not, after all, have Spanish blood, and neither was he brought up in Colombia, which is what he told me. However, it's safe to say that the Latin lifestyle gave him the opportunity to reinvent himself. 'He would have been shucking off a whole identity and getting the chance to be somebody quite different, which would have been very appealing,' agrees Antonia.

In 1952 he took leave from Venezuela and married an old schoolfriend of Antonia's, Rosemary. They'd met a few years earlier when Tim was still in the army and the relationship had slowly blossomed into romance. Antonia herself was unhappy about the union. 'Roz and I were sharing a house together. She was an art-school student, amusing and very talented. Not beautiful, but very attractive, very sociable. Whereas Tim was not sociable.' Roz did, though, share a similar background to Tim – her father was with the British Indian police under the Raj – and it must have given them a bond. Maybe she mistook that for love because when they married in Jamaica – chosen, apparently, for its glamorous setting – she was already regretting her decision. 'She realized halfway across the Atlantic it was a mistake but she couldn't get out of it,' Antonia recalls. 'As for Tim, I think he was lonely and Roz was my best friend.'

From Venezuela, Tim was transferred to the island of Borneo in the South China Seas. It's unclear how long he worked there, but at some point he parted company with Shell and seems to have gone through a transient period subsequently, moving from Borneo to Canada, where he got a position with Transcontinental Pipelines, and then leaving that after a relatively short time. With his career in the doldrums, he set about applying for other jobs, during the course of which he was asked to do an aptitude test. It revealed that he had a phenomenally high IQ; it also revealed, ironically, that he was more suited to academia. By this time, he and Roz were living in Vancouver and had a baby girl, Belinda. With a family to support, university wasn't an option. Tim was forced to take whatever work he could get, which was probably when he sold silk stockings door to door, a tale he regaled my Auntie Judy with. Perhaps due to financial pressures he returned to the oil industry, accepting a job in Colombia. He and Roz headed to South America again with their young daughter, to face what must have been Tim's most challenging post of all.

'He was managing an exploring oil company called Caltech. He was very young to be doing it. It was a terrible place at the time and he was dealing with difficult stuff.' Antonia denies that Tim was directly involved in guerrilla fighting, as hinted at in the newspapers: 'It would have been the aftermath of their activities. It came out in court because when he was asked how he knew Tina was dead, he said, "Well, I've seen death often enough." There was guerrilla fighting going on, and he saw people who were dying and dead. As manager of this oil company he had to deal with local politicians and so on, and local employees. It was a very violent time in Colombia.'

Balancing running an oil exploration company while negotiating with Colombian warlords took its toll. Tim was drinking heavily and his marriage was in difficulties, despite the fact that Roz was expecting their second child. To add to the strain, his mother had been diagnosed with terminal cancer. Perhaps it was in Colombia, rather than in the army, that he witnessed his friend Jack being blown up; assassinations and terrorist bombs were plentiful enough. Or perhaps it was simply the stress of daily life in such an unpredictable and dangerous environment, but something traumatic seems to have happened to Tim in Colombia because in 1958 he flew back to England, jobless and suffering from a severe nervous breakdown following the death of his mother. 'He could hardly speak when he came off the plane,' Antonia remembers. 'I think more went on in South America than we ever knew about.' She believes it was made worse by the fact that he hadn't allowed himself to grieve properly for his mother. 'If family life has not been good, it's worse than for somebody who has had a close relationship, because what the mother's death means in that case is the end of *ever* having the possibility of having a mother, which, really, he never had.'

Somehow Tim pulled himself through by sheer strength of will, despite the fact that he needed alcohol to keep himself functioning. Within a short time he had landed a job with Urwick Orr, one of the top four management consultancy companies in the UK at the time. 'If he'd had less resources to keep himself going in that sick state he would have broken down completely and had to get help. It would have been a lot healthier. Instead of which, he used his intelligence to defeat himself the whole time,' Antonia says, with professional insight. She knew he was drinking heavily but didn't want to take responsibility for him. Their father was suffering from depression and had been briefly admitted to a mental hospital. Having nursed her mother through the end stages of cancer, Antonia was finding it a struggle to keep her own life together. Typically, he turned for comfort to another, beginning an affair with a married woman some years younger than Roz, by whom they had actually been introduced. The Franklins were now living in Guildford in Surrey and had another daughter, Julia. Roz knew about the affair and was surviving on tranquillizers. 'I was appalled at Tim's behaviour and told him so,' says Antonia.

Tim began travelling internationally for Urwick Orr, gaining an impressive reputation as a consultant. It must have been particularly satisfying for a man with such an intellectual thirst, though, prompted by his lack of academic qualifications, he was tempted to embellish his achievements. The company sent him on a management course at Harvard which, by the time I met him, had become a first-class degree in business studies. I don't know whether he told other people this, though I doubt they would have disputed it; Tim's ability to convince was second to none. It was almost hypnotic: 'He told me his job was properly done if, when he'd finished, people said, "Oh we didn't really need you, we've solved it ourselves,"' recalls Antonia. She didn't approve of Tim's sleight-of-hand technique. 'It meant he hadn't been absolutely open with people and it would have been much better if they did know his intervention had been significant, because otherwise they were left slightly blind. It struck me as a questionable use of his power.'

It was a power that had long since lost its charm for Roz. Tim's drinking made him violent and, like his father, he had a vile temper. Having stuck out ten years of marriage to

Tim, the humiliation of his affair and the mounting domestic abuse had become too much to put up with. Belinda, their eldest child, whom I interviewed briefly, remembers this period, starting back in Colombia. 'He was well respected at work, but not for the way he treated my mother, or other women.' We compared notes on the psychotic state Tim used to drink himself into. Belinda's description of the switch in Tim was horribly familiar. She says, with some understatement, 'At that point I don't remember very happy things about him.' The cycle of drinking and violence continued in England until eventually, she says tellingly, 'My mother decided it was just too dangerous to live with him any longer. She took us away.'

Not long after that, Urwick Orr sent Tim to Jamaica, the Caribbean island where he and Roz had had their glamorous wedding. Perhaps, subconsciously, it was that association that made him fall for Tina Strauss, a chance to replay the romantic fantasy, to get it right this time. Except that he didn't.

CHAPTER SIXTEEN

It was, I believe, Fyffes, the banana company, that commissioned the survey that took Tim to Jamaica in 1963. In the early 1960s the banana industry had become extremely lucrative and in 1964 a 'banana war' broke out between Fyffes and rival Geest, though whether Tim's recommendations as a consultant influenced this, I can't say. Tim remained there for some considerable time – five months – but it seems likely that pleasure, as much as work, may have been the reason he stayed so long. Richard Strauss, who was connected with the industry, had befriended Tim, and they got on well. Tim was a clubbable type, at ease in the ex-pat community, and Richard Strauss must have been confident in his trust in Tim to suggest that his wife work for him. The Strausses, who had left England in 1956, two years after their only daughter was born, had lived in Kenya prior to Jamaica. They epitomized the colonial lifestyle, a lifestyle that much-travelled Tim had been born into. As far as Richard was concerned, Tim was one of them.

Richard Strauss was extremely wealthy and Tina would have had no need to earn a living, and certainly not as a secretary. Possibly she was bored and wanted the intellectual stimulation, but I think it's more likely that she just wanted Tim. There was a big age gap between the Strausses – Richard was fifty-four then, nineteen years older than Tina – and Tim was a handsome, physically impressive man her own age. It seems inevitable that these two attractive, clever people working closely together by day in this lush climate and socializing with the island's smart set by night would fall for each other. Tim, who was not yet divorced, had no scruples about having affairs with married women, but this does seem to have been a love-match. In leaving her husband and giving up her home, Tina was relinquishing much of her financial security; a risky chance to take with someone she'd only known for a few months.

As for Tim, he seems to have been utterly smitten. After all the bitterness with Roz, he had finally found his soulmate. Even the fact that the three of them – Tina had custody of her daughter – were forced by circumstances to live with Tina's aged mother couldn't dampen that, although the arrangement was clearly far from ideal. Whether they made a pretext of functioning separately at that point, I don't know, but there appears to have been some wrangling over Tina's alimony and, by the sound of it, they felt they never had enough money to live the life they, or at least Tina, desired to lead. They were desperate – or greedy – enough to make a false insurance claim on some of Tina's jewellery, to the value of about £3,500 (around £33,000 at today's rates). This was something I learned from the detective who arrested Tim. I don't know when this claim was made, but it perhaps fits with an odd memory of Belinda's. She remembers that, 'The last time [as a child] I saw my father he had a suitcase full of his stuff and he threw it down the stairs – my parents must have been screaming at each other – and a whole load of jewels fell out and they all belonged to Tina.'

From Urwick Orr, Tim was headhunted by Pickerings, a lift manufacturing company he had originally worked for in 1961 as a consultant. He had so impressed John Fothergill, who then ran the family business, that he created an entirely new arm, calling it Pickerings Export Company, just to get round the restriction of poaching Tim away from Urwick Orr (consultants were not allowed to work for existing clients). John Fothergill's son, who was also called John but went by his second name Christopher, went on to be joint managing director with his father and formed a close bond with Tim, who was ten years his senior. Tim, he says, taught him financial acumen and had a genius for management science, but the relationship went beyond business. 'He was like a professor to me, and also like an elder brother.' He and his wife were good friends with Tim and Tina, so much so that when the couple relocated to Teeside, they offered to share their house in Nunthorpe, south of Middlesbrough, with them.

Christopher describes Tina Strauss as 'tall, slim, attractive, well-dressed . . . she was a great reader and could talk about anything. Socially she was very adept. She supported Tim. They looked a good couple.' He confirms Tim and Tina were 'very much in love', adding that he and his wife never heard a loud word heard between them when they lived together (the couples had half the house each, sharing a joint staircase). He also confirms that Tina had downgraded her circumstances for Tim. 'She gave me the impression she was living well below her standard of wealth.'

It was a productive time for Tim and Christopher. Tim had single-handedly created an export market for Pickerings, winning contracts in Malta, New Zealand and Iran, but the engineering side of the business couldn't keep pace and the export company folded. Pickerings itself nearly went bankrupt, but working 24-hour shifts, the two of them turned the company round and back into profit within just six weeks. 'Tim's dedication,' says Christopher, 'was beyond belief.' The next five years saw Pickerings going from strength to strength as Tim forced the old-fashioned family firm to modernize its practices, an enterprise that won him respect among the more forward-thinking, and not a few enemies.

Service manager Derek King, who was one of Tim's

admirers, remembers him losing his temper more than once during these clashes with the diehards and having to calm Tim down. 'He could be very violent,' he says. Tim was known as a tough nut even then: he was reputed to have served in the SAS (a rumour that I suspect he spread) and everyone in Pickerings knew the story about the time he was set upon by a gang of muggers in Guildford and hospitalized all four, earning a commendation in the local paper for his bravery. Manifestly, it was a brave or foolish man (or woman) who messed with Tim Franklin, but his aggression was, as always, tempered by his charm. 'He used to come in to Pickerings with his hands full of sweet peas that he'd grown in his garden and give a huge bunch to the receptionist, who was always highly delighted,' remembers Derek.

Tim's success as a director of Pickerings meant he was able to afford a property of his own and in 1966 he bought The Garths, a well-appointed house in the village of North Otterington. Derek King, who lived in nearby Northallerton, spent many an evening there socializing with Tim and Tina and would often stop by in the morning to pick Tim up en route to a site visit and share a bacon sandwich. He remembers the extension on the side of the house, with the stairway going up and the concealed doorway at the top of the landing leading off into Tina's room, but says they did not give an impression of living together under any secrecy. The separate accommodation was a contrivance they did not bother to maintain among friends, and the two of them were completely open about their relationship in his presence. 'It was volatile, always on or off,' he recalls. 'They could be extremely fond of each other one minute and very loving, and the next minute there was feuding. I'd go in there some days and you could feel the atmosphere.'

By the late sixties, the bad days outnumbered the good and Tina was growing increasingly unhappy with their life. She wanted to move to a hotter climate and had her sights set on Spain, which seems to have had associations for the two of them (this was where the *matrimonial* was bought). However, at the age of forty Tim had found a home and a sense of belonging for the first time in his life. He enjoyed tending their large and colourful garden and he'd got a job he found challenging and enjoyable. He did not want to leave, and said so. A thwarted Tina put pressure on him, and that's when the rows turned nasty. Antonia recalls Tina phoning her on a number of occasions after they had settled in the North Riding. 'She said the tensions were tremendous. I remember twice advising her to leave him. And her reason for not doing so was the property. If she left the house she would never have a hold over it. She was very, very conscious of property.' She says there was 'some difficulty' about whose house it was, and it appears that Tina was in the process of purchasing her portion of the house from Tim. Had she walked out, she felt she would forfeit that investment, or that Richard would get his hands on it. Apart from the maintenance payments, which were nominally for her daughter's upkeep, it would seem her only capital was in the house. She was tied to the house, and the house was mortgaged to Tim.

Whether or not Richard Strauss had commissioned spies to check up on Tina's living arrangements, keeping that money stream going was vital to her, despite Tim being on a director's salary (this was why she consistently refused to marry Tim, because it would have meant losing Richard's fortune). They must have believed the threat was real because this was the reason for the separate accommodation, even if it was in name only. I imagine that, before they knocked through the wall, having such a solid physical barrier would have caused problems for Tim, given his possessiveness. Maybe Tina wanted some space and he was afraid of her excluding him. One night he came upstairs after Tina had gone to bed and put an axe through the cupboard next to her bed in the place where the doorway was to go. The cupboard was smashed to pieces. When Tina rang Antonia and told her this, Antonia sensed danger. 'I said, "For God's sake, Tina, get out. That's a pretty clear message." And she said, 'Well I can't, the house, the house . . .'

By now, Tim was once again drinking heavily and the pattern of alcohol-induced psychosis and violence that had frightened Roz into leaving him was being repeated. 'He'd been concealing his drinking, but he was drinking enormously,' remembers Antonia. 'He was quite out of control.' She didn't realize how much alcohol Tim was consuming until after he was arrested, when, on a visit to sort out the house, she discovered his secret stash crammed behind a partition at the end of the garage. It was full up to head height with empty whisky bottles. It's amazing that Tim managed to cover this up, let alone do his job, but he was practised at such deception – he had managed to pull it off at Urwick Orr – and at this stage his work doesn't appear to have suffered.

It was a different story at home. Tim made Tina's life a misery, even stalking her, and in desperation she rang Antonia again. 'She said, "I can't stand it. I go to the hair-dressers and his car's outside. He's one step behind me in the kitchen. He'd dogging me all the time." Which is something I remember from childhood ... It was that feeling that you could not get away from him, not for a minute. When we'd had a row, what you want to do is go. But to him, no. I suppose it was his insecurity.' She says she doesn't believe Tim actually struck Tina, but not long before the murder there was an incident that she took to be another warning, and said so. 'Tina rang and said he'd thrown all the things out of the kitchen – the washing machine, the fridge, the cooker, every single piece of equipment. And I said again, "Tina, he is doing his best not to hit you." He had thrown all the books from the shelf, and then the bookshelves, too. It seemed to me that he was really at the edge of violence, of hitting her. But he didn't, actually, until he killed her.' She was so concerned about what Tim might do that she wrote to her brother telling him she'd advised Tina to leave. I can imagine Tim's wrath at receiving this. He would have found the fact that Tina had talked about their private life to Antonia humiliating. Humiliating Tim was something you did at your peril, and Tina would have been circumspect about any further communication. Besides, the advice from Antonia would have been the same. 'She knew that I thought she was completely crazy to stay with him.' Antonia heard no more from either of them until she received the news of Tim's arrest for Tina's murder, seven months or so later.

What happened during this time? The facts of the murder have been well documented in the press, but a welter of speculation remains. In trying to discover the truth, I hired a private detective, David Farrar, an ex-police inspector and member of CID who worked in York for thirty years. As I'd hoped, he remembered the case, though he hadn't worked on it personally. With David's help I found Arthur Harrison, the detective superintendent who led the investigation. Mr Harrison, who had been promoted to Detective Chief Superintendent and was head of CID for North and North-east Yorkshire Police, now in his eighties, felt unable to contribute. However, his colleague at the time, a detective inspector called Strickland Carter (who went on to become DCI and succeeded Harrison as deputy when he was promoted to CID), turned out to be a friend of David Farrar's and was happy to talk. I also received help from former PC Harry Codling, who was on attachment to CID at the time.

'Strick' Carter remembers the Timothy Franklin case well. So well, in fact, that he's given talks to the WI, among others, about it. It's one that stands out in his memory because of its unusual features – 'There was the intrigue of the two parts of the house connected by the two mirrors; how often do you come across a thing like that?' – and because, despite what he learned about Tim's character, he rather liked him. He describes him as 'a good-looking, Errol Flynn type, handsome, militaristic, the type of person I would warm to'. Tim, he says, warmed to him, too. 'We were the same types.' Their exchanges were courteous. 'I always found him to be calm and polite. He maintained that charm he had throughout.' There was also the fact that, as Strick Carter puts it, 'our luck was in'. It could, he admits, so easily have turned out differently.

Tina Strauss had been friends with a farmer and his wife, who owned a farm just down the road from The Garths. Whenever Tina had gone abroad in the past – which she had done several times, house-hunting in Spain – she had sent them a postcard. This time she hadn't, and her unexplained absence had them concerned enough to mention her disappearance to John Scull, the local sergeant. Carter and Harrison were not directly involved at this point and John Scull is now dead, but Harry Codling, who assisted Sergeant Scull with the legwork, was able to fill in some details for me. It appears that Tina had confided in the farmer's wife about problems at home and this, on top of pressure from Shirley Green, another worried friend, was enough for Scull to consider the matter worth looking into. (I suspect these two ladies were connected with the church where Tina was the key-holder, which is how that story arose, although I haven't been able to confirm this.) Questions were asked of Tim, who had filed a missing persons report on Tina a few months earlier in January 1970. At the time, his story that Tina had gone off suddenly, probably to Spain, had been accepted by uniform and not investigated. He had not counted on the fact that Tina had such influential friends: Shirley Green was a detective constable's wife and was pushing for a full investigation, with the result that CID took over the case.

Now that inquiries were being made, Tim started to produce postcards from abroad claiming they were from Tina. The farmer and his wife also received one, although it did nothing to allay their suspicions. Tim's job involved a considerable amount of foreign travel and the possibility that the cards were forgeries could not be ruled out. They agreed to have their postcard sent off for analysis, along with a sample of Tina's handwriting. The result came back: no match. It was now August and it was at this stage in the investigation that DI Strickland Carter and DS Arthur Harrison were brought in. Until then there had been no evidence to suggest that anything was seriously amiss, but the postcards and the diligence of Tina's friends were enough to bring out CID's big guns. 'I suppose Tim's arrogance was such that he felt he could get away with it – after all, this was seven months later,' says Strick Carter. 'It could have gone on. You can just imagine, if this farmer hadn't said anything . . . a lot of people have grave suspicions but don't want to get involved . . . Ultimately, they could have left The Garths behind, and no one would have known.'

Carter and Harrison paid an informal visit to the house, where they found Tim with Tina's daughter. Tim told them that Tina had gone off to Spain to look for somewhere to live and find a finishing school for the girl, but an instinct told the two detectives that something wasn't right and they returned the next day for more explanation. This time Tim said, 'To tell the truth, we've had a bust-up and she's left me.' He added that Tina's mother had received a telegram from Malaga for her birthday and a postcard. Strick Carter went to Stratford to interview Tina's mother, who, fortunately, had kept them both. There was also a letter from Tina's accountant about her financial affairs and some other correspondence. Again, there was something that didn't ring true so they went back a third time with more questions. Tim, as usual, had his answers prepared. 'You know how plausible Tim was. He was very convincing. He could persuade people of anything,' Strick Carter reflects. 'Still, Arthur told him not to leave the country and Tim said he and [Tina's daughter] were going to go to Malta in a couple of days' time. We'd already established that they'd been on holiday together to the Canary Islands. And because he said he was going to Malta, Arthur said, "Let's see your passport." '

The passport Tim handed Arthur Harrison was full of entry and exit stamps on every page, so much so that he must have assumed the detective would miss the stamp for Malaga. Harrison did not, and when they returned to the station, he double-checked the date against the telegram. It was the same. Through Interpol they got on to the Guardia Civil, who traced an airport official who remembered Tim, having had an altercation with him at the airport. Sure now that the telegram had been sent by Tim and that the other correspondence had been forged, the detectives returned again, determined to find Tim's typewriter. He denied that he'd ever had one, but Tina's daughter, who was being interviewed separately, told Strick Carter that it was in the office. By now, Tim, who was hoping to get away to Malta, had become quite agitated. After conferring in the car, Harrison and Carter decided to search the house. They didn't find the typewriter, but what they did find was felt to be sufficient evidence to arrest him on a holding charge. Tina's daughter, who turned sixteen the same day, 27 August 1970, was taken away to stay with friends and Tim was driven to Northallerton police station.

A lengthy interrogation followed which went on throughout the night. 'He was calm, but sweating a lot,' remembers Strick Carter. 'He was so convincing, but we never doubted that there was something wrong because of the lies he had told and going to Malaga. All he would say was, "Superintendent, you are making a grave mistake." He kept repeating this. Then, as daylight broke, he said, "Superintendent . . . ", and we thought the same thing was coming, "can I have your assurance [Tina's daughter] will be taken care of if I tell you what really happened?" We said yes. Then he said, "We had an argument, she hit me over the eye with something, kicked me in the balls and the next thing she was lying dead on the floor." After confessing, he was quite jolly.' Strick Carter asked Tim to draw a map of the windshelter and mark the spot, which was under a rosebed, then he and Arthur Harrison called up Chief Inspector Tim Coffee of the forensic science lab and 'Prof Gee', the pathologist, and gave them the location. 'It was a real macabre morning. It was dank and foggy, just like a television drama – two detectives setting forth with spades and shovels. We met at the scene and started to dig.' Tim Coffee had a broom handle, with which he tested for the corpse by inserting into the hole and sniffing it. 'He kept saying, "You're nowhere near yet,"' remembers Strick. 'We thought Franklin was having us on. We had to go back to the cells and ask him, and he said, "You're too far over to the left."' More hands were called on to help, including John Scull and PCs Tom Pearson and Dirk Ireland. After moving over to the right and and starting to dig, they didn't need Tim Coffee's broom handle to detect the body. For the last two feet, the smell was appalling, so bad that Pearson's sinuses suffered for a long time afterwards as a result, according to Harry Codling. Even so, John Scull was up to his neck in the hole before he hit something solid with his spade. It was the inside of Tina's knee bone. Dirk Ireland, who once, coincidentally, had a meeting with my husband, relayed this story to him telling him the corpse 'exploded', from which I take to mean the blow released the pent-up foul gases. It was a horrendous undertaking for all of them, particularly the young constables, and they were glad to let the experts take over. 'After that, Prof Gee got down there with his brush,' says Strick. 'It was like an archaeological dig. It took all day.'

The rest we already know – how Tina had been strangled with a length of blue clothes line, the remainder of which was still hanging from the windshelter, how she'd been wrapped up and a cloth (Strick Carter thinks it was a headscarf) stuffed in her mouth. Forensics found the microscopic blood splashes in the back hallway, under the stairs, and Tim admitted to burying the iron bars in a different part of the garden, which were also retrieved. A search of the house revealed many of Tina's personal possessions still in place; possessions which, had she really moved abroad, she would surely have taken with her. The detectives also discovered the 'hole' in the wall, which was quite a large space about three bricks thick and had hinged wooden doors on either side. To Carter's eyes the space had a rough, unfinished appearance: it had not been panelled and the brickwork was still showing, although Tim's colleague Derek King claims that the decision to leave the bricks exposed was part of the decor. Both doors opened about nine inches off the floor, requiring one to step into and out of the space, and had full-length mirrors attached. To the casual observer – or even a snooping investigator – they would have looked like part of the furniture.

Tim always denied striking Tina, and he stuck to that story. It made proving a motive – not essential, but helpful in a murder inquiry – impossible. The detectives researched Tim's background, talking to his former headmaster at Tonbridge, who, Strick Carter says, described him as 'a very intelligent man, extremely ambitious with excellent leadership qualities but very aggressive with a very bad temper'. In other words, a man of outstanding abilities but with a low flashpoint when it came to violence. The ambitiousness, in particular, was noted: having spent a week in London with Tina Strauss's solicitors, Strick Carter and John Scull discovered that she had left everything to Tim in her will. The possibility that she had been killed in a quest for money could not be ruled out. It wasn't just Tina's estate that Tim stood to benefit from. He was, as Strick Carter puts it, 'fully aware of [Tina's daughter's] financial benefits'. The press had quoted her as being an heiress to almost £500,000 of her father's property (roughly £4.5 million in today's money) but the real figure may have been much higher. The detectives, taking into account her aunt's estate, which she was also due to inherit, estimated it to be more like £1.5 million (the equivalent of £14 million today). The fact that Tim had hidden Tina's jewellery in a drawer in his Stockton office before his arrest was seen as a further incriminating factor, as was the fact that he had cashed post-dated cheques from Tina after the murder and continued to bank the alimony payments of £200–£300 a month (worth around £1,900–£2,850 today).

Antonia says her impression was the cheques 'were to do with settling the business of the house' and that Tim cashed them to maintain the deception that Tina was alive. This would have been true of his continuing to accept Richard Strauss's money on Tina's behalf, too, although Tim claimed he never spent any of it. However, the revelation about Tina's will came as a surprise even to Antonia. 'I'm astonished that somebody as careful with money as Tina would have left it . . . I would have thought she would have changed it by then. She was intent on leaving him.' She concedes that the financial incentive had to be considered: 'There was a hell of a lot of money involved with this. It's only natural to think that's what the motive was. But I don't think it was. I think the money was incidental.'

There is a second, more controversial theory that the police considered: that Tim had struck up a relationship with Tina's daughter before the murder, and that Tina found out. However, she denied having had a sexual relationship with him. Strick Carter says the teenager never reacted to anything they put to her, including questions about the nature of her relationship with Tim – 'She was flat, on one level the whole time.' Antonia says, 'She was an emotional teenager at an age when mother and daughter are often at loggerheads, when indulgence from somebody could win her over completely . . . She might have appeared quite sophisticated, the way teenagers do – they like to seem perfectly grown-up and in control when everything is going to pieces around them – but I think she was just a desperately needy girl.' Carter confirms that the mother-daughter relationship had been 'a bit frigid', something they had learned from interviewing the girl's close friend, and Antonia doesn't dispute this. 'She hadn't had a good relationship with her father, or her mother. She thought her mother had been prepared to leave her, and I think she probably was, because she was threatening to send her to boarding school. She wasn't proposing to take her with her, wherever she was going.' Antonia also states categorically that the girl was not in any way involved in the murder. 'She may have known in the way that one knows something one doesn't want to know, but she didn't know her mother was dead. I'm quite clear about that.'

Christopher Fothergill also heard this theory. From his own point of view there was never any indication that Tim had acted improperly. He believes the press understated how bad that final fight was. 'It must have been a gruesome battle for life. Tim was injured too. He had scratches and a deep cut on his forehead, which he said had been caused by running into a tree. But she [Tina] was no weakling.' After that, he remembers, Tim's performance at work declined rapidly. He was drinking heavily throughout the day and unable to concentrate, performing so badly that they even considered sacking him. This was put down to Tim's depression over Tina leaving him and Christopher says the first he knew of the murder was on his return from holiday in August 1970. 'The police barged in and gave me hell. They thought there had been some sort of a cover-up.'

Ultimately, he rejects any suggestion of Tina's daughter as a possible factor in Tim's motivation and the potential financial motive. 'Tina leaving him was the third scenario – that he took a swipe at her and damaged her so badly he had to go through with it. I would say that's the most likely one . . . For my own peace of mind, that's what I've always gone for.' Although he describes what happened as 'a horrible accident', he is sure the guilty verdict was correct. 'It couldn't be manslaughter, when you consider that he buried her. It was murder. But murder can be an accident. It's the last blow that's the killing one.'

If one is seeking a motive, the possibility that Tim killed Tina in anger at her leaving him, either out of retribution or jealousy, is certainly the simplest explanation, especially if there was another lover in the picture (which Tim hinted at). Tim told Antonia and Belinda that he'd been drunk when the murder happened and, given his propensity for violence and the warning shots that Antonia had identified in his previous fights with Tina, it seems within character. The police didn't know how out of control Tim's drinking was, and although Strick Carter smelt alcohol on his breath during several of their interviews, he did not suspect him to be an alcoholic. It was not a subject that was brought up by the defence, for obvious reasons, and since Tim had been forced to dry out on remand he would, anyway, have presented a picture of sobriety. Neither would he allow his mental state to be put forward for consideration. Antonia recognized that he was 'badly disturbed' and felt initially that he should have been in a psychiatric prison, but despite the letter that Tim wrote to her on his arrest, he refused subsequently to acknowledge there was anything wrong with him. He was examined by the defence psychiatrist before the trial, who pronounced him fit, while privately admitting to Antonia, 'The trouble is, he can run rings round all of us.'

So, was it a fight that went too far? Did Tim, in disarming Tina, find himself wreaking revenge with the iron bar? Did he, on finding her unconscious and horrifically wounded, finish the job by strangling her, first with his tie and then with the clothes line? If that was the case, then premeditation would have been involved, at least in the latter stage. That was the prosecution's argument, and the judge's reminder to the jury that in self-defence, 'you are not entitled to . . . use the occasion to take vengeance' seems to me more significant than any pauses. Look at the context: Tina had been threatening to leave Tim for a year before he killed her. That is a long time for resentment to build up. Tim's anxiety, and his anger, have been demonstrated by his obsessive behaviour, the stalking, the incidents with the axe and the furniture. He was a man who, from childhood, had an acute fear of being abandoned, and not only was Tina blatantly planning on leaving him (possibly for someone more powerful, which would really rub the salt in), she was also taking her daughter away. Having already lost his own family, to lose his surrogate family too would, I imagine, have been unbearable, particularly if he had developed an attachment to the young girl. And the pain at the subconscious level would have cut even deeper. Antonia recognizes that, 'What Tina had done that was fatal to her was to say that she was leaving and putting a girl in boarding school, because that's exactly what our mother had done.'

Whatever the detectives' private suspicions were, there was no evidence to support these theories or any others and they had to go with the story Tim told them – for which, after all, there was some evidence. This is what Antonia and Belinda believe and there is nothing to gainsay it, except Tim's repeated assertion to me that he'd lied to protect somebody. When I tell Strick Carter this, he looks intrigued. 'That statement is something that was always at the back of our minds.'

Antonia believes the person he was lying to was himself. 'He might have thought he was lying to protect [Tina's daughter] from the truth that he'd killed her mother, which was part of his motivation. He couldn't face telling her, couldn't face her knowing. So I expect it did feel to him as if he was protecting her from the truth.'

And here we have the conundrum: how can one ever believe a liar when they tell you what they say is the truth, and afterwards tell you the truth is that they lied? The fact that they've lied is all you can believe of them, which makes a mockery of everything else. Tim told so many lies, so convincingly, throughout that entire period, that to believe his story requires a degree of credulity few would entertain. Even Gilbert Gray, the QC who was Tim's defence at the trial, says, 'There was a great deal in the narrative of what happened that could not be easily explained except on the basis of the most audacious hypocrisy.' I had tracked down Mr Gray with David Farrar's help. It turned out that he lived behind the Minster, just a few doors away from where we used to live in York, a coincidence that ought to have surprised me but doesn't because there have been so many of them in this story. Like Strickland Carter he found Tim 'a most engaging fellow', and planned to use this to his advantage. 'It was my hope that his pleasant personality would overwhelm the unpleasant nature of the narrative. That's really what I was basing it on. Because the bald story, simply told, took a bit of swallowing. It required a willing suspension of disbelief and was certainly theatrical in scale.' However, far from persuading the jury, Tim's personality worked against him. 'He did not, when he was giving evidence, prevaricate or shilly-shally. He looked the questioner in the eye. He did not display the classical symptoms of a liar. But that, in a sense, made all the more believable what he'd done. They were saying he was a conman, a smoothie and everything else, and to some extent he proved it with his performance.'

And a performance it undoubtedly was. After sentence was passed, Strick Carter remembers Tim turning to the jury, bowing, and saying 'Thank you for your kindness in your deliberations', and then turning round and bowing to the public gallery at the back, as if taking a curtain call. 'He smiled, though I don't think it was at anyone in particular,' he says, when I tell him the papers mention a woman. I suspect it was Antonia, who attended the trial throughout, though her memories are vague. 'To me, the room looked enormous. I was in a very spaced-out state . . . That time was so traumatic, my mind went into a sort of clench.'

There's a certain heroic quality to this bowing and smiling and courtesy when you've just been found guilty of murder, and it calls to mind the only bit of (cod) Latin Tim ever taught me: '*Non illigitamus carborundum*', which means, 'Don't let the bastards grind you down'. It could, I suspect, have been his motto in life, though it was no practical use against twelve sceptical Yorkshiremen. Even before Tim had uttered a word, the jury had a firm view. Geoffrey Baker was thorough and fair. It was his first murder prosecution leading brief and he was 'a very enthusiastic and zealous prosecutor', according to Gilbert Gray. 'The atmosphere in court was astonishingly hostile,' he recounts. 'I've never forgotten when I called Tim to the stand he had to walk across the front of the jury box, and as he passed the juror on the second row on the end, he winced, pulled what was plainly a hostile face and leant away from Tim as if he couldn't bear the proximity. Not a good sign.'

I was surprised at just how well Gilbert Gray remembered the case. It was the first murder trial he defended, but that's not why it stays in his memory. 'I've had many murders since then, but there was something particular about that.' It was, he says, the challenge that appealed. 'And the nature of the challenge was to overcome the shock-horror and the initial revulsion [that] was manifest on the face of the jury.' Although there were elements of the murder that 'lacked charm', as Mr Gray, with exquisite understatement, puts it, he found Tim's 'intelligence and audacity' impressive. 'With many murders it's brute force and ignorance and there's no subtlety about it. That's not a murder trial, it's a waste of time. A true murder is a different quality altogether and sometimes in such cases you feel you're almost in the presence of evil. I didn't do so with Tim. I thought I might be shaking hands with a guilty man, but I didn't feel he was thoroughly evil as some murderers are. I think it was rather like Macbeth. Having waded in so far, he had to wade on. In the end, I'm prepared to accept that he believed it in its entirety. A capacity for self-delusion undoubtedly existed there.'

With the hostile atmosphere in the court – the public gallery was packed – Gilbert Gray wasn't in the least surprised that Tim was found guilty. 'I can't say even to this day that I would have found him an absolute liar,' he admits, 'but I think he was lying about the crucial bits.' The strangulation was one of them. According to Gray, Professor Gee, a man he calls 'almost too saintly' to be a pathologist, had erred on the side of caution when he said there was no evidence to prove that the ligature had been applied before or after Tina's death. Gray maintains that in the locus – the site where the ligature had dug into her neck – there were signs of a vital reaction or bruising, 'proof positive' that she was alive at the time. Tina may have been unconscious, but she wasn't dead. And to finish her off instead of calling for help is a calculated act of murder. Tim never admitted to this and Gray went with his claim of self-defence. 'I didn't have to believe it or not. That's what he told me, so we had to run it. There was nobody on the other side to say, "No, it's not." He got some injuries, as I remember, which were consistent with that, but they might have been self-inflicted. You never know.'

Gilbert Gray went on to represent Tim for his appeal, which was based on the allegation that the judge, Mr Justice Griffiths, had led the jury by his 'dramatic' pauses. 'I can't say my heart was altogether in support of the submission . . . He was first, last and all the time a very fair judge.' Tim lost the appeal, which was not unexpected, but his persuasiveness was such that Mr Gray confesses he entertained 'a few misgivings' about the conviction. When I tell him about Tim's history of alcoholism, his violence towards Roz and Tina and his mental disturbance, he says the information eases his mind. 'I've often thought about the case,' he admits, adding, 'I still ride in a few Pickerings lifts. My mind goes right back to it.' For an eminent silk whose cases include Matrix Churchill, the Birmingham bombing, the Black Panther and the Brinks Mat robbery, the 'Body in the Garden Trial' is one that, astonishingly, continues to haunt.

CHAPTER SEVENTEEN

Prison life suited Tim. Any other company director locked up in a maximum-security jail – he was sent to Wakefield Prison – on a wing full of lifers with, arguably, less finesse, might have cracked up, but Tim adapted swiftly. He excelled in structured environments and was used to asserting himself in the company of other men, displaying a talent for leadership that seems to have garnered the respect of both inmates and staff. On one occasion he went on hunger strike in protest at the lack of adequate dental treatment in the prison, which prompted the rest of the wing to agitate for a riot in his support, a tactic he successfully talked them out of. Antonia was told this by the assistant governor of the prison, who made a point of commending her brother's good influence. 'He said Tim had got the wing functioning in such a way that they didn't riot or chuck food down the well and he argued their point and was able to represent them.' She recounts the story of how she was contacted by a career criminal – 'an armed robber sort of bloke' – who told her how much Tim had done for him inside and said he'd do anything for him in return. Tim's charm, it seems, was undiminished by incarceration.

It wasn't long before Tim had established a niche for himself running the prison library (I had a copy of Eliot's *Four Quartets* that he must have lifted, because it was stamped 'Property of Wakefield Prison' on the flyleaf). He began studying for an Open University degree in Philosophy and Psychology and relished the intellectual stimulation. Ironically, it had taken a jail sentence for him to explore this side of himself, a side that the aptitude test years ago had identified as his true calling. And it wasn't just Tim who was benefiting from learning: his skill in teaching others was soon marked and he was offered a job teaching business studies to prison officers. It didn't work out, apparently because the college was sited across the road and the principal objected to one of his staff turning up in handcuffs. Since Tim was the source for this titbit it may be an apocryphal tale, but it makes me smile anyway.

Antonia visited Tim whenever she could, travelling up from Cornwall for whole weekends, but his only other visitor at Wakefield was Christopher Fothergill, who came to see him once a month. He brought in treats and news of the outside and made a point of keeping the conversation upbeat and forward-looking. It was a practical way of repaying Tim for Pickerings' success, he says. 'We never spoke about the past. We always spoke of the future. I never asked him about what happened. He trusted me to be honourable.'

After four years at Wakefield, Tim was transferred to Portsmouth Prison, which had a less harsh regime. His ankylosing spondylitis had begun to manifest itself by then, which was when he received the radiation therapy to prevent curvature of the spine. He served two years there before being moved again, this time to an open prison, also in Portsmouth, where he was treated with leniency because he was a model prisoner and reckoned to be harmless. A punishing regime of physical exercise was necessary to stop his back seizing up and, whenever possible, he spent all day labouring in the prison gardens. Given that he'd buried Tina under a rosebed in his own garden, it's ironic that digging would, in a strange way, become his salvation. He was suffering from chronic stiffness, the result of a radical procedure that had fused his backbone into a vertical rod. (Radiation is no longer used to treat AS because of the high incidence of leukaemia it causes.) It ensured Tim wouldn't develop the classic stoop of advanced AS sufferers, but there was a payback in pain. After his early battles for survival in the prison pecking order, he now had an even bigger fight on his hands: a battle to survive at all.

Tim was released on parole in 1978, having served just eight years. The reduction in his length of sentence – he was expected to serve at least fifteen – was a result of a campaign by Antonia, who recruited her local MP, Jeremy Pardoe, to petition for Tim's early release on health grounds. Her argument was that the longer he remained in prison, the more likely he was to become crippled by the spondylitis, which would ultimately result in him being unable to earn a living. She was supported by Christopher Fothergill, who wrote to the prison authorities with the commitment that Pickerings would employ Tim on his release. This was not, he insists, a promise he had made with Tim from the outset, but rather a late development to facilitate parole. Tim had already begun the rehabilitation process at this point, and was working at an old people's home on day release from the prison (where he was, typically, conducting an affair with one of the nurses). With Antonia volunteering herself as a stabilizing influence on Tim, plans were drawn up for his parole. He went to live in north Cornwall, near Antonia, in a house she purchased on his behalf with the money left to him in their father's will, Boun having died while Tim was in prison.

Belinda, who came to visit him in Morwenstow, admits to an initial nervousness about being around Tim. She had been forbidden from mentioning his name at home, but after her stepfather died (Roz had remarried not long after Tim met Tina) she had tentatively made contact. 'I wanted to know him,' she says. 'He was my dad and I loved him.' A reunion had been arranged while Tim was still in prison, but it was an unnatural situation, cloaked in subterfuge –

the press, alert to his imminent release, were back on his case
– and not enough to reassure her of her safety alone with
him. 'I was worried when he came out of prison. My
mother was a right scaremonger but she had reason, and as
a mother myself I'd feel the same. But I knew he'd never
hurt me as a child and I couldn't see why he would hurt me
as an adult. All the same, I was careful, I really was.' Her
knowledge of the events surrounding the murder was
sketchy, pieced together from newspapers bought surrepti-
tiously on her way to school as a teenager. One night,
encountering Tim in the kitchen, she plucked up the
courage to tell him she needed to know what he'd done. He
sat her down and told her about the argument with Tina,
describing how he'd swung her round and smashed her
head against the wall in 'a moment of madness'.

'I felt better for hearing it,' Belinda admits. 'I knew it, but
I needed it out of his mouth . . . My mother always said
Tim was after Tina for her alimony, and that that's why he
couldn't let go of [Tina's daughter], because she was heir to
the money. But I don't think that's particularly true . . . It
was not in any way premeditated. He was drunk, or he'd
never have done it.' She says her relationship with Tim
afterwards involved a lot of catching up. 'We did our best,
but obviously there's a limit to how much you can do with
somebody who is so damaged, and I was damaged as well.
It's affected everyone's lives pretty dramatically.'

While Tim and Belinda were taking their first tentative
steps towards resuming their relationship as father and

daughter, Tim was also trying to find his feet again in the world of work. He had asked Christopher Fothergill to give him manual work to help with his back, and it was arranged that he would start out with Dave Upton, a service engineer in Bristol, which had the advantage of enabling Tim to learn the engineering side of the business. This partnership, more than anything, was what rehabilitated Tim and his friendship with Dave remained throughout his life, to the point that he was the one Tim chose to confide in the night he died. Dave, a blunt-speaking, down-to-earth chap, took Tim as he found him, refusing to be intimidated by his notoriety. When, after a short while working together, Tim asked him, 'Am I what you expected?' he replied, 'Well, if you thought I was looking for someone packing two pistols, you've got it wrong.' His directness was appreciated, and although they often disagreed about things, Tim accepted his discipline. The fitter's mate job and workman's clothes were to some extent a cover-up, designed to give him a low profile – in reality, Tim was conducting time and motion studies, reporting to Christopher Fothergill – but he did do some manual labour and Dave's role as his boss was not just for show. He ordered Tim never to turn up for work so much as smelling of drink, made him wear work boots whether he liked it or not and even sacked him on one occasion for allowing an accident to happen in a lift shaft.

Dave remembers Tim with enormous fondness, calling him 'an inspiration' to be around. 'He taught me a lot. He was so clever – I don't think a lot of people ever appreciated how clever he was. He was always five streets ahead of you. He could take anything in his stride. I really liked him. We had a lot of fun over the years.' He admits Tim had an aggressive side but never felt he was any kind of threat. Despite their clashes they always parted friends and, more often than not, Tim would have talked him round to agreeing with him. 'He could have told you white was black and you would have believed him when he was finished,' he laughs.

Dave's family liked Tim too, and he got to know the Uptons well, becoming a frequent visitor to their house and inviting them over for impromptu barbecues in return. 'He was a bloody good cook,' Dave says, recalling sunny evenings in the garden eating steak followed by strawberries. The Uptons, who had three young children, weren't the only family to receive Tim without prejudice. Christopher Fothergill, who had remarried since their early, house-sharing days together and was now living in Switzerland, negotiated for Tim to be permitted a passport and flew him out to stay with him and his wife. Tim spent a happy fortnight with them, integrating into family life and pushing a pram by the shores of Lake Geneva, the picture of a man who had survived the worst and come through smiling. But however much he may have given the appearance of a genial uncle, the obsessional, fixated side of him remained unchanged. Something was brewing in the back of his mind, a plot that I suspect had been simmering away for a while and a few months after his release from prison he was rearrested in dramatic fashion.

I have few details about what happened, other than the fact that it involved Tim breaking a restraining order. What I do know is that someone accused him of abducting and terrorizing them and that, as a consequence, Tim was considered so dangerous that his house was cordoned off and encircled by police marksmen. Antonia, who returned home from work to find armed police at her door, was shocked by the news. She insisted on accompanying the officers to Tim's house, where she volunteered to go through the door first, hoping to defuse the situation. She found Tim coming out of the kitchen, carrying a plate of food he'd just cooked. He gave no sign that anything was wrong and does not appear to have been anticipating the police's visit. 'When I told him they'd come to arrest him, he went grey,' Antonia recalls. 'Whether he thought he'd get away with it, I don't know.'

Tim was taken straight back to prison. When Antonia went to see him, he told her he was going to kill himself. It's a mark of how serious his alleged crime was that his own sister debated over whether to warn the prison authorities of his intention. 'I thought, he has the right. Because I couldn't see him ever getting out.' She did, however, and although the prison officer she spoke to was dismissive, an extra check must have been made. Tim was discovered with his throat and both wrists slashed, just in time to prevent him from bleeding to death. Even then, says

Antonia, 'I didn't know whether I'd done him a service or not. It was an absolutely desperate time. I thought, that's it, for life. And then, they released him.'

This is quite astonishing, and Antonia certainly found it so. 'It terrified me. As far as I was concerned, what had happened was the totally irresponsible, out-of-control side of Tim and if that was what he was going to do, then he was a danger, he was a risk.' The reason for this turnaround was that a witness had come forward with evidence to contradict the accusation that had been made against Tim, although Antonia didn't credit it. 'Personally, I believe the accuser.' I cannot be certain of who 'the accuser' was, and Antonia does not feel that part of the story is hers to tell. Bearing in mind the sensitivity of the case, it would be wrong to speculate, although I believe I have an idea of the accuser's identity, based on things other people have said to me. However, it's fair to ask whether that person was more likely to be someone from his past or from his new life, post-release. Christopher Fothergill says he never questioned Tim about it, believing the incident to be an overreaction on the part of the police. Antonia did not view it that way; she refused to take responsibility for Tim again, insisting that he be supervised by someone else. She did, though, stipulate that Tim must not be left on his own and so he was released to a bail hostel. He was not suspended from his job with Pickerings and must have found a way of carrying on with his work without informing Christopher that he was based in a hostel for homeless people, because

Christopher never knew about Tim's temporary accommodation. After a few months there he started at Exeter University, where he was given a room at Barton Place, a hall of residence for male post-graduates. This was in October 1979, two years before I came to Exeter. Although her trust in him had been broken, she wanted to believe he could reform. When he came out of prison the second time, he had told her, 'That bloke is dead', meaning that he had killed the violent man inside him. He seemed to be on course, at last.

Once at Exeter, Tim formed a relationship with a young girl, an undergraduate of eighteen or nineteen. I don't know who this girl was, but it could have been the ex-girlfriend he mentioned to me a couple of times. Once again, he seems to have become obsessed, and when the girl tried to break it off he began spinning elaborate plots to keep her. Antonia spotted the switch in him and became perturbed. 'He was lying to me. And the way he was behaving – all my alarms went off. I thought he might harm her.' She decided to confront him and did so, inviting him over to Lower Cory. Leo, her husband, insisted on being present, concerned that Tim was so unbalanced he might vent his fury on her. When Antonia warned Tim that she was going to write to his probation officer, he was predictably furious. 'He said, "If you do that, our relationship will change." And the way he looked at me. God he was angry . . .' She did write to his probation officer and it did change, and they saw little of each other after that. Tim's liaison with the girl was terminated and although he befriended Ginni after that, it was not a sexual relationship (she had a boyfriend in the Merchant Navy) and appears to have had none of the destructive possessiveness that was his usual form. And then, in October 1981, he met me.

Nobody warned me about Tim. I do feel angry about that now, but I'm not sure I would have listened at the time. Antonia wasn't aware that I was quite so ignorant of the facts of his crime. She assumed that because my father was a police officer, he would have looked into Tim's case and that I would have been wise to the potential danger. After her clash with Tim over the previous girlfriend, she was loathe to interfere again, although she continued to be anxious about his relationships with the young girls he met at Exeter. It explains her rather unbending attitude the one time Tim did take me to meet her, about which she admits, 'A lot of my body language would have been wanting to convey to you that it was not safe.' I, of course, remained oblivious of this, primed by Tim that his sister was bound to disapprove because of my age, and defiant in my love for him. As to the lack of paternal protection, my father had had no reason to suspect anything untoward about Tim at that point because I hadn't told him anything about his past. He genuinely liked Tim. Everybody did.

Dave Upton recalls the first time he visited Tim at Barton Place and realized just how popular he was. 'We were walking up the driveway and all these students were talking to him, saying hello, asking how he was. You'd have thought he was the Pope.' And that's how it was. Tim was a star. And, like all stars, he stage-managed his appearances and edited his past, careful to keep that other persona of his hidden away (at least until he got into an intimate relationship). He was open about being a lifer, and that honesty – as far as it went – brought him respect. It also deflected difficult questions: no one, seeing him wince as he gave a perfunctory explanation of what happened, pushed him further. The fact that it had apparently been a terrible accident and that, according to Tim, he should never have been found guilty in the first place, only made him more iconic. The subject of his thesis, 'Scapegoating in the Criminal Justice System', was the summation of this, a logical proving of his victimization. It was also the ultimate in self-delusion, arising as it did from the false proposition that because he'd *said*, 'X is true', X *was* true. Black is white. Believe me. Here's the proof. QED.

'The trouble is, he can run rings round all of us,' the psychiatrist said. Such intelligence is rare and it was Tim's blistering intelligence that both dazzled and drew one to him. But however brilliant he was, he lacked emotional intelligence. The charisma was a cover for a man with an emotional age of six who was still trying to control his four-year-old sister in every unhealthily obsessive relationship with young women that he had. Put together with his skill at manipulation, his pathological lying, his arrogance, his violent and sometimes uncontrollable temper, his aggressiveness and isolation as a child, his drinking, his history of promiscuity, his criminal past (and apparent inability to learn from the experience, if the abduction incident is true) and, notably, his failure to accept responsibility for his own actions, and you have the main characteristics of a psychopath.

CHAPTER EIGHTEEN

Handsome, charming, US serial killer Ted Bundy was a psychopath. So was Hannibal Lector, the charismatic cannibal in *Silence of the Lambs*. One was real, one is fictional, but both were dangerous, remorseless, cunning individuals who did evil, unimaginable things. The word 'psychopath' is a loaded one, especially in popular culture, and it weighs heavily in the balance of notorious murderers. It is so loaded with opprobrium that nowadays the term 'sociopath' is generally used instead, along with 'anti-social personality disorder' (ASPD), although experts dispute their interchangeability. Whichever word one uses, the image doesn't, on the face of it, seem to fit Tim Franklin, a man whose preferred pastime was growing sweet peas — sociopaths tend to be risk-takers who need constant stimulation – nor would it appear to describe a man who was loved and respected by so many people.

Certainly it was not something that ever occurred to me when I was with Tim, nor to anyone else in my immediate family. When I went back to my diaries to write this book, it was easier to be analytical about Tim's behaviour. That fraught twenty-year-old netted in his schemes was like a trapped butterfly; however hard I beat my wings against the glass he was not going to let me escape. I hadn't wanted to, at first. I was happy in the bell jar that was Tim's world. But it was a world where everything referred to him and I was brainwashed into thinking that the things that happened were my fault. I had no hope of gaining objectivity. Two decades later, reading that stuff, I began to suspect he might have had some sort of mental problem, but I wasn't sure what it could be. It was only when I interviewed Antonia and she mentioned his 'disturbance', that I realized I wasn't the only one who had dared to think this. Even so, her description of Tim as being virtually psychopathic was one that shocked me, because I had the same preconceptions about psychopathy as everyone else.

'I think he was borderline psychopathic, but very well managed,' were her exact words. She is well informed on the subject: Antonia worked with psychoanalyst R. D. Laing in the 1960s and he became a personal friend. He took great interest in Tim's case, although he never met him personally or made a clinical evaluation. 'He would always make time to see me to talk about Tim because he was interested in people on the outside edge of sanity, the extremes,' she says. By 'borderline' I take her to mean that Tim was verging on being psychopathic, or possessed certain psychopathic tendencies, rather than having full-blown psychopathy. His whole life was a balancing act, a wire walk over a canyon. For much of the time he kept his balance and we applauded his skill and bravery, but when he stumbled he fell a long, long way and the chasm was deep and black.

So, was he psychopathic or not? On the psychopathy checklist (PCL-R) formulated by Dr Robert Hare, a standard method of evaluation that is used particularly in the US, Tim scores highly. I have spoken to two professionals who have both described Tim as a sociopath. One of these, a psychiatrist, met Tim several times socially and formed this opinion without knowing anything about his background; the other, a clinical psychologist, is the husband of a friend who has heard me recount Tim's story endlessly over cups of tea and delivered his opinion unprompted by my asking. When I went back to him later and asked why the definition seemed, at an instinctive level, to go so against the grain, he stressed that a severe personality disorder such as ASPD or sociopathy doesn't tell the whole story of a complex person. In other words, the fact that Tim liked gardening was one aspect of him and (to me) a redemptive one, but it doesn't mean he *wasn't* a risk-taker; the fact that he chose to argue self-defence rather than provide a motive for provocation does. That he was arrogant enough to think he could get away with this high-risk strategy is telling: grandiose self-worth, having a very assured, opinionated or inflated view of one's abilities, is number two on Hare's psychopathy checklist, and one that Tim's fantasies about the SAS, the concentration camp, Harvard, being 'a published poet' (he wasn't, it turned out) would seem to fit. Number one is the ability to charm, which was perhaps Tim's most attractive and disarming characteristic and one that he employed equally successfully with men and women.

There is, though, a crucial feature of psychopathy that I am unsure whether Tim had or not, and that is a lack of guilt or remorse. I do not remember him expressing regret or sorrow about the murder, but then we didn't talk about it, so it's not surprising. He did talk about 'the burden' he carried with him, but this was usually when I was depressed, which was something he couldn't cope with. It was always 'What about my pain?' as if he had to go one better, and Antonia confirms this. 'He didn't have the capacity to care in a way that wasn't narcissistic about other people. He could only care for people if they were "for" him.' (This lack of empathy is, actually, very much a part of the psychopathic make-up, as is the narcissism.) Perhaps Tim did feel guilt after the murder – he certainly went to pieces for a while – though this could have been due to anxiety about getting caught. So-called 'primary psychopaths' do not, apparently, suffer from nervousness or doubt about their actions, which is why they are seen to be lacking a moral conscience, and Tim wasn't one of those. There is, however, another category of 'secondary psychopaths' who do report feelings of guilt and might fear the consequences of their wrongdoing. They are daring, adventurous, unconventional people who expose themselves to more stress than the average person but are as vulnerable to that stress as anyone else (witness Tim's 'episodic' alcoholism and panic attacks). They make up their own rules early in life, are strongly driven by a desire to escape or avoid pain but are unable to resist temptation. Typically they continue to act in antisocial ways post-release – criminal versatility is pretty much a 'given' – due to their poor impulse control and rapidly fluctuating moods. It's a definition that does, I think, describe Tim accurately.

What, then, of Tim's ability to captivate people, to earn not just their respect, but their love? People weren't blind to his faults. They knew and accepted him, despite his past; they suffered his tongue-lashings, his criticism, his palpable aggressiveness. Was it all a con-trick? Were we all fooled? In his book, *Without Conscience*, Dr Robert Hare writes that anyone can be duped by a psychopath. Even so, it is hard for me to credit that this side of Tim was just an act. He had a powerful and alluring personality – 'he could really sparkle when he wanted to', as Christopher Fothergill put it – but I never got a sense that it masked a cold or indifferent person underneath. He *could*, it's true, be very cold towards me, and his indifference to what I was going through, especially in the latter stages of our relationship, was very hurtful; nonetheless, I didn't see it as a vein that ran through him. That qualification of Christopher's, 'when he wanted to', is significant, though. Christopher was very perceptive in his remarks about Tim. He said Tim could 'vary his charisma' to suit the level of a workman or influence a prime minister, adding, 'Whatever the person he met, he had the ability to impress them. Whether they impressed him to a similar degree is debatable.' When I think about Tim helping my mum with the quick crossword, or teaching Dave Upton problem-solving techniques in a lift shaft or arguing Wittgenstein in the pub with Nigel or charming the detective who arrested him – not to mention getting a wing of hardened lifers on his side – I can see this is true.

Was it genuine? I don't know. It was for us. Our university friends, Tom and Chris, keep Tim's photo pinned up on the noticeboard above their computer and refer to him fondly as 'Uncle Tim'. Chris is still angry at Tim for killing himself before she could show him their first child. Ginni remembers Tim as 'the perfect gentleman' and talks equally generously about how he helped her through a time when she was very vulnerable. My mother has Tim's camera, which he left her, and won't let anyone else use it. She says she still hears his voice in her head, helping her when she gets stuck on an anagram. Dave Upton, I discovered, keeps Tim's tie in his wardrobe, and takes it out every so often to get it dry-cleaned and pressed. When he told me this in his West Country accent, which is as thick as clotted cream – 'I said, "There you are, Tim, I'm looking after it for you"' – I found such a huge lump rising in my throat that I couldn't swallow. It's been many many years since I've cried for Tim, and I hadn't shed a tear throughout writing this whole book, but the interview with Dave, which I conducted just before I began this final chapter, opened the floodgates. I couldn't stop crying, not just then, but afterwards, and again writing up my notes, and even now, if I'm honest, the tears are pricking at the back of my eyes. Because it touched me so deeply that Dave, who is now sixty-one, had loved him. Not only that, but it made me remember the good things about Tim, which I'd started to forget in the course of this investigation. At times it's been as if I've been writing about two other people, characters in a story, not him and me. Not intentionally – I have striven always to be honest, to keep telling myself 'keep it real' – but I recognize that subconsciously distancing myself has helped me survive this emotional rollercoaster ride. So, when the tears came at last, I had to admit that whatever Tim was, whoever Tim was, and whatever he did, he inspired people, and that is a great gift not just to possess, but to receive.

My talk with Dave Upton proved to be a revelation in more ways than one. Dave was the last person to see Tim alive, the person to whom Tim had given his 'confession', and I was hoping he held the key that would unlock the mysteries still surrounding Tim. Securing the interview was a long job, which was why I didn't talk to him until this late stage, but when I got him to open up at last, it was worth it.

We chatted about how they'd worked together and Dave's memories of Tim, and then moved on to that final evening in Bristol. Dave said Tim had phoned him up when he was on a job in Cornwall and asked he come to see him at his hotel in Bristol. Dave was tired after his long drive and didn't much fancy it, but Tim persisted, calling him several times. 'He wouldn't be put off,' Dave recalled. 'He said, "I've got your tea over here." So I stuck my head under a tap and went on over.' Tim had the meal laid out in his room, a feast of smoked salmon and all his favourite delicacies. 'Not my sort of food,' chuckled Dave, 'I said, "I don't like that, it's horrible." ' He sat down and ate it anyway and listened while Tim made phone calls bidding people goodbye. Everyone thought he was going to start a new life in Spain, which was what Dave believed, too, so there was nothing especially unusual about this, although he was puzzled about why Tim was flying from Bristol instead of Gatwick, which would have been the more logical choice from Oxford. Tim, of course, had a satisfactory explanation, although the next day, when Dave found out that he was dead, he kicked himself for not having made the connection. However, he insisted there was no sign that Tim was planning to kill himself: 'We sat there and had a laugh and I arranged to meet up with him again in Cornwall.' He said he was there for about two hours and left the hotel about 12.30 a.m. Tim was drinking Coke, as always, and although he did see him take painkillers during the evening, it was only a single dose. Dave sighed, remembering. 'When I went to the coroner's court, I was screwed down to the floor. And I thought, well, it's done now, he's out of his agony . . . but I suppose really I should have seen something there.' He paused, then he added, to my surprise, 'I don't think he died a lonely man.'

'No?' I asked, not knowing what to think.

'No. He spent half the night talking about you. Your age, why you'd finished. He thought the world of you.'

That overwhelmed me, because Tim and I had been apart for fifteen months by then and I had no idea he still felt that strongly about me. The letter that he left for me was friendly, but not romantic or sentimental, and in the light of everything I now know about Tim I had begun seriously to doubt whether he really had loved me. It seems, perhaps, that he did, and I am grateful beyond words for that insight because it helps. It helps not just to restore my faith in what we had, but to regain a sense of proportion. Tim was severely disturbed, but he wasn't a madman. Underneath it all he was an extremely vulnerable person, ultimately more vulnerable than me. I have survived. I was the strong one, after all.

This wasn't the only insight I gained from my conversation with Dave. There was another, in many ways more disturbing one, to do with Tim's crime. Dave said Tim told him most of what happened, but he wouldn't repeat it because Tim told him in confidence. When I told him Tim's assertion that he'd lied to protect somebody, he confirmed that he'd said this to him. Apparently Tim hinted at more than one affair going on, but he mentioned no names.

323

'When you listen to Tim, he would only give you half the picture,' Dave said. 'You had to try and fit it all together.' Tim trusted Dave with his personal papers (it seems he didn't burn everything from his past at Devonshire Place after all), but Dave wouldn't reveal their contents, except to say, 'There are certain things he wrote that I think were wrong.' Those papers have long since been destroyed so there is no hope of finding any clues now. I was left with Dave's cryptic conclusion: 'I think Tim felt guilty, but not 100 per cent guilty.'

I have chewed over this conversation endlessly since then, without coming up with any real answers. It may have been that something happened that gave Tim a *motive* for murdering Tina Strauss, but even if there was someone else present, that doesn't make them an instrument, at least, not directly, although failure to act or intervene would be a criminal offence, as would any involvement in the disposal of the body and the deception that followed. However, it does not absolve or excuse Tim from committing the crime in the first place. As to any peripheral stuff about other affairs, that is speculation and even though it's since been suggested to me from another reliable source – someone, significantly, who did not get the information from Tim – it does not, in any case, appear to have a direct bearing on the murder.

As Dave said, 'There's much more went on than we'll ever know', and perhaps that is all we can say. That, anyway, is what Tim would like us to say. But whether there is an unsolved mystery, or whether it's a case of Tim wanting people to believe there is an unsolved mystery are two very different things. I can't understand why a man who was about to kill himself would lie, particularly when he trusted his confidante to keep his secret (which Dave has). What advantage is there in that? But then my mind doesn't work like Tim's. To someone who is sociopathic, not accepting responsibility for one's actions is a classic motivating force, as is the need to have others look up to you. Pathological lying is a way of achieving this. Dave accepted Tim for who he was, he didn't need to see him in a 'better light', but I suspect this wasn't enough for Tim. Ultimately, he needed to convince *himself* that he wasn't to blame, or at least not entirely. Tim's allusions sound like spin from beyond the grave, which is a clever trick to pull off in anyone's book, even in this day and age.

What am I to make of all this? When I asked myself, back at York Crown Court, whether I'd have found Tim guilty if I'd been on the jury, the answer is probably yes. Certainly now, knowing what I know about Tim – which is a great deal more than the jury ever got to hear about him – I can answer in the affirmative. I don't think anything excuses what he did, and I don't just mean the murder. But there are so many frustrating loose ends. An Agatha Christie novel would tie them all up nicely at this point; Hercule Poirot would assemble the company and explain it all and one could close the book with a satisfied sigh. But this is not a novel. It's a true story. And real life is messy. People have agendas, pasts, reputations to protect. I didn't set out to expose any sort of scandal; I started this book as a memoir, although it became something of a detective story along the way, much more so than I ever intended. I could go on peeling away the layers, but what purpose would it serve?

The only person who might be able to give me any meaningful answers is Tina's daughter. I'll never know the truth about Tim's feelings for her, but I suspect, for all her wealthy upbringing and apparent sophistication, she was a needy and vulnerable child who had been caught up in a terrible tragedy. I did try to find her, with no success. She's been using a forwarding address ever since that time, and even her best friend hasn't heard from her in twenty years. That friend who had played with her in the garden at The Garths during the summer of 1970 and has clear memories of Tim, emailed me and said that Tina's daughter had married, which would have been a long time ago now. It's encouraging news. Antonia says she passed her in the street in London once, but neither of them acknowledged each other. Antonia thought it for the best; the girl – by then a young woman – had made her own life, and any association with Tim's family would not have been helpful. People need to move on, though how you get over an experience like that, I don't know. I hope she has. I hope she's escaped from Tim's shadow. It took me long enough.

It is time to draw a line under this now. When I spoke to Belinda, she told me what a damaging effect Tim had had on her life, to the extent that she's given up on relationships now. 'I was always looking for the father-figure that I wanted him to be.' She's had extensive therapy to try to deal with her issues and sees the process as ongoing: 'I'm keen the buck stops with me.' Belinda has two children, now grown up, and she's taken pains to ensure she didn't pass her own emotional damage on to them. It's something I feel the same about. My daughter is six, a lively, outgoing, happy little girl with strong ideas about who she is and what she likes. If there's one thing I can pass on to her, it's building on that positive image of herself, so that she'll never allow herself to be manipulated like I was. Every time she hugs me and I look into her dancing eyes I feel hope. And I wonder. If Tim had been loved as a child, if he'd had even a little of the parental love that I feel for her, would he have turned out differently?

I asked Antonia that question, whether Tim was simply a victim of his upbringing, the lack of proper parenting, the harshness of boarding school life, being effectively abandoned at such an early age. She thinks it is significant, that his psychopathy was created through having no founding in relationships – 'You have to invent an awful lot about yourself' – but agrees it doesn't justify his extreme behaviour. Tim wasn't the only child to suffer such privations in the name of a 'good education', and although such an experience undoubtedly scars, the establishment would collapse if everyone turned out like Tim. 'I believe we have a choice,' Antonia says, 'and Tim didn't choose to deal with his background.' She urged him to have therapy many times, but he consistently refused, and she believes his choice not to confront what happened to him as a child is fundamental. In psychoanalytical terms, it means Tim never grew out of the childish conception that he could wield power without taking responsibility for the consequences, that process we call socialization. And as a result, emotionally, he never grew up.

This explains something to me. The times when Tim and I were at our happiest, our most carefree, were when we were playing our infantile games. Then we were 'P' and 'B' and our playmates were the toy animals: Bwian the lion and Lottie the otter and Wol the owl and Syd the cat and the cubs Bertwum and Bertweece, who, Tim said, jumped in the car at Kingston Bagpuize and refused to get out. If it sounds like *Winnie-the-Pooh*, that's because it was. In Tim's fantasies, he and I lived in a perpetual hundred-acre wood where booeys darted in the dark and rabbits rode magic carpets and a noble St Bernard with a plumy tail came bounding to the rescue of a timid squirrel. When Tim left me that card, saying, 'Thank you for the happiest years of my life', I didn't understand how they could have been, but I do now. I joined in his game. I was the little girl who did what he said, who didn't desert him in the playground – not, at least, for four years. When I matured and left him, he tried to find a replacement in Lucy, another teenager. It was pathetic, and not just in the ludicrous sense. I feel pity for him now because he couldn't see it, and that wasn't Tim's fault. It was all he knew.

Boun, Tim's father, was a womanizer. He was promiscuous, irresponsible, unfaithful to his wife and neglectful of his family. Shortly before he died at the age of seventy-three he went on holiday to Spain with a twenty-four-year-old girl. He was, like Tim, suffering from ankylosing spondylitis, but that didn't prevent him from enjoying the company of young women. He was charming company and although sex wasn't involved by then, he obviously appreciated the female form. (Tim used to tell a story about his father hanging around outside Fortnum & Mason, offering to buy apricot silk underwear for girls he took a fancy to, which explains why Tim wanted to get me these items the time we went there.) 'It was the same pattern,' says Antonia, comparing her father and Tim, 'girls getting younger and younger.' Boun, the 'bad boy', had a terrible temper and a cruel streak. He was brilliant at management but was also emotionally repressed, a depressive and had suicidal tendencies. It all sounds very familiar.

Perhaps it was the Russian blood, some intense, brooding fatalism in the genes passed down from Tim's aristocratic but equally feckless grandfather that made Boun and his son so alike. Antonia's comment about parts of her family coming 'straight out of Dostoevsky' is telling. But it was obviously more than that. Children learn by what they experience early in life, which is why abused children often grow up to be abusers and children of alcoholics show a greater-than-average tendency to become drinkers. Tim rejected his parents when he grew up, but he held on to their values, with the result that he was almost doomed to repeat the pattern set out by his father. Was it some sort of subconscious competition to beat the man who hit him for his table manners and crushed his self-confidence? Father-son rivalry is not uncommon and the parallels are too obvious to ignore. If it was, I don't think Tim realized it. If you don't look inside yourself, you can't counter that sort of influence. It makes no sense to take on the very characteristics one hates, but that was exactly what Tim did, even with the manner of his death.

Tim's suicide – I am quite sure it was that – left a great many people bereft. It wasn't just the loss; we felt personally to blame. There was a sense that, in taking his own life, Tim was saying, 'You didn't want me', but I don't think it was revenge. Deep down, Tim hated himself more than anyone else. To live alone, without a partner and a job, meant he would have had to fall back on himself and that yawning black hole inside him would have swallowed him up. Tim couldn't be alone. Being alone, to him, was worse than death. I don't know why. Perhaps it was because his past crowded in on him, or more likely it harked back to being abandoned as a child. He could have got himself another girl if he'd gone to Spain, but I think he was tired of all that, of the running, of reinventing himself. It was, quite simply, time.

When Christopher Fothergill asked him to retire, Tim having become a liability at work, it was the cue for an action Tim had long planned. Christopher certainly felt himself 'a factor' in Tim's suicide and seems to bear the responsibility heavily. And it isn't just Christopher. Antonia had lost her husband, Leo, only six weeks earlier. To find his sister, who had always coped, so utterly devastated, removed the only sure thing he had left. She was the rock he had always returned to, his strength and security in all the madness, and she had crumbled completely. 'I took away something that was very important to him. I was his prop. And because of that, my collapse may have been a factor in his suicide, too,' she says.

I tried not to feel guilty. In fact, I was determined not to feel guilty. After all, we weren't together when he did it. But when he left me that letter, calling me his '*espousa*', it was almost impossible not to feel like his widow, and therefore as if I'd abandoned him too. After I'd scattered his ashes at Exmouth I lived in a fog of misery and self-recrimination until the day, three months or so later, I took the things that he'd left me out of storage. Packed in the splintery tea-chests between the crockery and the linen were two slim volumes of Philip Larkin's poetry and a couple of yellowed newspaper cuttings. One was an article on living with chronic pain; the other, an appreciation of Larkin with another poem, 'Aubade'. 'Aubade' describes a visceral awareness of death pressing against the curtains in the dark, the pre-dawn dread of dying: 'This is a special way of being afraid/No trick dispels'. It is the starkly honest acknowledgement of an atheist with no comfort of a world hereafter, and his description of the 'furnace fear' of facing up to the inevitable is one I recognize in myself, though I had no idea Tim felt that way. Death was something he seemed to have no fear of. But then no one, however arrogant, can surely be that blasé. Can they? In the last verse of the poem daylight breaks, 'and all the uncaring/Intricate rented world begins to rouse'. In Tim's hotel room, by the time the morning commuters clogged the streets, the light behind the curtains could not have roused him. I hoped that, before he lost consciousness, he had glimpsed the first rays of the new day, that there had been, literally, a little light at the end of the tunnel.

As for the newspaper article about pain, I think it was Tim's way of saying that he was suffering more than any of us realized. His quality of life had begun to deteriorate to what he regarded as an unacceptable level; not only was he having seizures, but the spondylitis was attacking other joints and affecting his digestive system. More importantly, his ability to perform mentally had been called into question. However vociferous he was in his public denial of this, he must have known, within himself, that his brain had become unreliable. He had never been going to see out his days in a nursing home. It was time to end it, and the pills and booze were all he needed to provide, in Larkin's words, 'the anaesthetic from which none come round'.

The two volumes of poetry that Tim left me were *High Windows* and *The North Ship*. They were crisp, their pages unmarked, their spines pristine. I checked the flyleaf on both: no inscription. Flicking through them, I recognized a

couple of the poems from *High Windows* – 'Annus Mirabilis'
and 'This Be the Verse' (of course). *The North Ship*, which
was Larkin's debut collection, published in 1945, was
unfamiliar to me, and as I examined it I noticed one of the
corners had been turned down, marking a page. I turned to
it and there I found what I had been looking for, at last.
Tim's farewell to me:

> Love, we must part now: do not let it be
> Calamitous and bitter. In the past
> There has been too much moonlight and self-pity:
> Let us have done with it: for now at last
> Never has sun more boldly paced the sky,
> Never were hearts more eager to be free,
> To kick down worlds, lash forests; you and I
> No longer hold them; we are the husks, that see
> The grain going forward to a different use.
>
> There is regret. Always, there is regret.
> But it is better than our lives unloose,
> As two tall ships, wind-mastered, wet with light,
> Break from an estuary with their courses set,
> And waving part, and waving drop from sight.

Permission to let go. How typical of Tim to leave it to me
in this secret, coded way. Nothing was straightforward with
him. You always had to read between the lines. I didn't
realize then what an achievement this was, to earn his

blessing. If that's what it was. Tim didn't let go of the women he loved without a fight, if at all. I should have known that. Even a poem about parting can seduce.

Perhaps I'm being too cynical. It's hard, now, for me to trust Tim's motives. Maybe I should accept it for what it is. It is possible that Tim got more from our relationship than I'm allowing myself to think. Perhaps, in setting us both free, he had finally learned what it is to love. If I gave him that, it would make it all worthwhile, all the angst and the rows and the tears. Because, above all, I loved him. I loved him with a passion I haven't experienced since and I don't want to experience again, because it brings the edge too close, the fall too far. Maybe we all need to feel that thrill once. But once is enough; you can't live like that, not without going crazy, and we were out of control, addicted to the rush. That is where it gets dangerous. I got out in time, but I tasted enough to get a feeling for how it can corrupt common sense, make the unthinkable thinkable, and not just thinkable but justifiable. That was how Tim lived and loved and, cocooned in his world, anyone who loved him back was at risk of becoming complicit. Love and need can be hard to differentiate and the line between passion and obsession is a thin one. The ability to kill is within all of us. You are lucky if you never find out what it takes to unleash it.

EPILOGUE

August 2003

Mars was shining brightly in the night sky when I went to bed. Our daughter had wanted to stay up late to see the red planet. I'd said no, it's too late and you'll be tired for school, but when I crept in to check on her at midnight, she sat bolt upright in bed and began chattering so volubly that I felt her forehead for a fever. We took her into our bed, then turfed her out again because, having told her not to talk, she started singing instead. An hour later, she was back again, bored. We still hadn't slept. It wasn't just her insomnia; my mind was buzzing and Stephen was tossing and turning restlessly, yanking more than his share of the duvet. At 3.30 a.m., I made tea for us and hot milk for our daughter, then

despatched her to her room again, this time with a Famous
Five story tape and her personal stereo. There were a few
precious hours to go before the alarm went off, and I was
becoming desperate. But sleep wouldn't come. It was as if
there was some vibrant energy, some force filling the house
that had us all in its grip. We even wondered whether Mars
was exerting some sort of weird astronomical hold over us:
was everyone in the country lying awake? It felt as if I
would never be able to sleep again. I lay there, puzzling over
this, when a sudden thought broadsided me. 'What date is
it today?' I asked.

Stephen groaned. 'Yesterday was the twenty-seventh.'

'What's the time?'

'I don't know. Early.' He reared up and peered at the
illuminated clock on his side. 'Ten past five.' He slumped
back down.

I felt a shiver run through me. Tim had been arrested on
27 August and they interrogated him all that night. He
confessed to the murder the next day at 5.10 a.m.

I never did get any sleep.

Tim has haunted me throughout writing this book,
dogging my dreams, giving me nightmares, still. More than
once I've dreamt that I've come across him laid out on the
grass, as if dead, and then he's opened his eyes and I've said,
'Why didn't you tell me?' and then I've begged him to give
me the truth. Sadly I can't remember whether he does or
not. In another dream I watched him beat up the hardest

boy in my school. All the kids were yelling, 'Fight, fight, fight' and I was screaming, 'Stop it! Stop him!' because I knew what he'd do, but they crowded me out. Afterwards, I was ostracized by classmates and teachers for having knowingly brought in a murderer. The big boy had been pulped. More recently, I found myself alone in a house with Tim. He said he was going to get me and chased me from room to room. When I ran outside and got into my car he leapt into another one and followed me. It seems, even now, I can't escape him.

It's not just during the night. Tim is still with me in other ways, and not good ones. I find myself anticipating his reaction even when I'm with Stephen, becoming instantly defensive when there's no need, waiting for the deluge of anger that doesn't come. I cannot get ready to go out without feeling Tim's mounting frustration, almost as if he's pacing the hall waiting for me. I told Antonia this and she understood. She talked about Tim's ability to brainwash people and admitted she would consciously 'debrief' herself after visiting him inside. But when you are young and vulnerable and unaware of being manipulated, it is easy to soak it all up, and I did. Tim invaded me, he re-routed my emotional wiring, and as a consequence it's had a damaging effect on my relationships. I realize now I was projecting my feelings about Tim onto Stephen and, knowing that, it's become easier to stop.

When Tim and I split up in December 1985, Mum said to me, 'I'm sure that if you'd known how things would turn out, you'd never have got involved with Tim.' Even though he'd nearly destroyed my sanity, I denied it vehemently. Tim had made me who I was; he'd educated me, taught me to think, opened up new possibilities for me. I was his creature. I suppose a part of me still is, though I like to think I'd have got here anyway, wherever 'here' is. But it's pointless to ponder. The important thing is to learn. I feel I've resolved certain issues, as well as gaining more self-awareness. I can understand how women get into abusive relationships, and how hard it is to get out of them. I can see how low self-esteem undermines and that gratitude is not a sound basis for love. As to my attraction to father-figures, I recognize that I colluded with Tim by playing the little girl to his pervy parent. It's easier to be with someone who looks after you and tells you what to do than embrace the big wide world of responsible relationships. Tim wasn't the only one who hadn't matured emotionally. It's taken a while, but I have now.

For one thing, I don't feel the need to define myself solely by a man any longer. One of the many reasons I love Stephen is because he gives me space to be myself, to have my own pursuits, my own friends. We're a partnership. We're not perfect, we have spats and niggles like anyone else, but we respect each other and support each other and the caring is genuinely altruistic, not a subtle manipulation of power. Being a parent has changed me, too. Self-obsession is an indulgence you can't afford with children; a whole new set of priorities takes over. I can stand apart from that relationship with Tim and be confident that I exist for someone who does, truly, deserve my devotion, my daughter. She is my beloved '*hija*'. Giving birth to her has given me a strength I never knew I was capable of, the strength to look death in the face. Once you've been there, the rest isn't so complicated. My love is about her, not me. Unconditional commitment to another, as Tim would say. He could say it; he just couldn't do it.

I thought I'd said goodbye to Tim when I scattered his ashes on that May morning in 1987. I was wrong. It wasn't farewell, it was simply a new phase in our relationship, one that's continued to give me heartaches over the years. But that's over now. A few days ago I went to North Otterington, the place where Tim and Tina lived, and finally, after all this time, made my peace.

It's just The Garths, the vicarage, the church and, further up, a country house hotel, which are set back off the busy A167 to Northallerton; not much of a hamlet, even. I pulled over outside St Michael and All Angels, the little church, and got out. It was a glorious day with big blue prairie skies and white cumulus clouds so puffy and precisely drawn they might have been slapped on by a weatherman. I opened the latch on the wooden gate and let myself in, scrunching up the path between overgrown graves. Part of the churchyard at the front had been fenced off with wire netting and there were sheep grazing between the lichen-yellowed slabs and wonky headstones. A sign in the porch said the churchyard was a sanctuary for wildlife. It was a sanctuary for lonely Tina, too, although it didn't save her. Another sign on the notice-board informed me that the villages of the Thorntons and the Otteringtons had approved a child protection policy, and that 'any concerns' should be reported to the parish protection representative. Had this existed back in 1970, would it have made a difference? Who knows? Solberg Hall, the hotel just down the road, was a police training centre back then, and nobody there noticed anything untoward. The outbuildings were (and still are) used by the dog section, and the police dogs were exercised in the fields at the back of the properties. No wonder Tim buried Tina so deep. She was literally under their noses.

The church door was locked. A shame; I would like to have gone in and said a prayer. I'm not sure who for. Tim? Tina? Myself? Turning round, I spotted some tins of food lined up on a wooden beam: oxtail soup, new potatoes, baked beans, tuna chunks. Who for? A tramp with a can-opener, I assumed. It was a nice thought. I sat on a stone ledge in the porch and watched the thistledown wafting across the churchyard. The seed heads must have burst all at once, for the summer breeze had sent them drifting thickly through the air like snowflakes in slow motion. There was a blurr of wings as a swallow dived into the porch, saw me and flew off again. I looked up and noticed two nests above the door and a third in the apex of the beams. The birds continued to buzz me so I took the hint and left. It was their home; I didn't need to stay there any longer. I stumbled along the squashy verge towards The Garths, grateful for my boots and trousers against the stinging nettles. A tall hedge shielded the garden from view, but I could make out a neatly trimmed lawn, bright flowerbeds, washing on the line, a toy tractor. I wondered where the windshelter had been. Strick Carter, who knew one of the previous occupants, had told me it had been stripped out years ago and that the annex and the house had been knocked through. I stood, indecisively, in the entrance to the drive. The profile of the house looked just the same as it did in those 'Body in the Garden Trial' logos. A woman with her back to me was retrieving shopping from the boot of her car. I ducked out of sight, not wanting her to think I was casing the joint, and retreated. It was not, after all, a venue for sightseers. All signs of Tim and Tina had gone. It was enough to know that life had moved on at The Garths; happy, ordinary family life, just as it should be.

When I got back into my car, a piece of thistledown floated in through the open window and I caught it in my hand. I examined it, stroking its delicate filaments, marvelling at its structure of fine, tiny threads. And it struck me that that's what this book is about: not just Tim, but about all the fragile threads connecting him to other people. Everyone's got a story to tell. This is mine. But I'm just one of the threads. As to the other stories, they don't belong to me . . . I uncurled my fingers and watched the thistledown soar away on the breeze, tumbling in the warm current as it lifted higher until finally, it disappeared from view.